Chapter 1

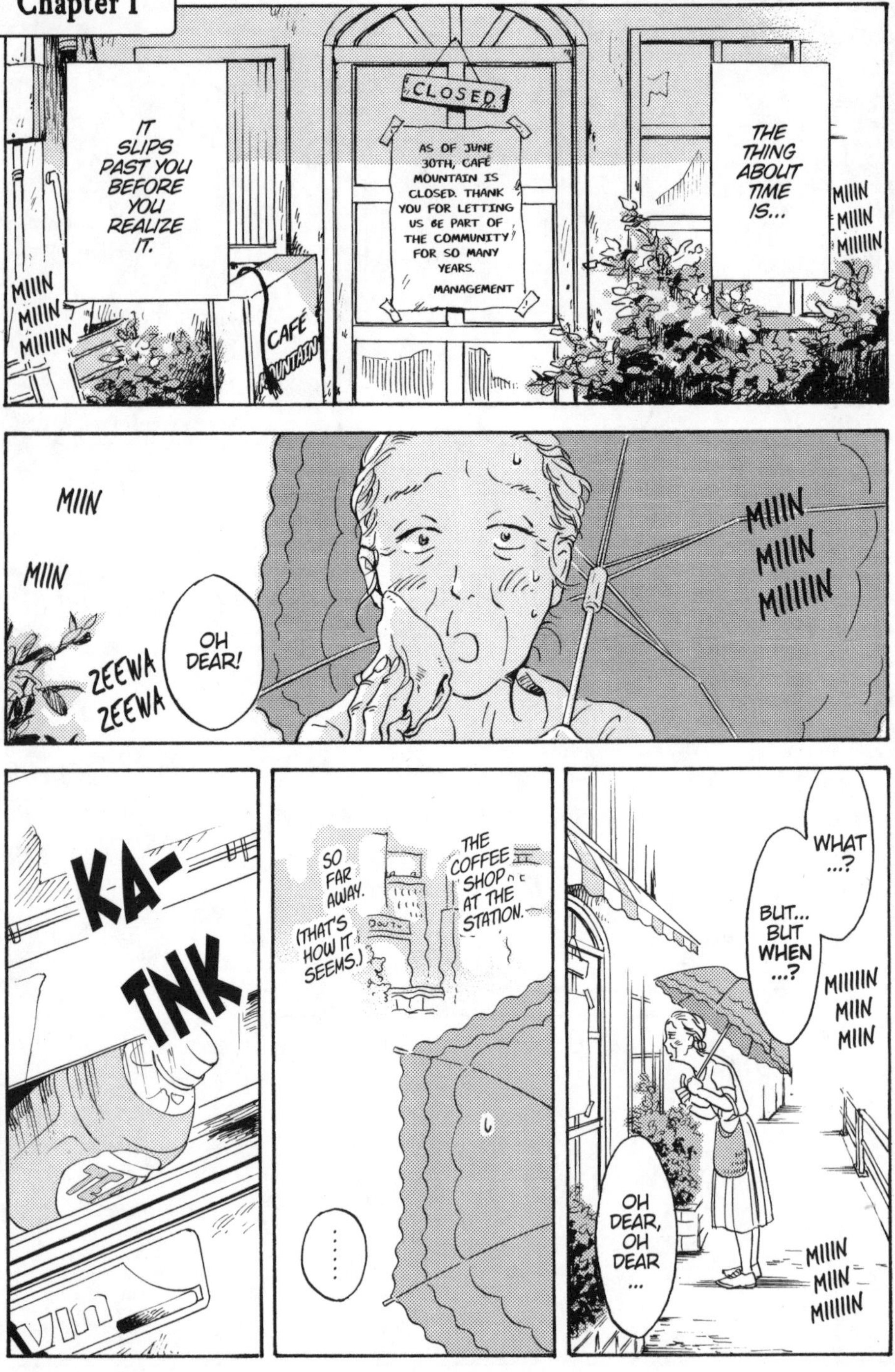
THE THING ABOUT TIME IS...
MIIN MIIN MIIIIN
CLOSED
AS OF JUNE 30TH, CAFÉ MOUNTAIN IS CLOSED. THANK YOU FOR LETTING US BE PART OF THE COMMUNITY FOR SO MANY YEARS.
MANAGEMENT
IT SLIPS PAST YOU BEFORE YOU REALIZE IT.
CAFÉ MOUNTAIN
MIIN MIIN MIIIIN
MIIN MIIN MIIIIN
OH DEAR!
MIIN
MIIN
ZEEWA ZEEWA
WHAT ...?
BUT... BUT WHEN ...?
MIIIIN MIIN MIIN
OH DEAR, OH DEAR ...
MIIN MIIN MIIIIN
THE COFFEE SHOP AT THE STATION.
SO FAR AWAY.
(THAT'S HOW IT SEEMS.)
......
KA-TNK

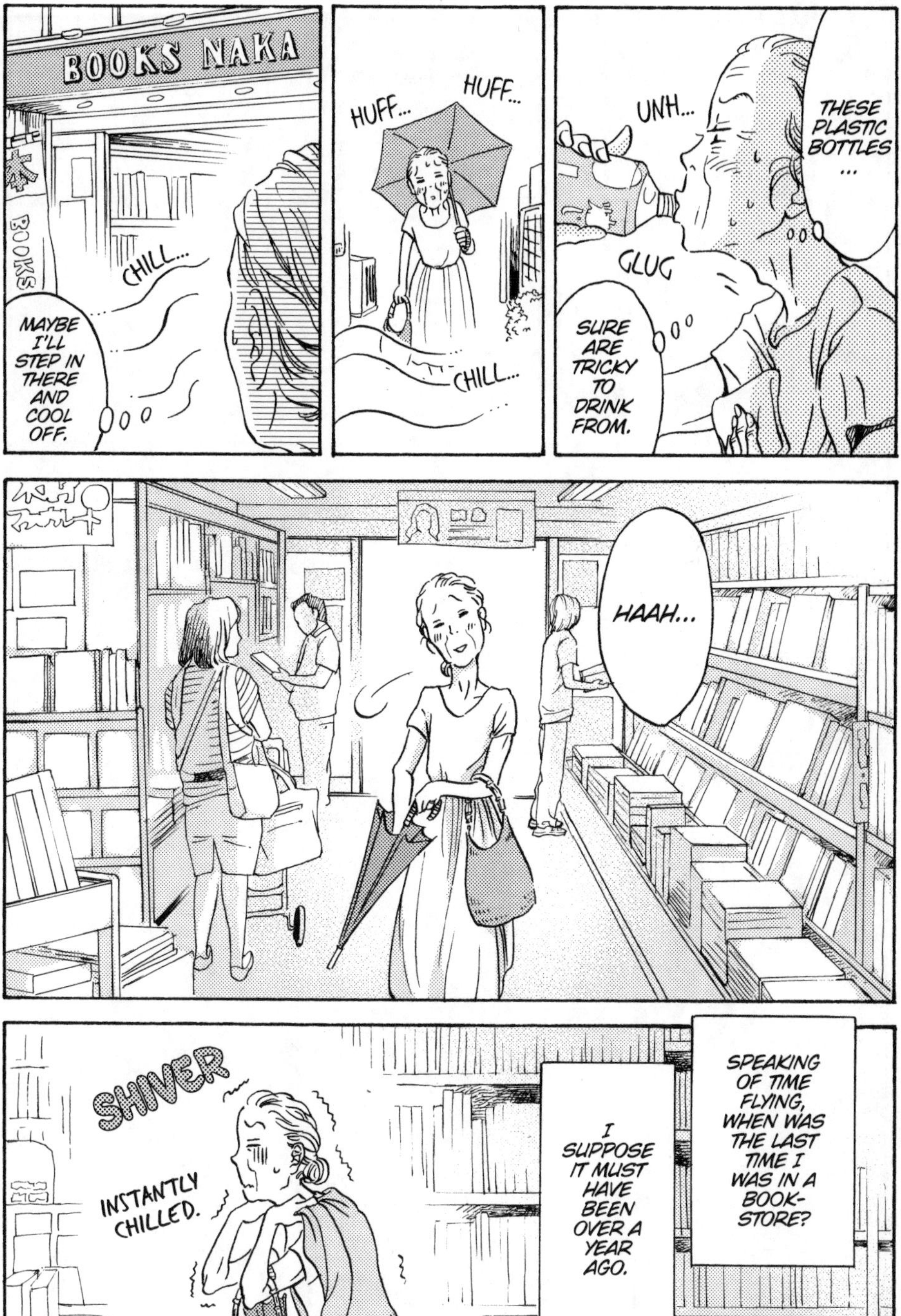
THESE PLASTIC BOTTLES ...
UNH...
GLUG
SURE ARE TRICKY TO DRINK FROM.
HUFF...
HUFF...
CHILL...
BOOKS NAKA
BOOKS
CHILL...
MAYBE I'LL STEP IN THERE AND COOL OFF.
HAAH...
SPEAKING OF TIME FLYING, WHEN WAS THE LAST TIME I WAS IN A BOOK-STORE?
I SUPPOSE IT MUST HAVE BEEN OVER A YEAR AGO.
SHIVER
INSTANTLY CHILLED.

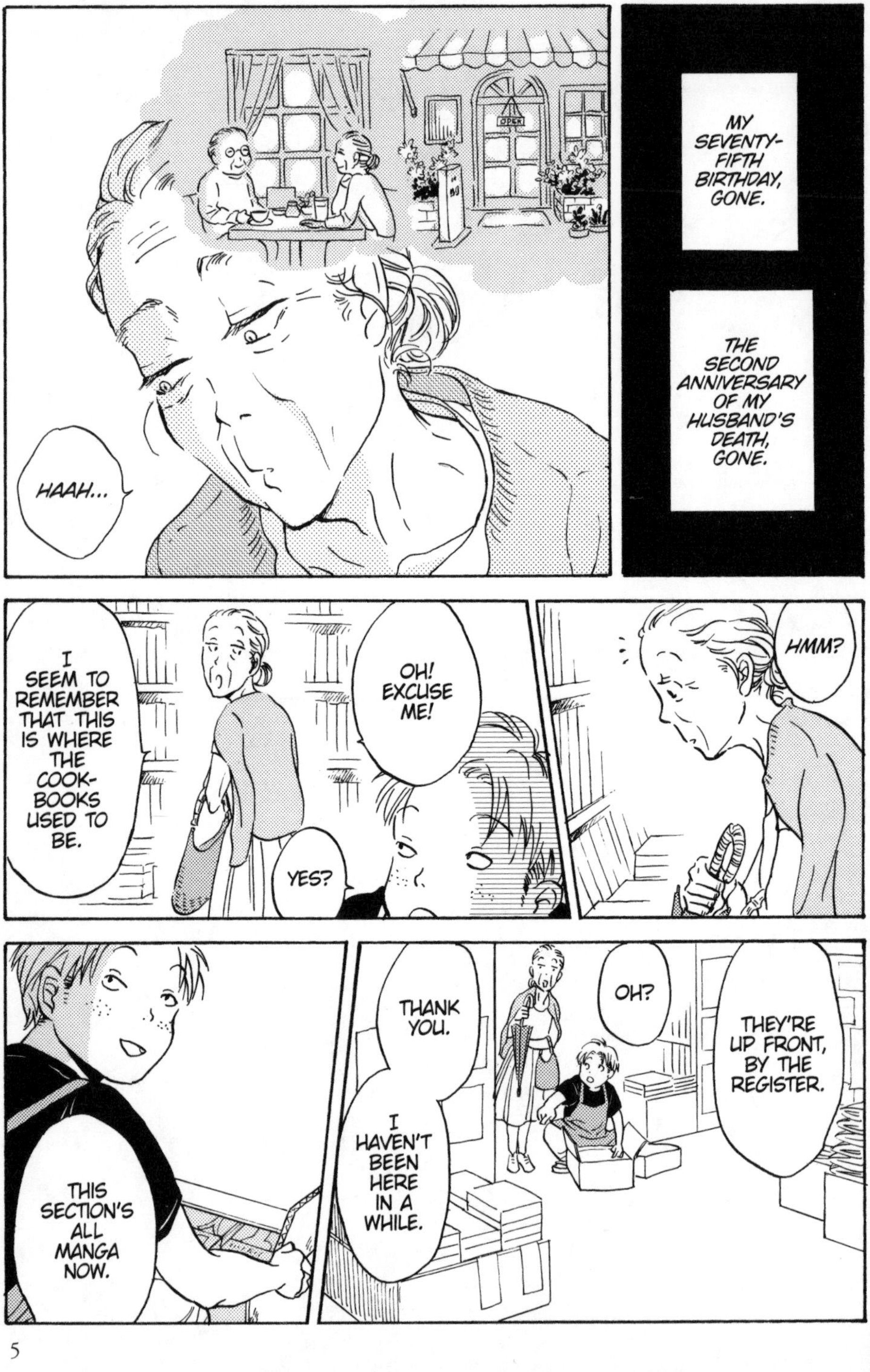
MY SEVENTY-FIFTH BIRTHDAY, GONE.
THE SECOND ANNIVERSARY OF MY HUSBAND'S DEATH, GONE.
HAAH...
HMM?
OH! EXCUSE ME!
YES?
I SEEM TO REMEMBER THAT THIS IS WHERE THE COOK-BOOKS USED TO BE.
THEY'RE UP FRONT, BY THE REGISTER.
OH?
THANK YOU.
I HAVEN'T BEEN HERE IN A WHILE.
THIS SECTION'S ALL MANGA NOW.

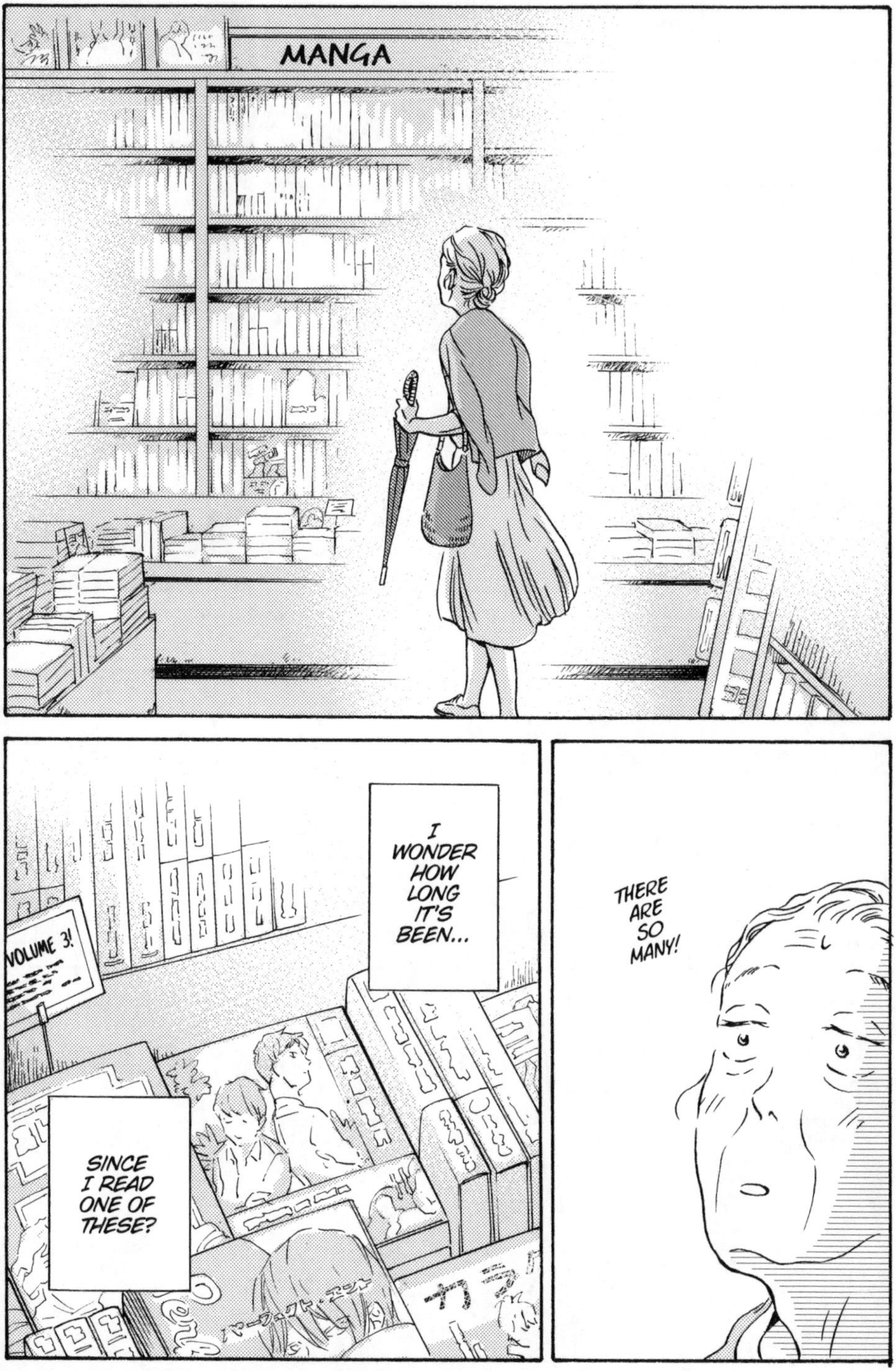
MANGA
THERE ARE SO MANY!
I WONDER HOW LONG IT'S BEEN...
VOLUME 3!
SINCE I READ ONE OF THESE?

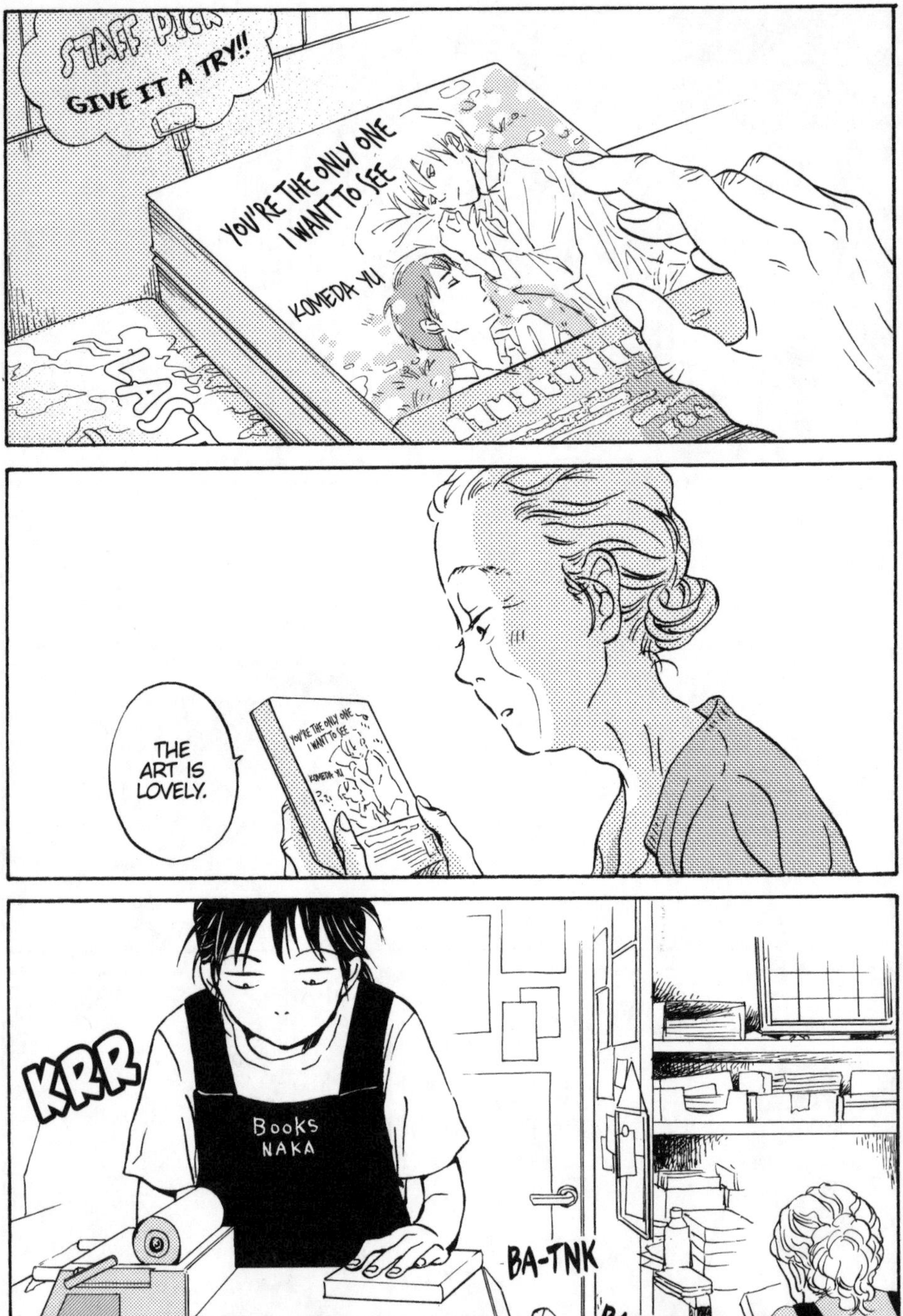
STAFF PICK
GIVE IT A TRY!!
YOU'RE THE ONLY ONE I WANT TO SEE
KOMEDA YU
THE ART IS LOVELY.
YOU'RE THE ONLY ONE I WANT TO SEE
KOMEDA YU
KRR
Books NAKA
BA-TNK
BA-TNK

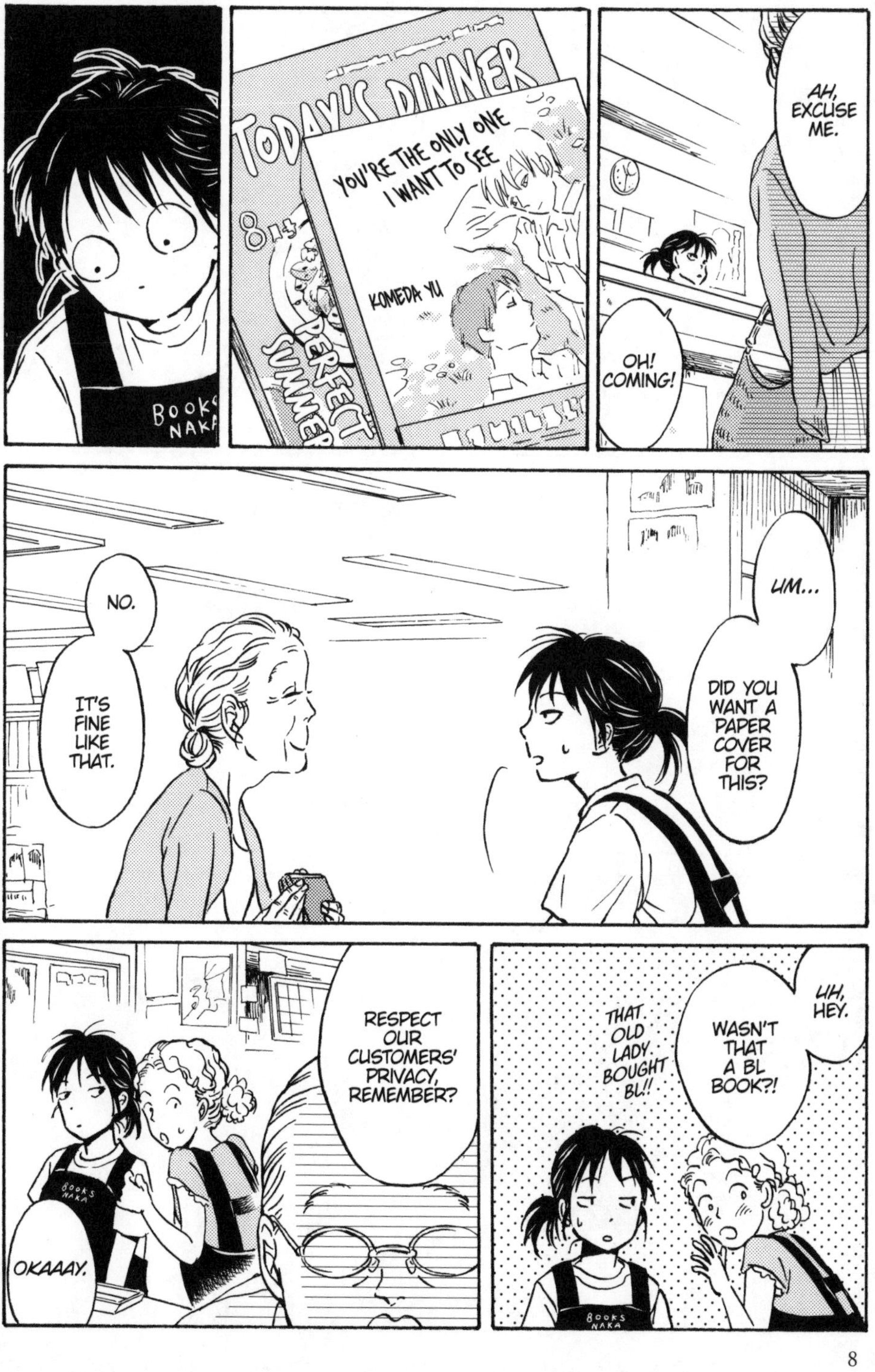
AH, EXCUSE ME.
OH! COMING!
TODAY'S DINNER
YOU'RE THE ONLY ONE I WANT TO SEE
KOMEDA YU
PERFECT SUMMER
BOOKS NAKA
UM...
DID YOU WANT A PAPER COVER FOR THIS?
NO.
IT'S FINE LIKE THAT.
UH, HEY.
WASN'T THAT A BL BOOK?!
THAT. OLD LADY. BOUGHT BL!!
BOOKS NAKA
RESPECT OUR CUSTOMERS' PRIVACY, REMEMBER?
BOOKS NAKA
OKAAAY.

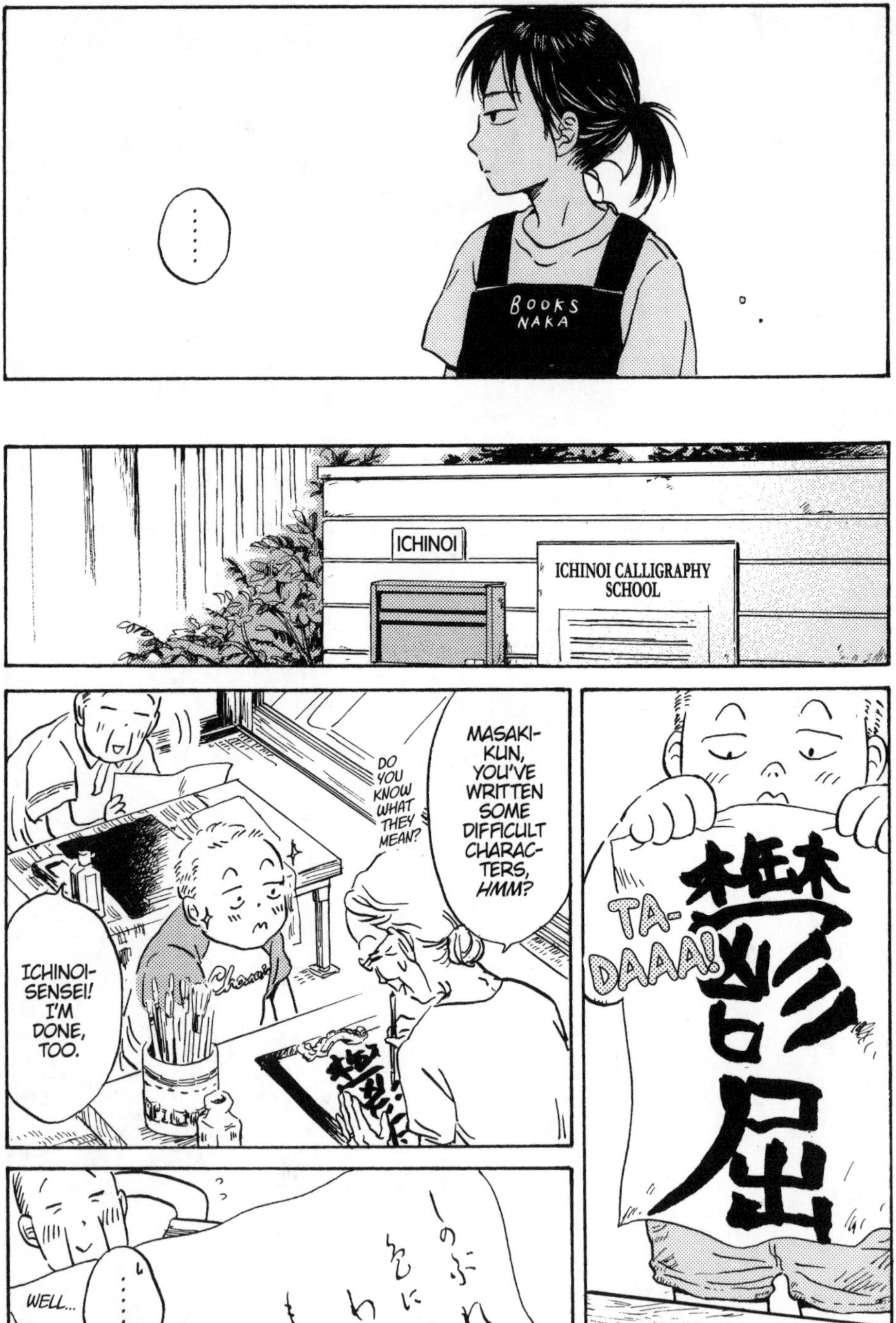
……
BOOKS NAKA
ICHINOI
ICHINOI CALLIGRAPHY SCHOOL
TA-DAAA!
MASAKI-KUN, YOU'VE WRITTEN SOME DIFFICULT CHARACTERS, HMM?
DO YOU KNOW WHAT THEY MEAN?
ICHINOI-SENSEI! I'M DONE, TOO.
……
WELL...

Paper: gloomy.

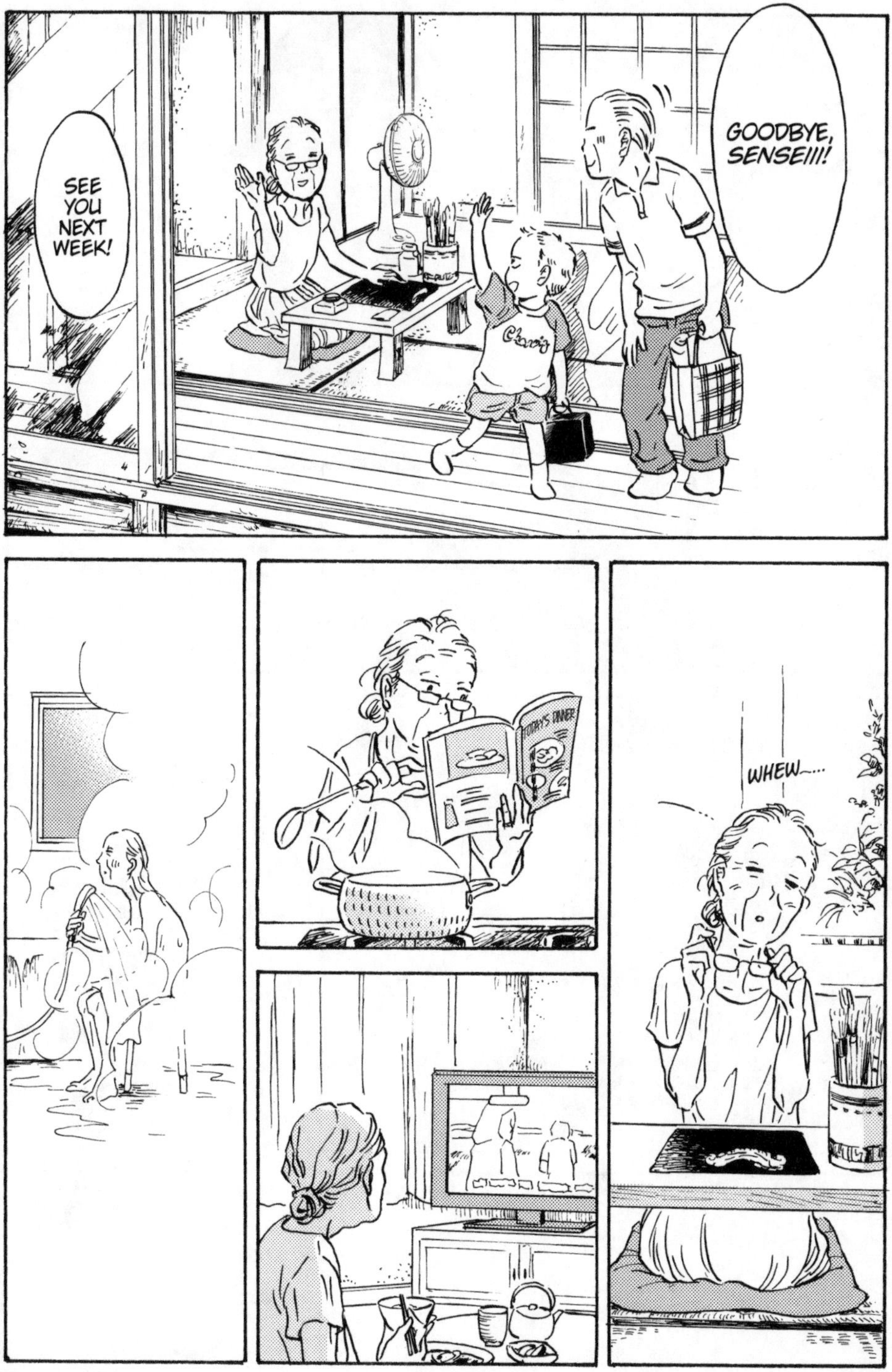
GOODBYE, SENSEI!!!
SEE YOU NEXT WEEK!
WHEW....
TODAY'S DINNER

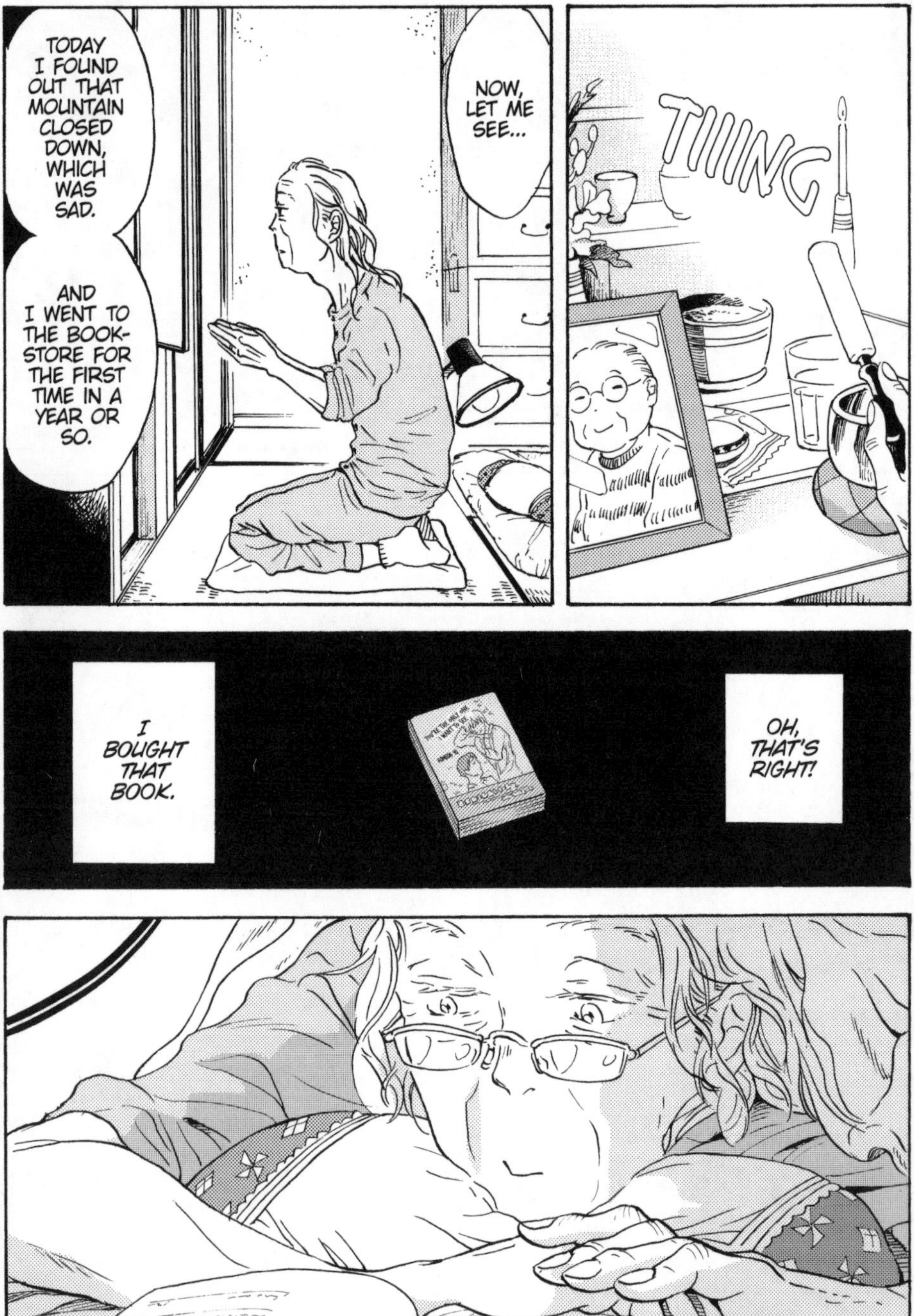
TIIING
NOW, LET ME SEE...
TODAY I FOUND OUT THAT MOUNTAIN CLOSED DOWN, WHICH WAS SAD.
AND I WENT TO THE BOOK-STORE FOR THE FIRST TIME IN A YEAR OR SO.
OH, THAT'S RIGHT!
I BOUGHT THAT BOOK.

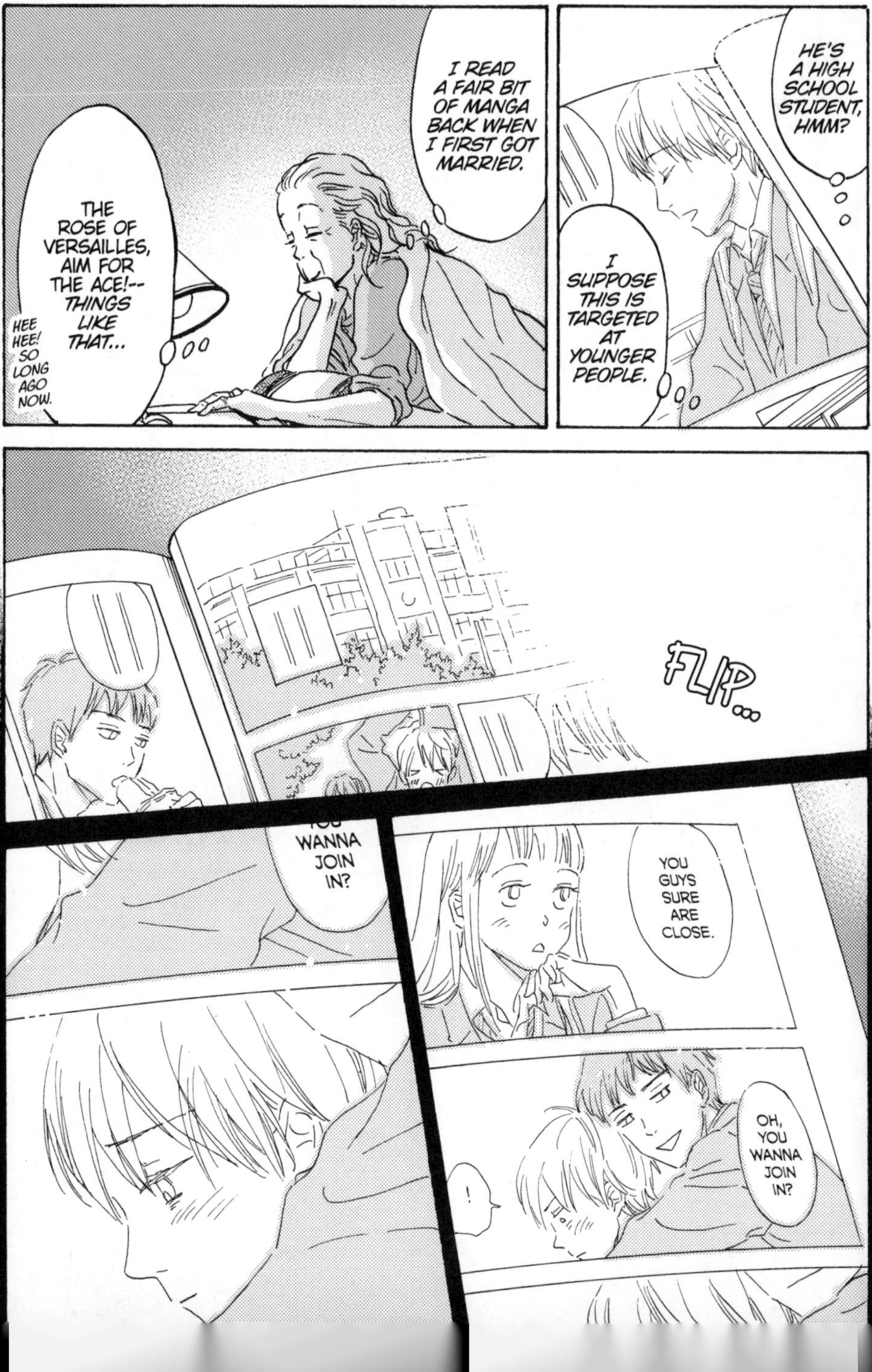
HE'S A HIGH SCHOOL STUDENT, HMM?
I SUPPOSE THIS IS TARGETED AT YOUNGER PEOPLE.
I READ A FAIR BIT OF MANGA BACK WHEN I FIRST GOT MARRIED.
THE ROSE OF VERSAILLES, AIM FOR THE ACE!-- THINGS LIKE THAT...
HEE HEE! SO LONG AGO NOW.
FLIP...
YOU GUYS SURE ARE CLOSE.
OH, YOU WANNA JOIN IN?
!
WANNA JOIN IN?

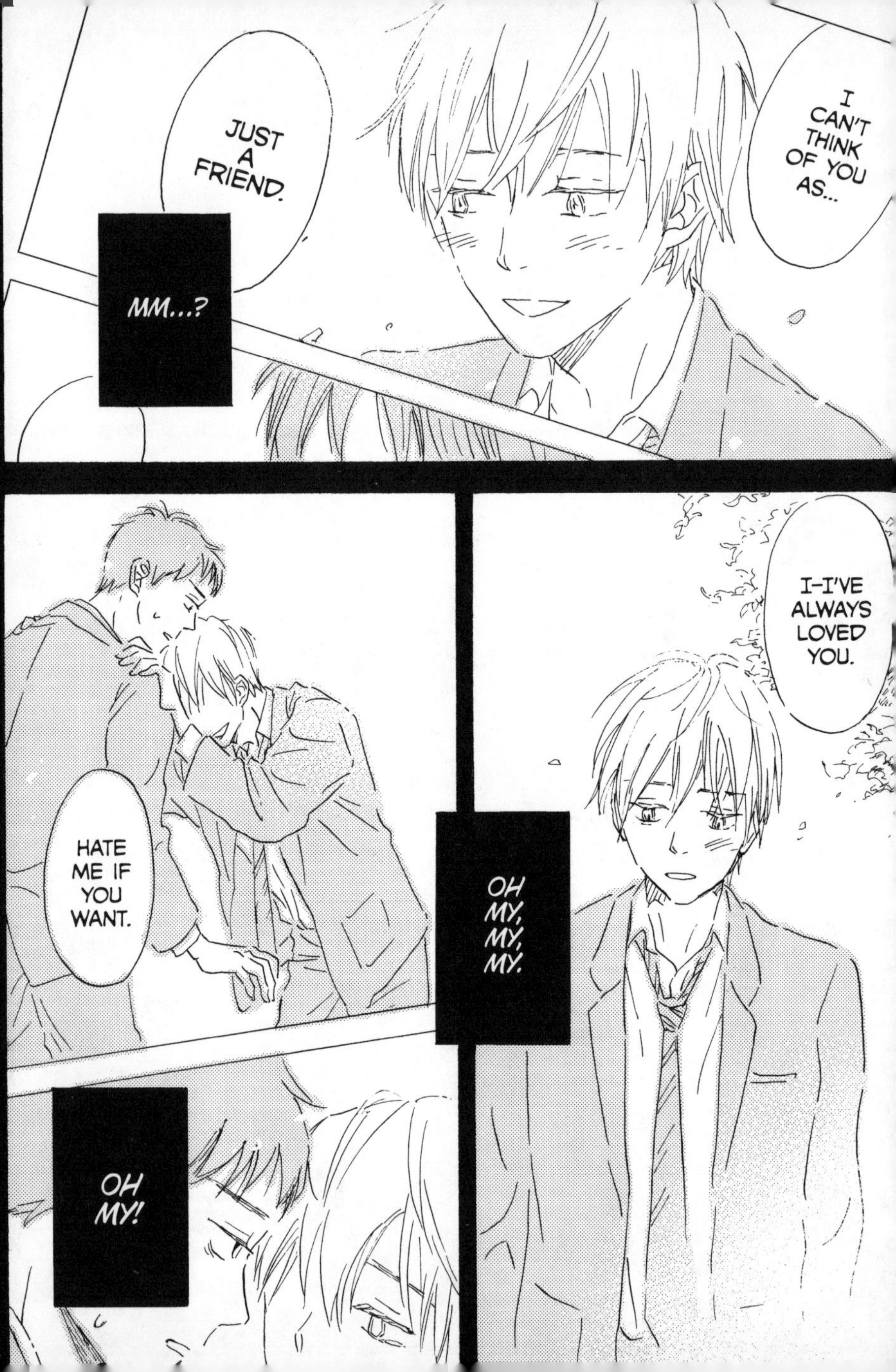
I CAN'T THINK OF YOU AS...
JUST A FRIEND.
MM...?
I-I'VE ALWAYS LOVED YOU.
OH MY, MY, MY.
HATE ME IF YOU WANT.
OH MY!

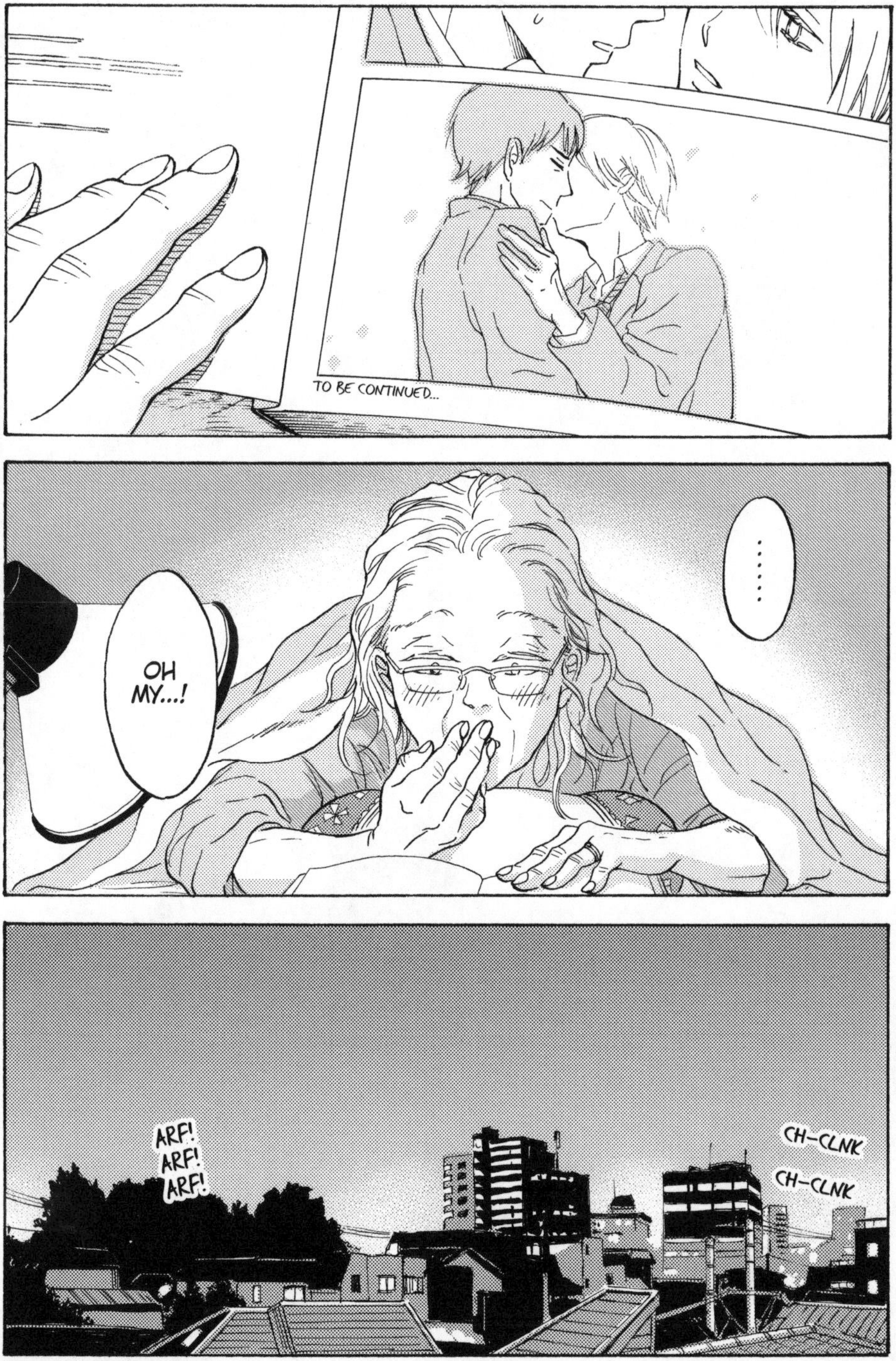
TO BE CONTINUED...
......
OH MY...!
CH-CLNK
CH-CLNK
ARF! ARF! ARF!

Chapter 1/END

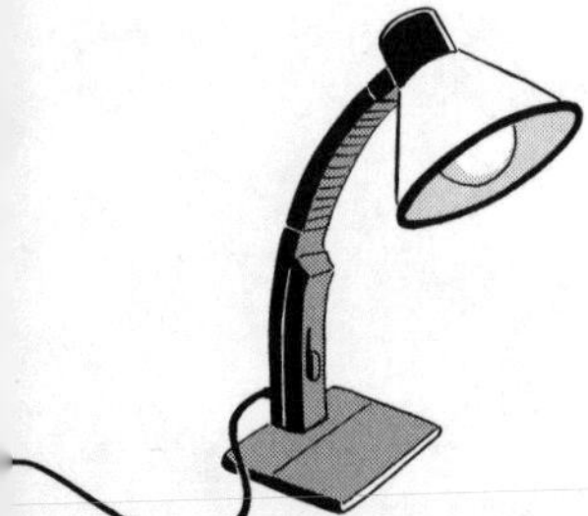

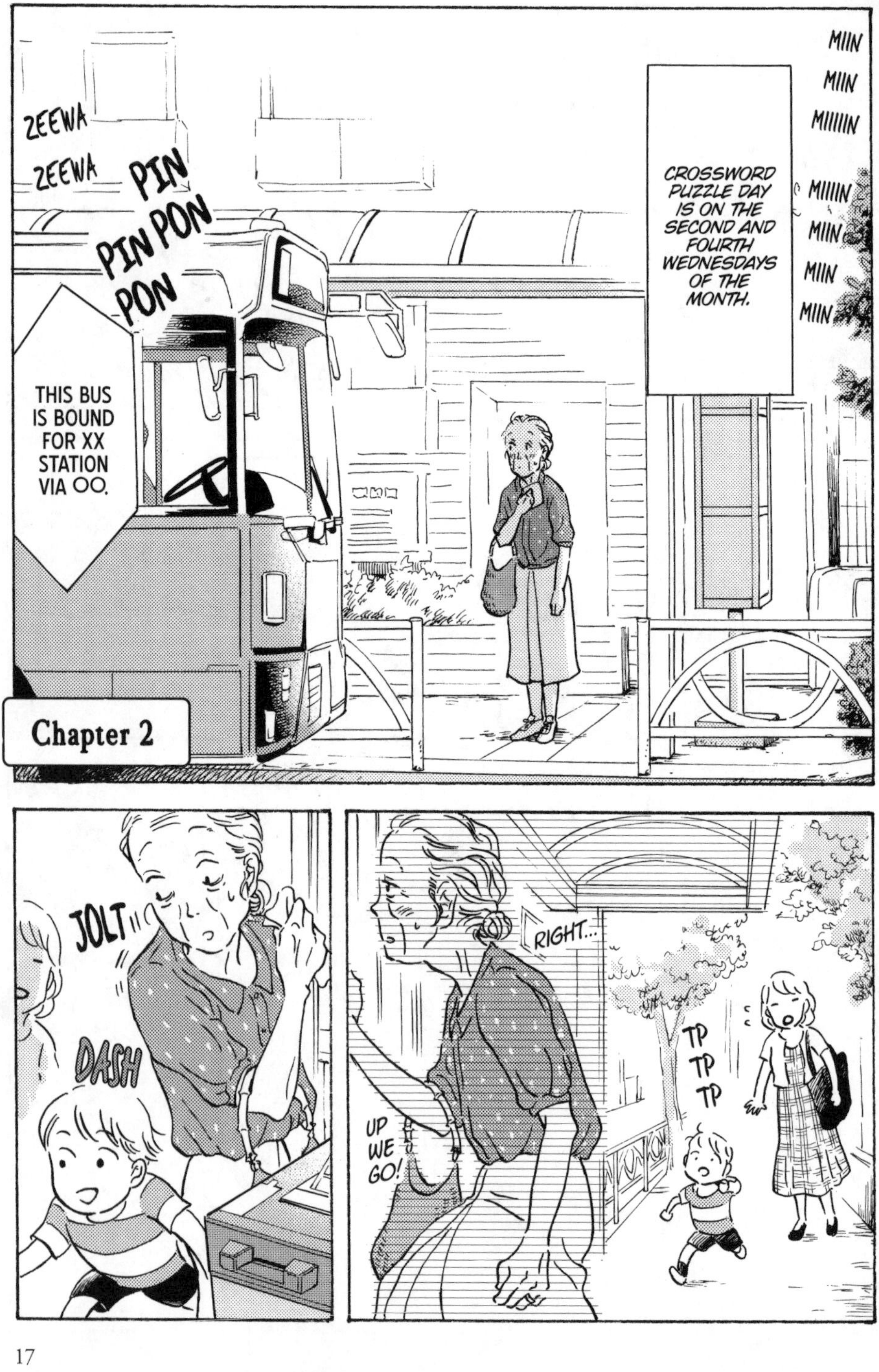
MIIN
MIIN
MIIIIN
MIIIN
MIIN
MIIN
MIIN
CROSSWORD PUZZLE DAY IS ON THE SECOND AND FOURTH WEDNESDAYS OF THE MONTH.
PIN PIN PON PON
ZEEWA
ZEEWA
THIS BUS IS BOUND FOR XX STATION VIA OO.
Chapter 2
RIGHT...
TP TP TP
UP WE GO!
JOLT
DASH

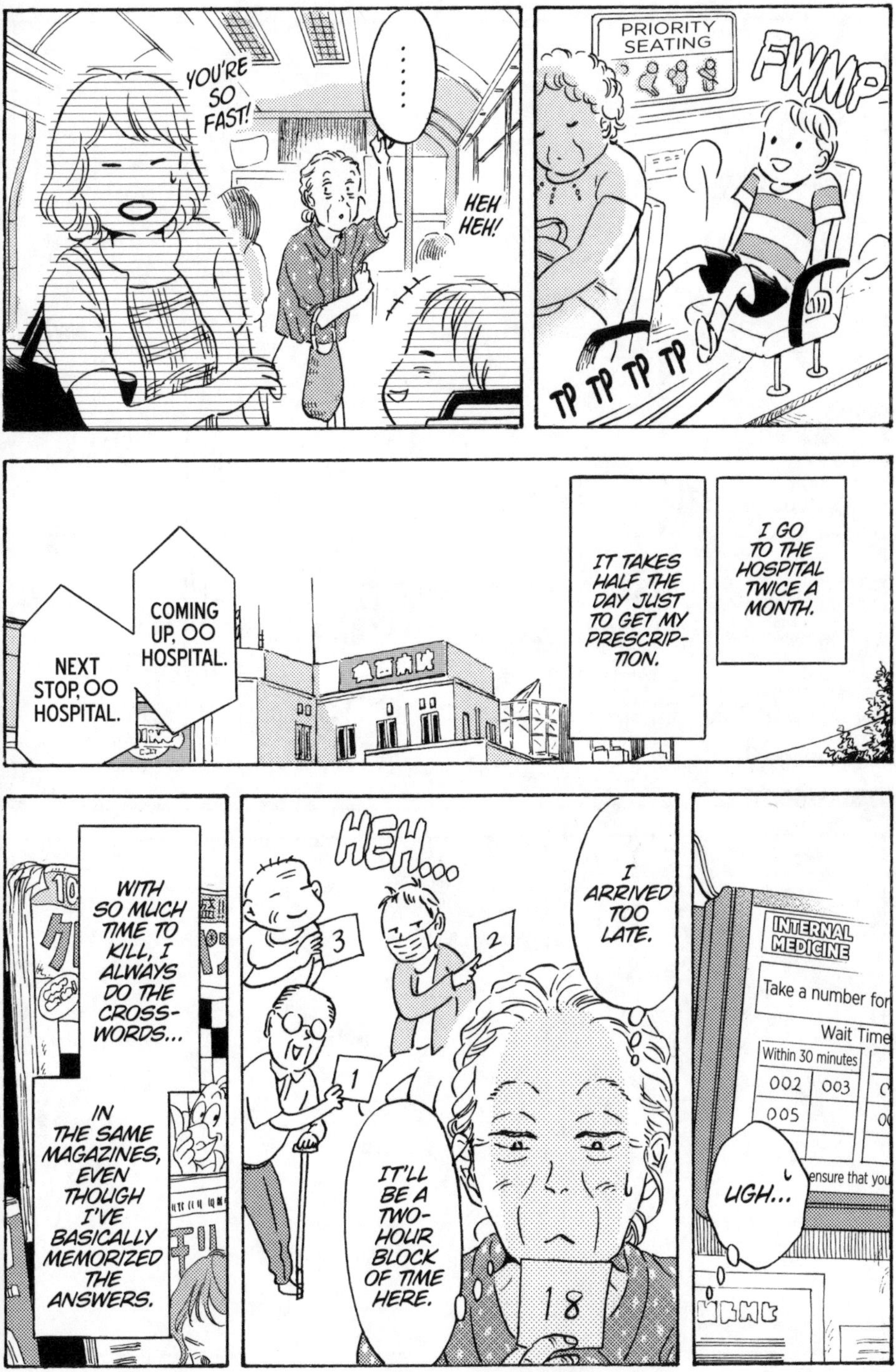
PRIORITY SEATING
FWMP
TP TP TP TP
......
YOU'RE SO FAST!
HEH HEH!
I GO TO THE HOSPITAL TWICE A MONTH.
IT TAKES HALF THE DAY JUST TO GET MY PRESCRIPTION.
COMING UP, OO HOSPITAL.
NEXT STOP, OO HOSPITAL.
INTERNAL MEDICINE
Take a number for
Wait Time
Within 30 minutes
002 003
005
ensure that you
UGH...
I ARRIVED TOO LATE.
HEH...
2
3
1
IT'LL BE A TWO-HOUR BLOCK OF TIME HERE.
18
WITH SO MUCH TIME TO KILL, I ALWAYS DO THE CROSSWORDS...
IN THE SAME MAGAZINES, EVEN THOUGH I'VE BASICALLY MEMORIZED THE ANSWERS.

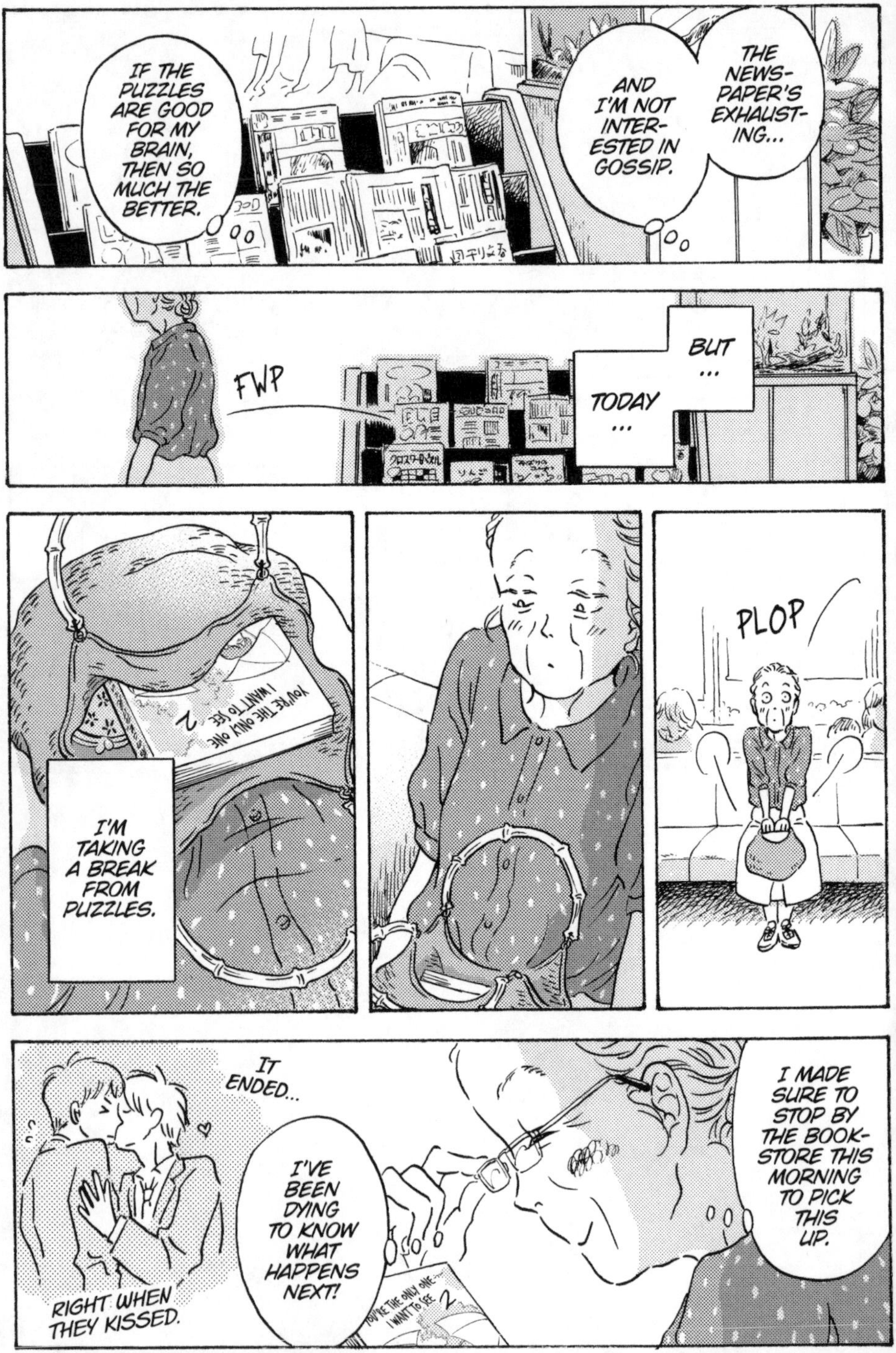
THE NEWS-PAPER'S EXHAUSTING...
AND I'M NOT INTERESTED IN GOSSIP.
IF THE PUZZLES ARE GOOD FOR MY BRAIN, THEN SO MUCH THE BETTER.
BUT ...
TODAY ...
FWP
PLOP
YOU'RE THE ONLY ONE I WANT TO SEE 2
I'M TAKING A BREAK FROM PUZZLES.
I MADE SURE TO STOP BY THE BOOK-STORE THIS MORNING TO PICK THIS UP.
I'VE BEEN DYING TO KNOW WHAT HAPPENS NEXT!
IT ENDED...
RIGHT WHEN THEY KISSED.
YOU'RE THE ONLY ONE I WANT TO SEE 2

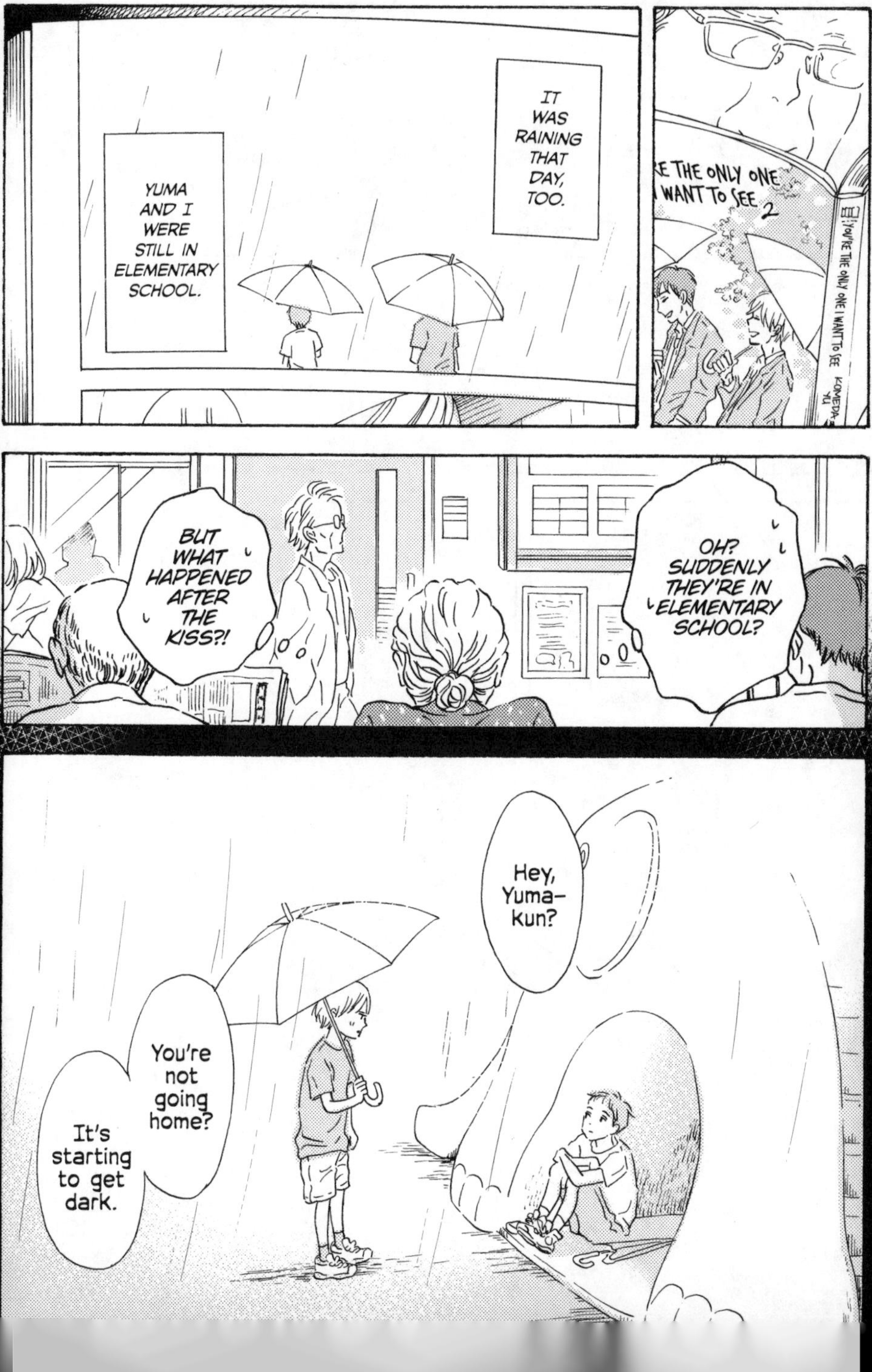
E THE ONLY ONE
WANT TO SEE 2
YOU'RE THE ONLY ONE I WANT TO SEE
KOMEDA YU
IT WAS RAINING THAT DAY, TOO.
YUMA AND I WERE STILL IN ELEMENTARY SCHOOL.
OH? SUDDENLY THEY'RE IN ELEMENTARY SCHOOL?
BUT WHAT HAPPENED AFTER THE KISS?!
Hey, Yuma-kun?
You're not going home?
It's starting to get dark.

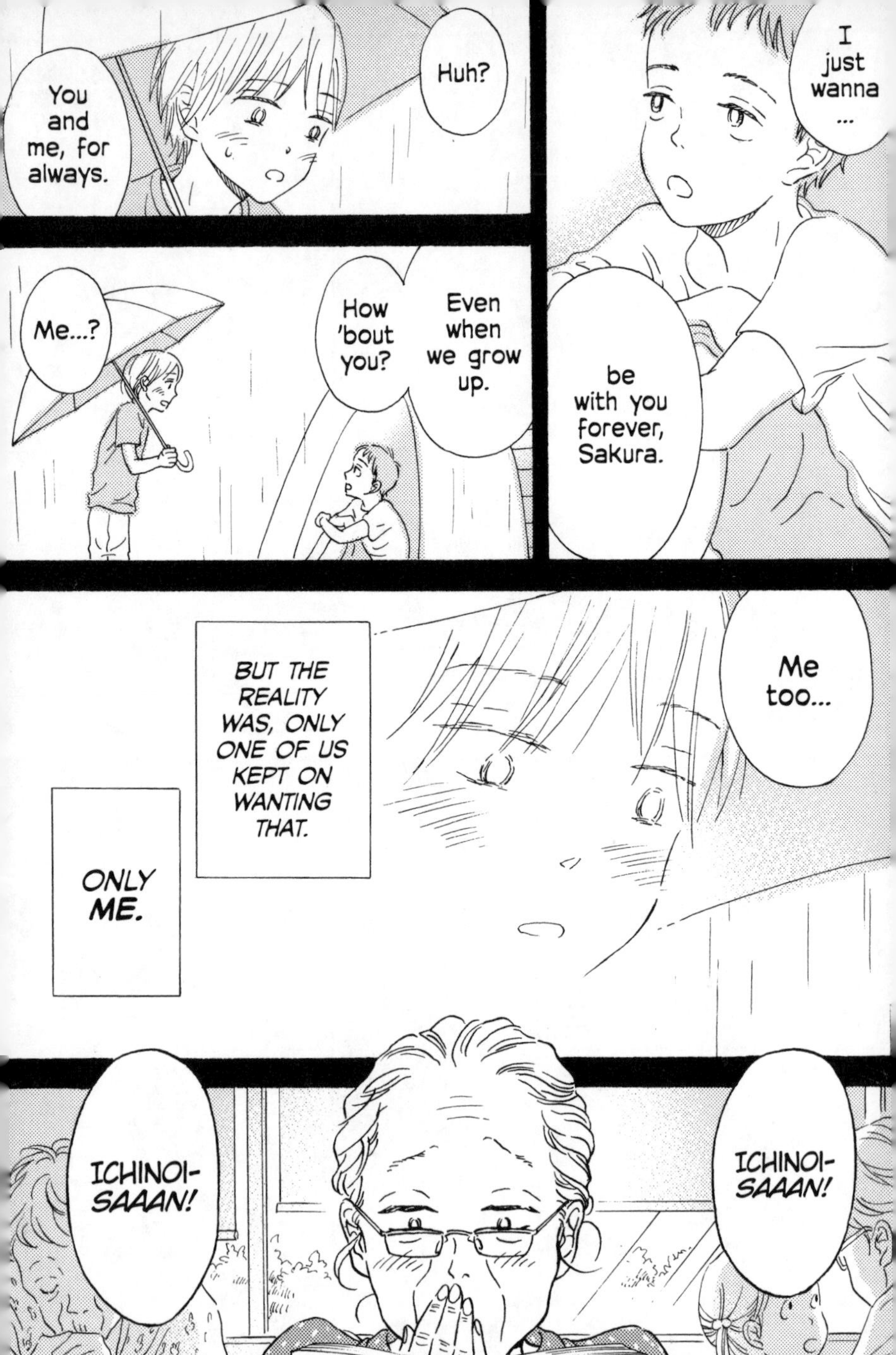
I just wanna ...
be with you forever, Sakura.
Huh?
You and me, for always.
Even when we grow up.
How 'bout you?
Me...?
Me too...
BUT THE REALITY WAS, ONLY ONE OF US KEPT ON WANTING THAT.
ONLY ME.
ICHINOI-SAAAN!
ICHINOI-SAAAN!

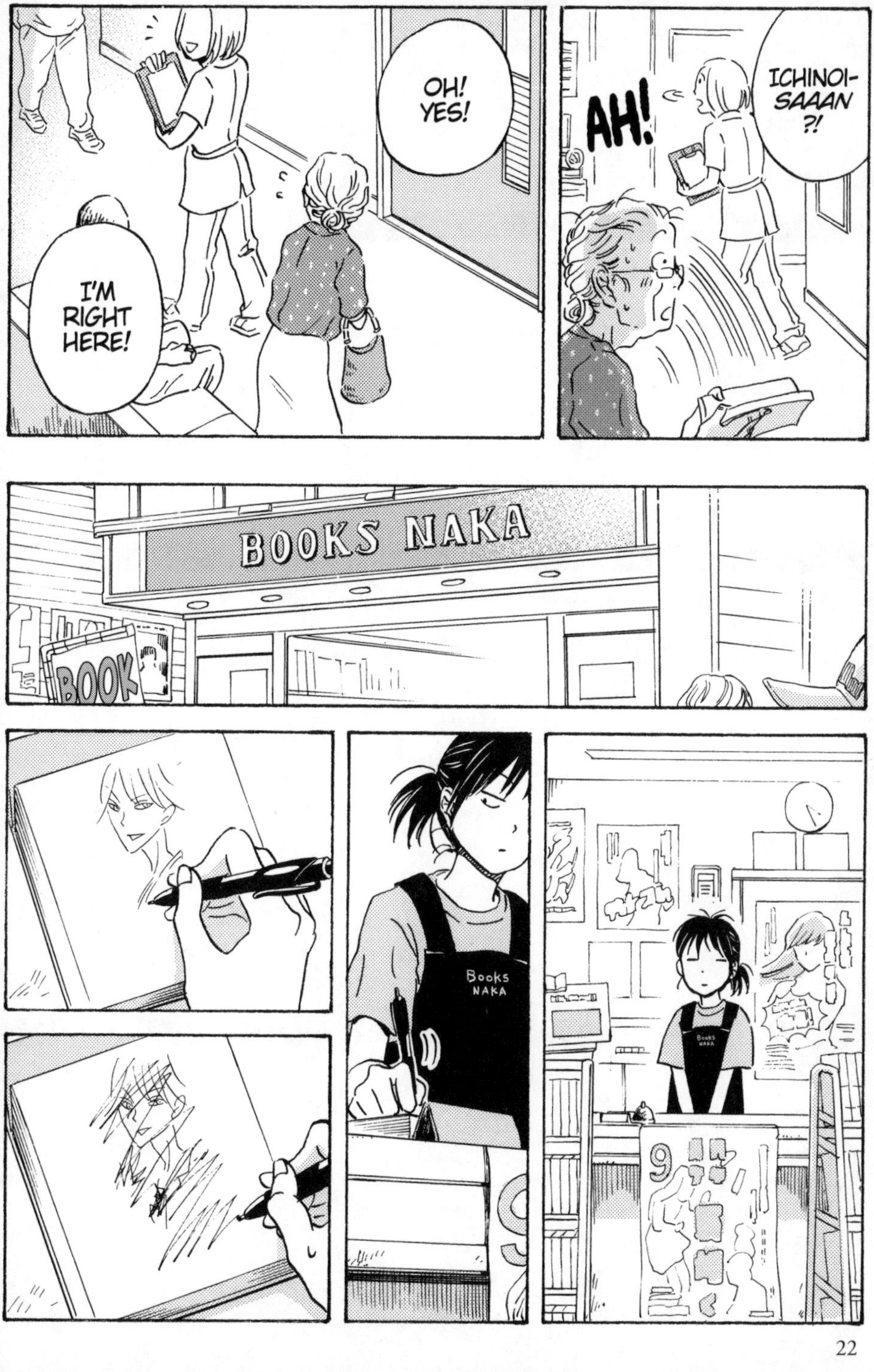
ICHINOI-SAAAN ?!
AH!
OH! YES!
I'M RIGHT HERE!
BOOKS NAKA
BOOK
Books NAKA

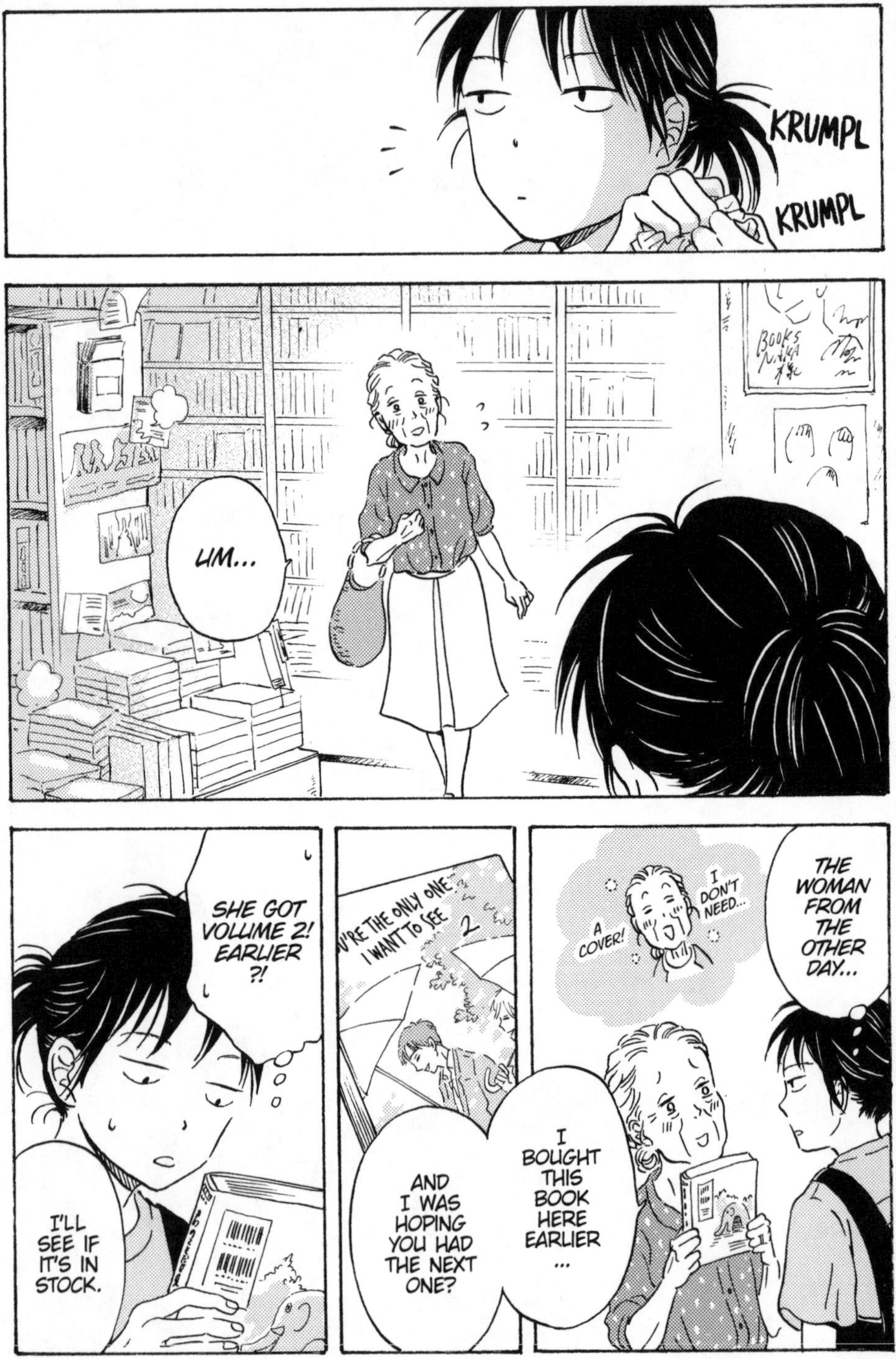
KRUMPL
KRUMPL
UM...
THE WOMAN FROM THE OTHER DAY...
I DON'T NEED...
A COVER!
I BOUGHT THIS BOOK HERE EARLIER ...
AND I WAS HOPING YOU HAD THE NEXT ONE?
'RE THE ONLY ONE I WANT TO SEE
2
SHE GOT VOLUME 2! EARLIER ?!
I'LL SEE IF IT'S IN STOCK.

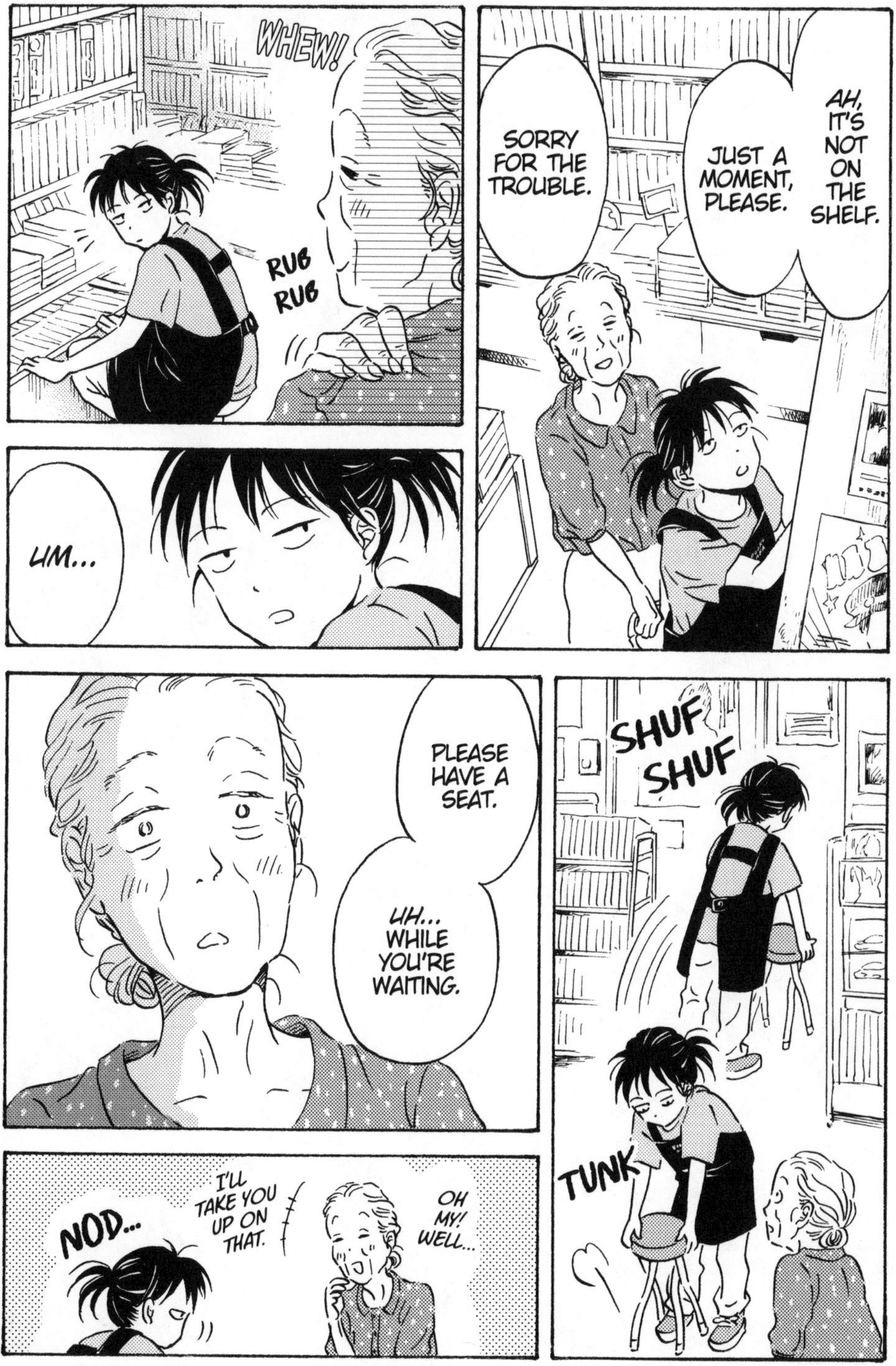
AH, IT'S NOT ON THE SHELF.
JUST A MOMENT, PLEASE.
SORRY FOR THE TROUBLE.
WHEW!
RUB RUB
UM...
SHUF SHUF
TUNK
PLEASE HAVE A SEAT.
UH... WHILE YOU'RE WAITING.
OH MY! WELL...
I'LL TAKE YOU UP ON THAT.
NOD...

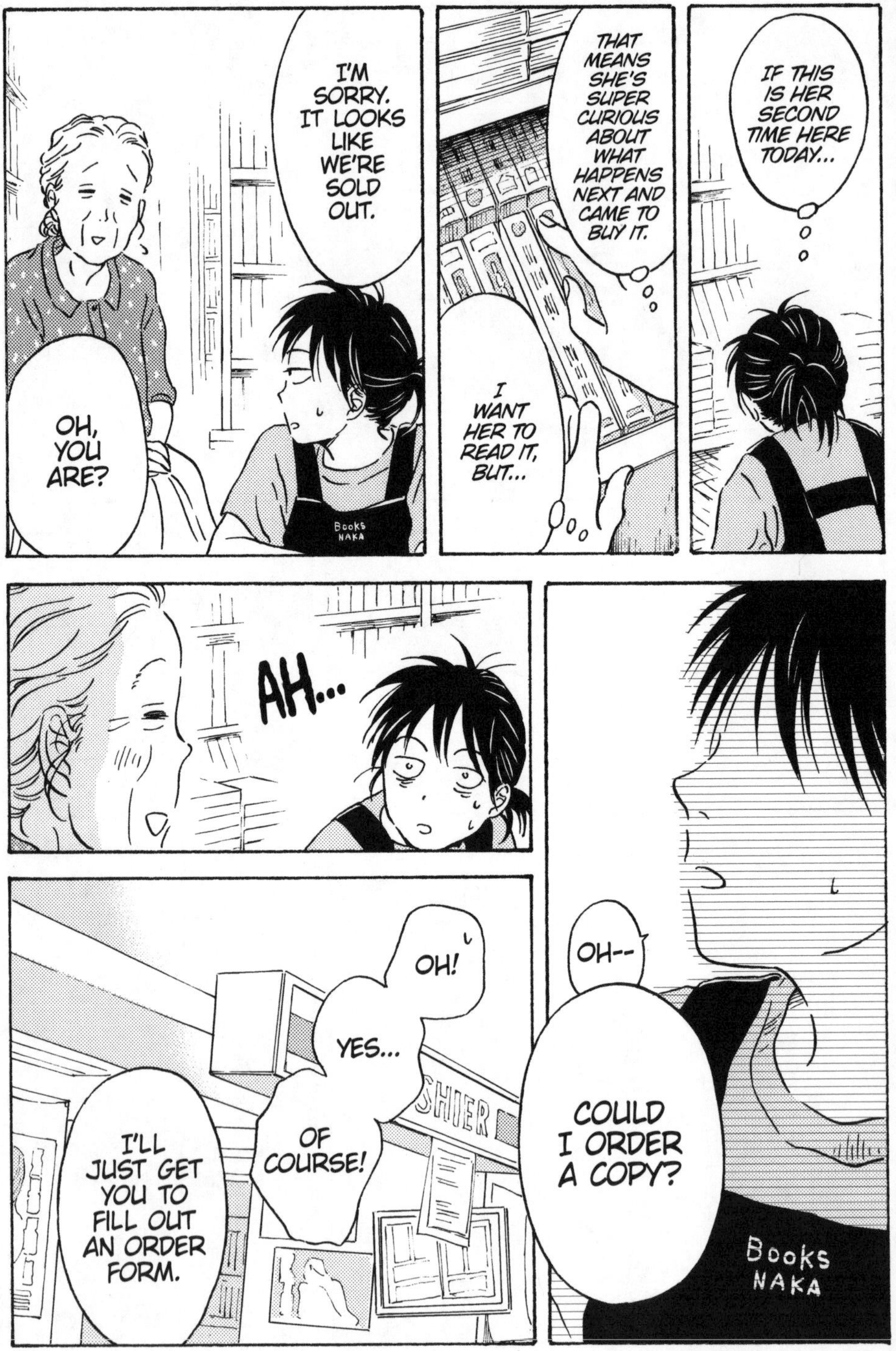
IF THIS IS HER SECOND TIME HERE TODAY...
THAT MEANS SHE'S SUPER CURIOUS ABOUT WHAT HAPPENS NEXT AND CAME TO BUY IT.
I WANT HER TO READ IT, BUT...
I'M SORRY. IT LOOKS LIKE WE'RE SOLD OUT.
BOOKS NAKA
OH, YOU ARE?
OH--
COULD I ORDER A COPY?
BOOKS NAKA
AH...
OH!
YES...
OF COURSE!
SHIER
I'LL JUST GET YOU TO FILL OUT AN ORDER FORM.

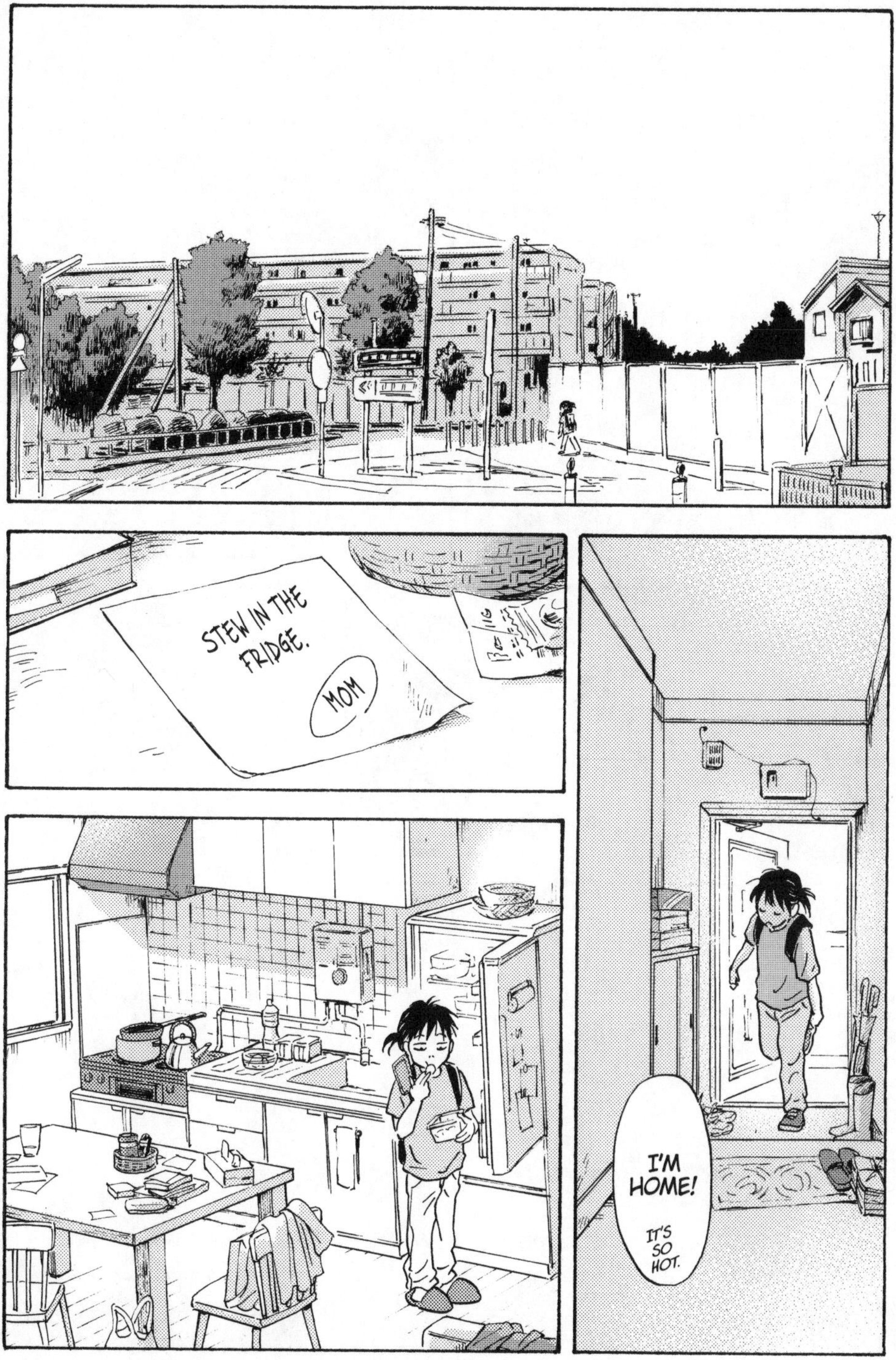
I'M HOME!
IT'S SO HOT.
STEW IN THE FRIDGE.
MOM

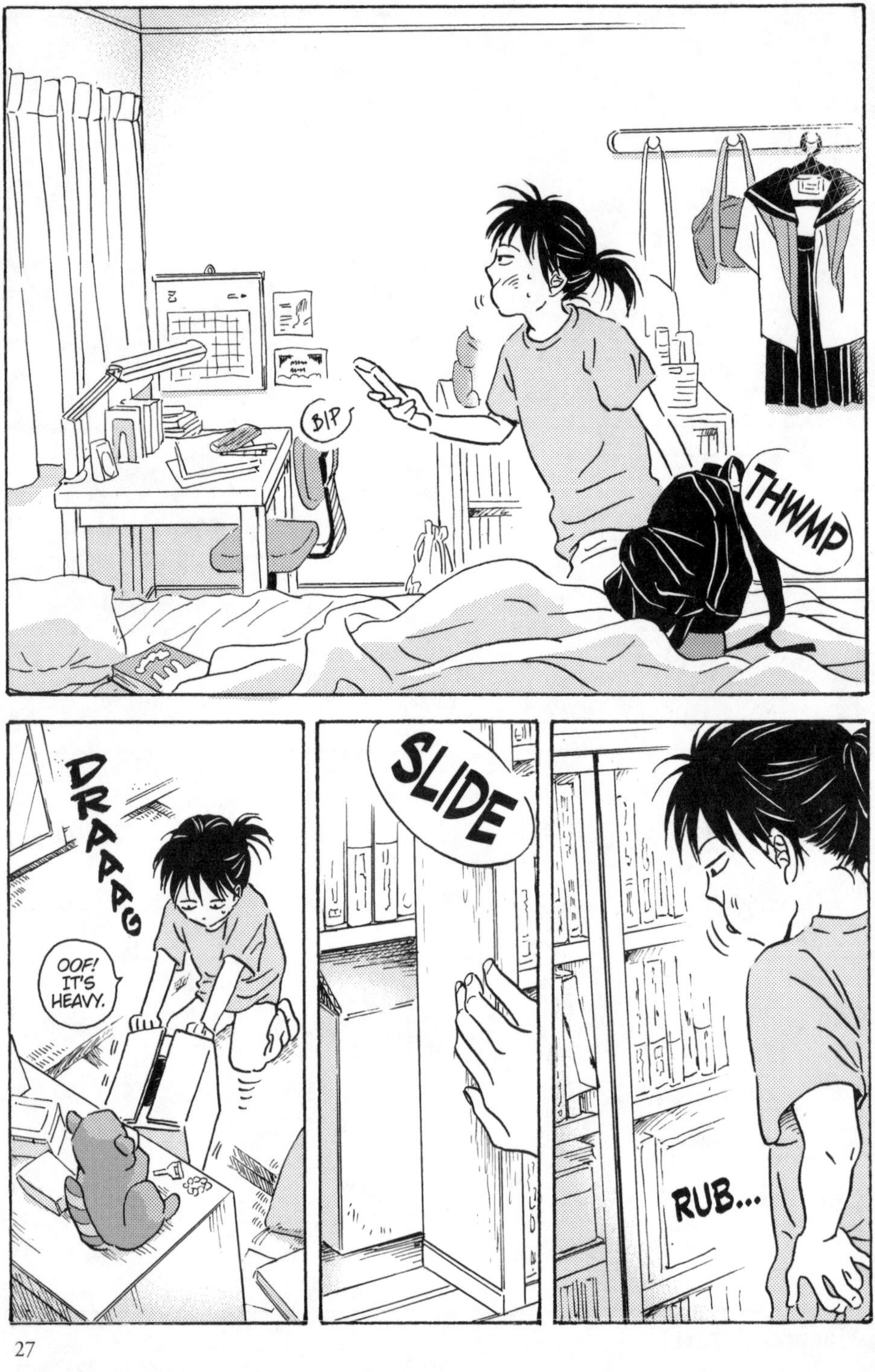
THWMP
BIP
RUB...
SLIDE
DRAAAG
OOF! IT'S HEAVY.

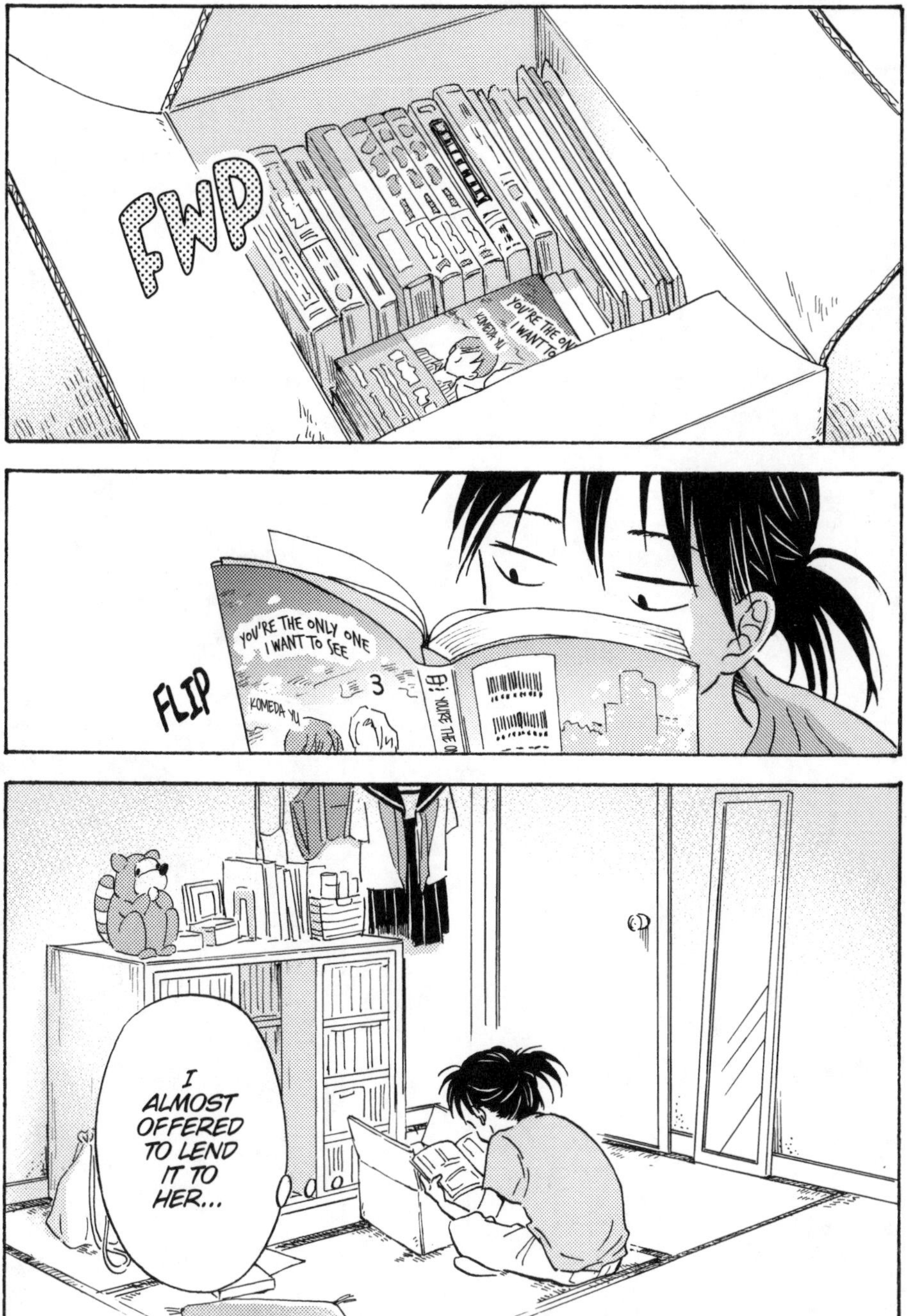
FWD
YOU'RE THE ON
I WANT TO
KOMEDA YU
YOU'RE THE ONLY ONE I WANT TO SEE
3
KOMEDA YU
FLIP
I ALMOST OFFERED TO LEND IT TO HER...

Chapter 2/END

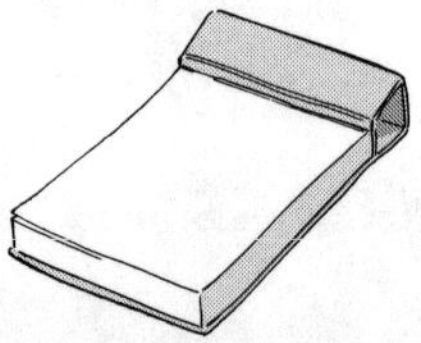

metamorphosis

Chapter 3

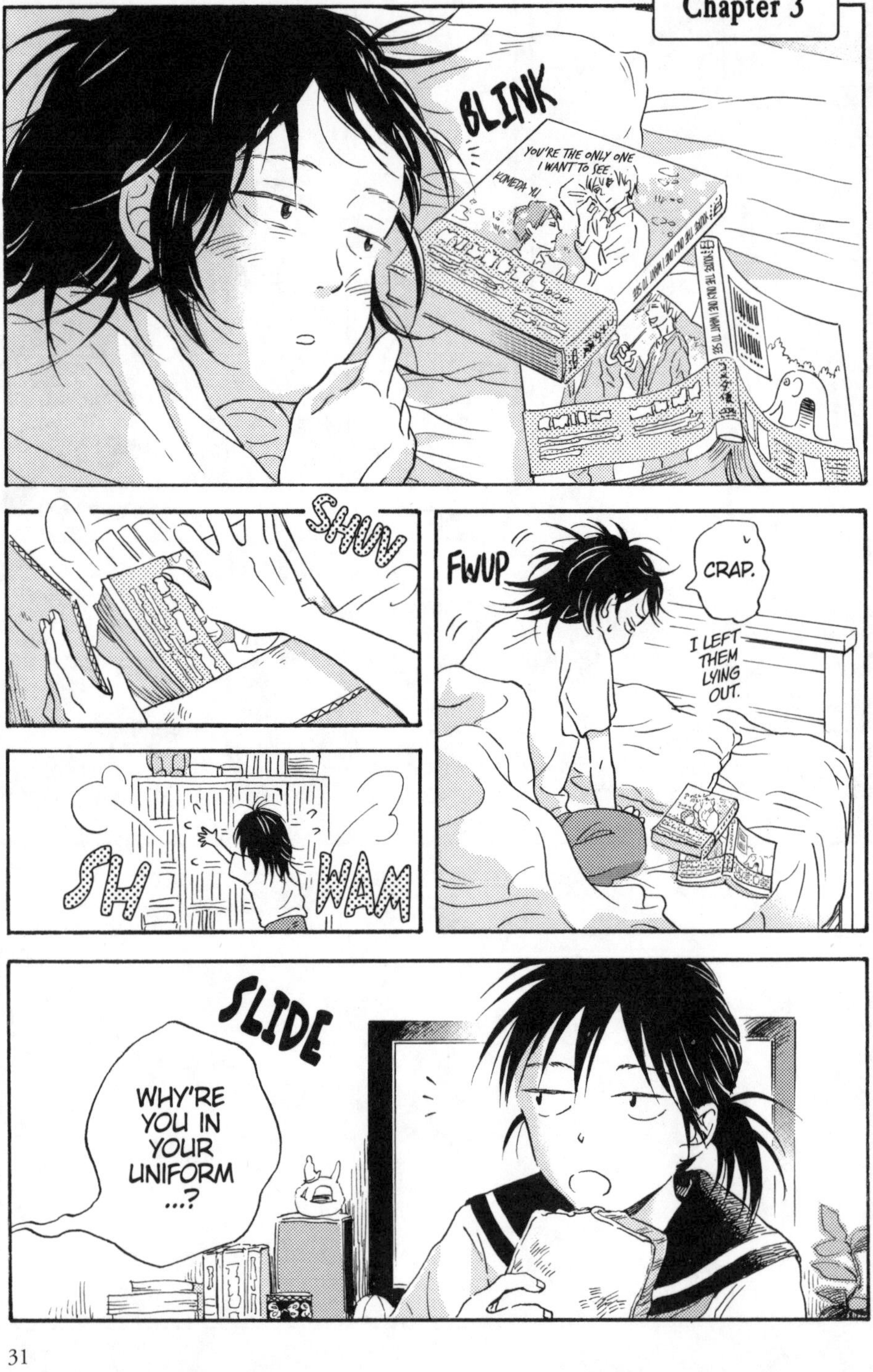
BLINK
YOU'RE THE ONLY ONE I WANT TO SEE.
KOMEDA YU
YOU'RE THE ONLY ONE I WANT TO SEE
FWUP
CRAP.
I LEFT THEM LYING OUT.
SHUN
SH
WAM
SLIDE
WHY'RE YOU IN YOUR UNIFORM ...?

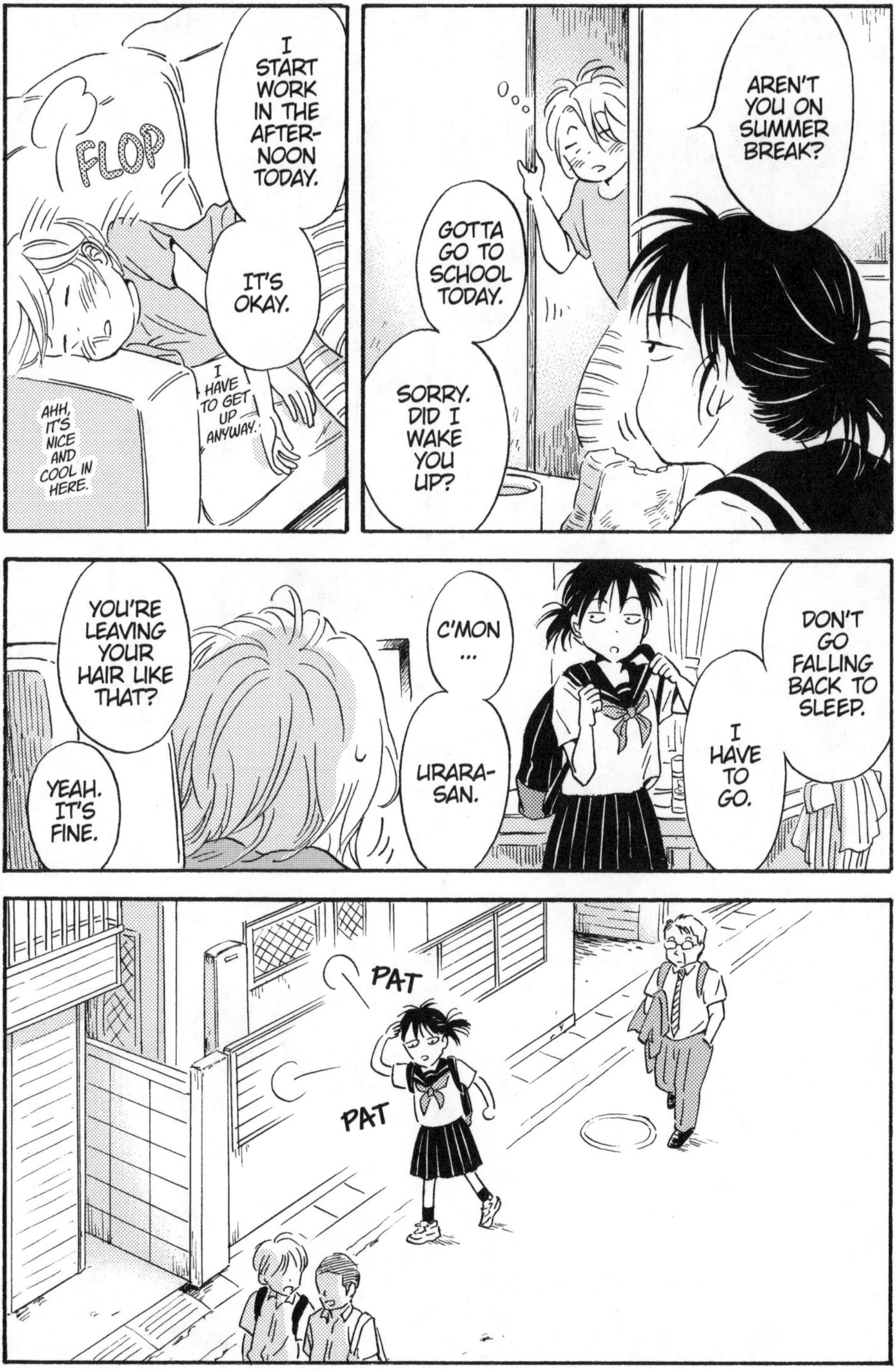
AREN'T YOU ON SUMMER BREAK?
GOTTA GO TO SCHOOL TODAY.
SORRY. DID I WAKE YOU UP?
I START WORK IN THE AFTER-NOON TODAY.
IT'S OKAY.
I HAVE TO GET UP ANYWAY.
FLOP
AHH, IT'S NICE AND COOL IN HERE.
DON'T GO FALLING BACK TO SLEEP.
I HAVE TO GO.
C'MON ...
URARA-SAN.
YOU'RE LEAVING YOUR HAIR LIKE THAT?
YEAH. IT'S FINE.
PAT
PAT

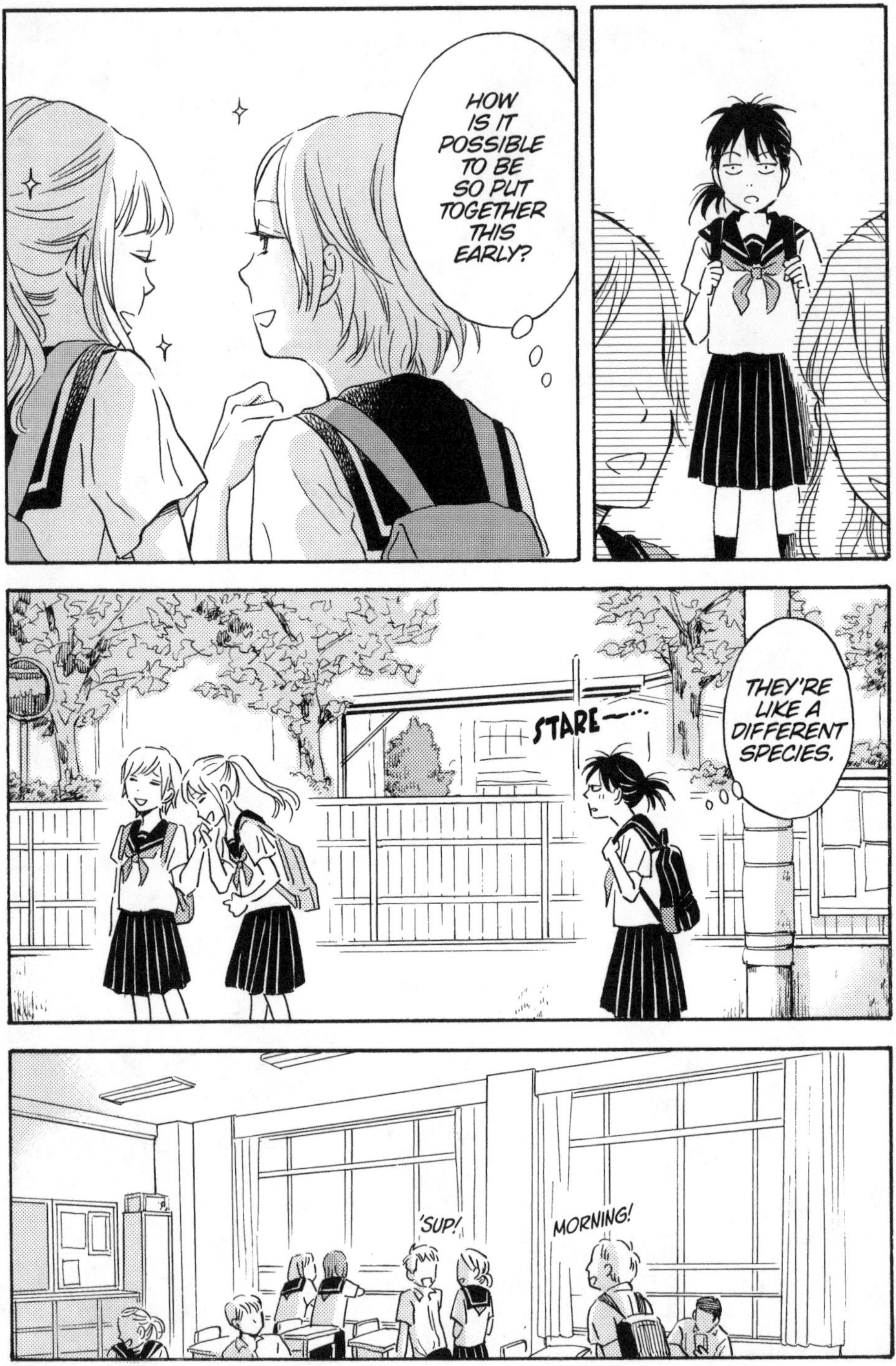
HOW IS IT POSSIBLE TO BE SO PUT TOGETHER THIS EARLY?
THEY'RE LIKE A DIFFERENT SPECIES.
STARE—...
MORNING!
'SUP!

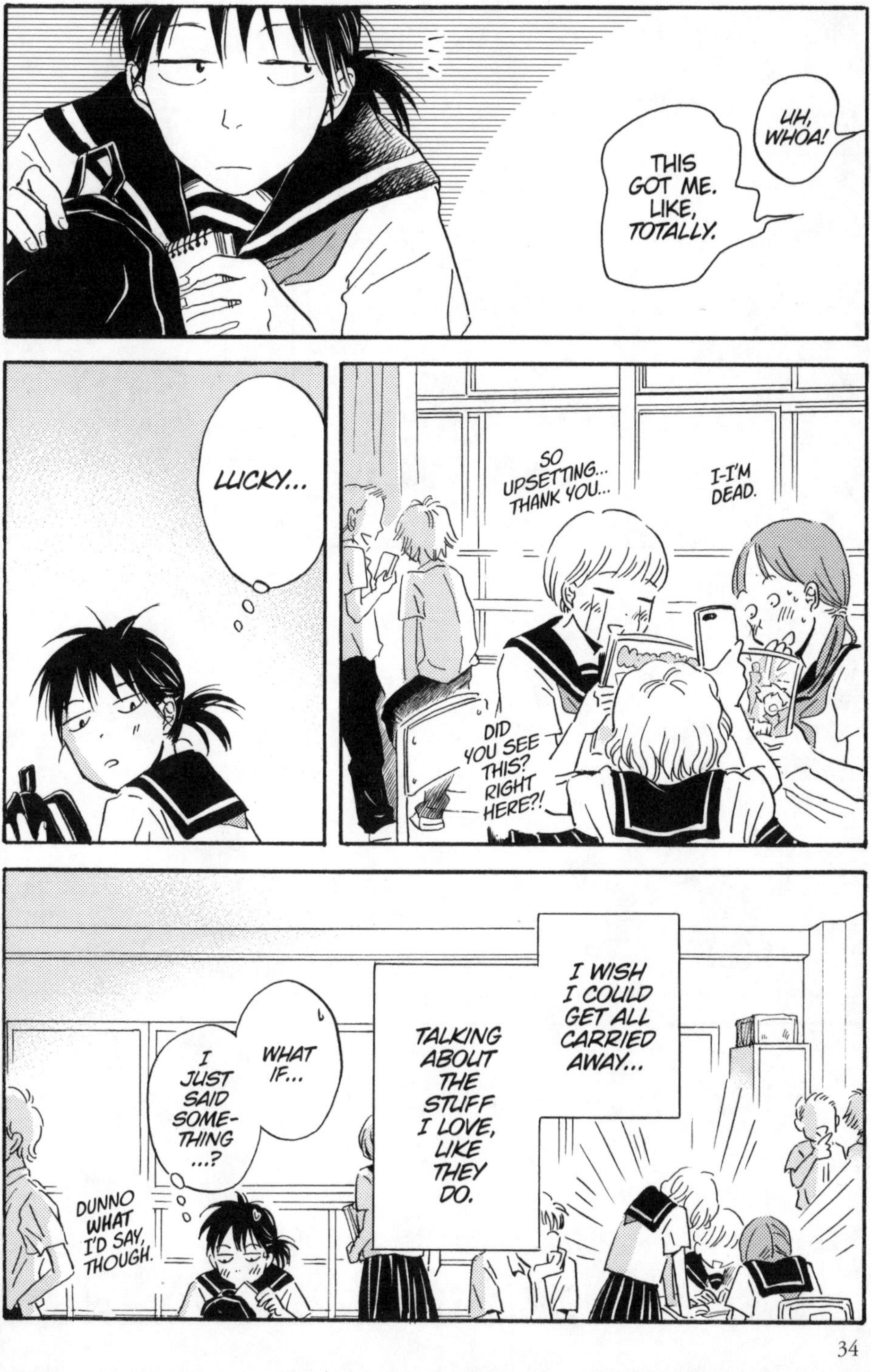
UH, WHOA!
THIS GOT ME. LIKE, TOTALLY.
I-I'M DEAD.
SO UPSETTING... THANK YOU...
DID YOU SEE THIS? RIGHT HERE?!
LUCKY...
I WISH I COULD GET ALL CARRIED AWAY...
TALKING ABOUT THE STUFF I LOVE, LIKE THEY DO.
WHAT IF... I JUST SAID SOMETHING...?
DUNNO WHAT I'D SAY, THOUGH.

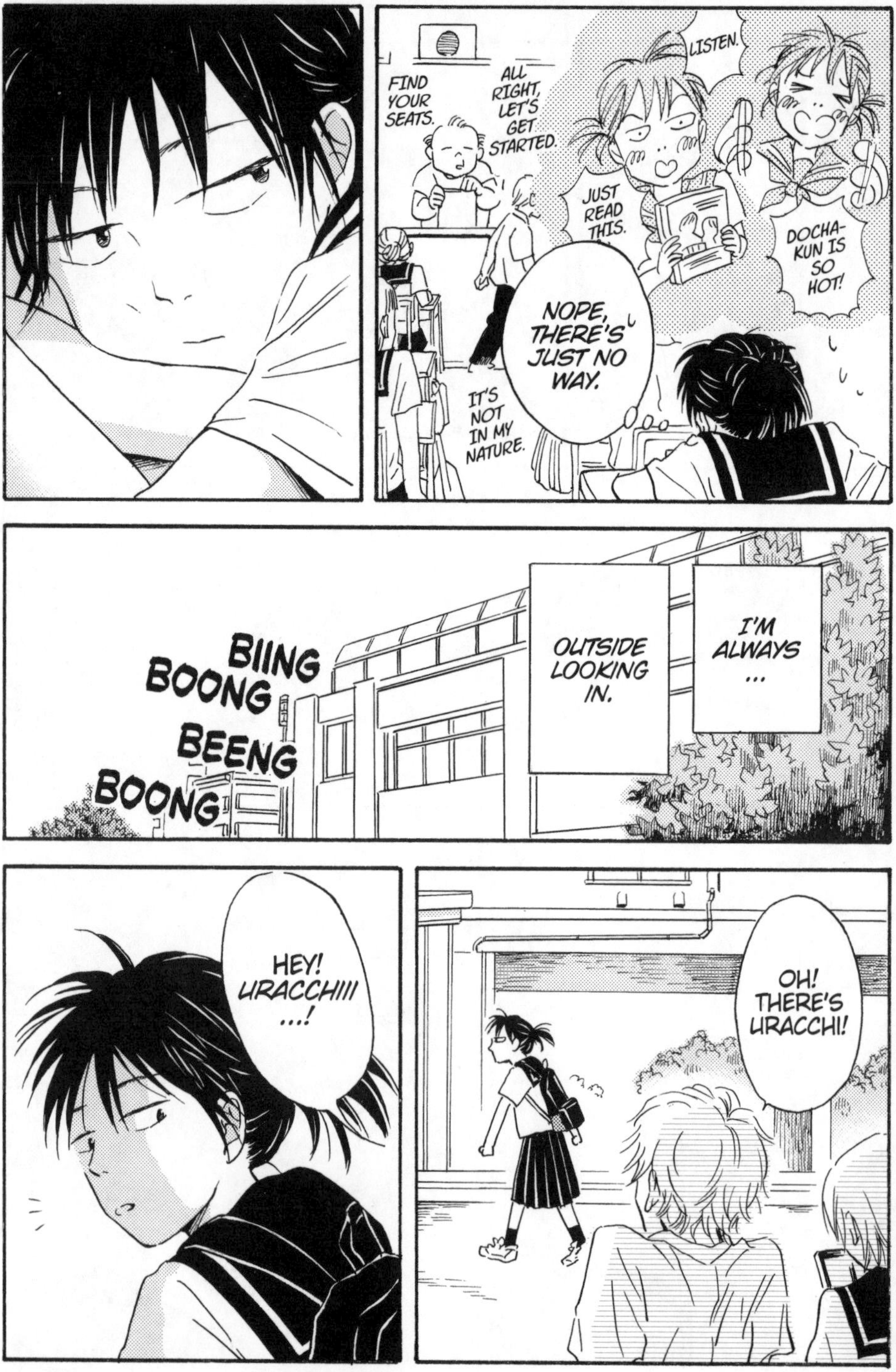
LISTEN.
DOCHA-KUN IS SO HOT!
JUST READ THIS.
ALL RIGHT, LET'S GET STARTED.
FIND YOUR SEATS.
NOPE, THERE'S JUST NO WAY.
IT'S NOT IN MY NATURE.
I'M ALWAYS ...
OUTSIDE LOOKING IN.
BIING BOONG BEENG BOONG
OH! THERE'S URACCHI!
HEY! URACCHIII ...!

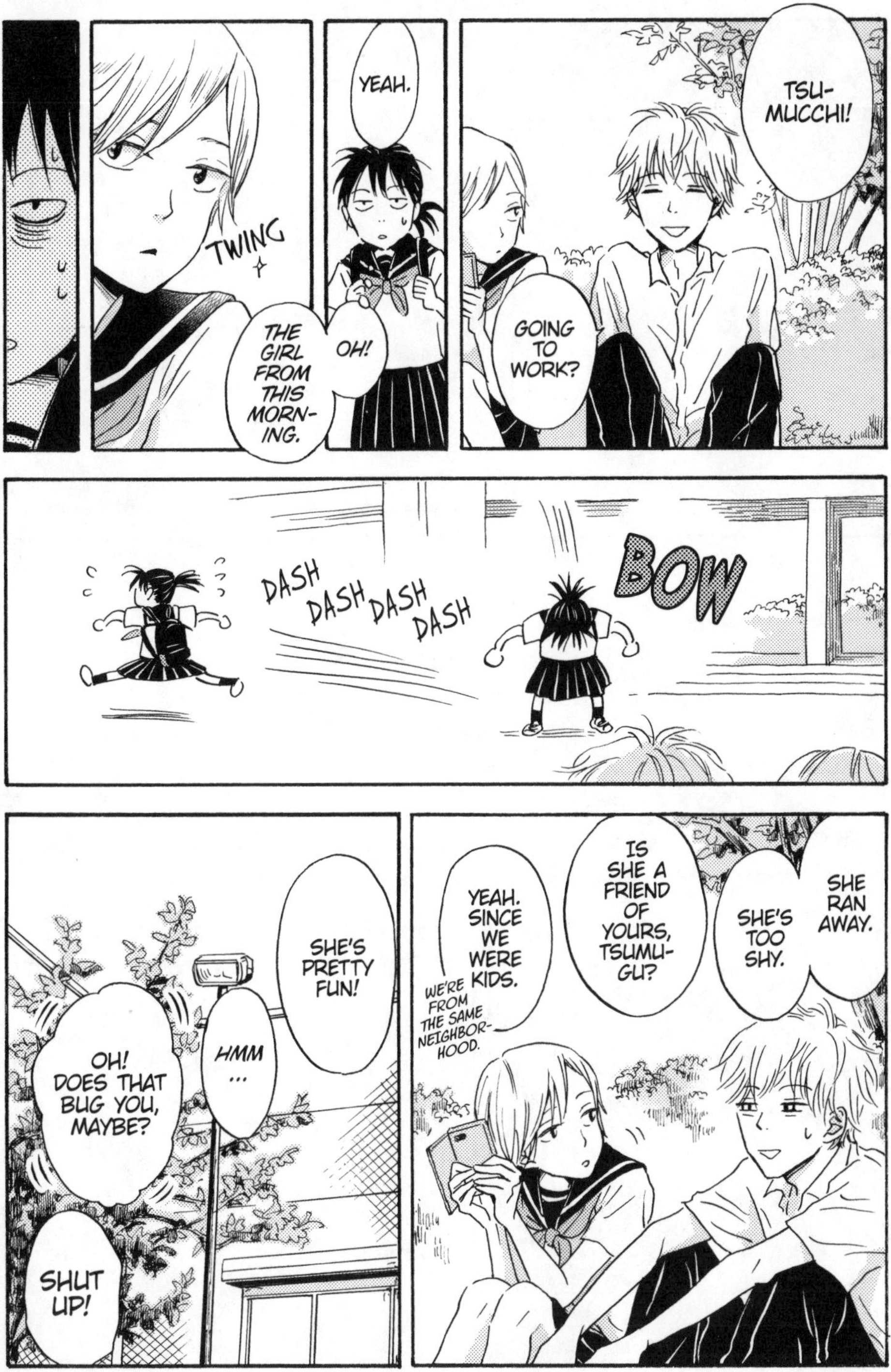
TSU-MUCCHI!
GOING TO WORK?
YEAH.
OH!
THE GIRL FROM THIS MORNING.
TWING
BOW
DASH DASH DASH DASH
SHE RAN AWAY.
SHE'S TOO SHY.
IS SHE A FRIEND OF YOURS, TSUMUGU?
YEAH. SINCE WE WERE KIDS.
WE'RE FROM THE SAME NEIGHBORHOOD.
SHE'S PRETTY FUN!
HMM...
OH! DOES THAT BUG YOU, MAYBE?
SHUT UP!

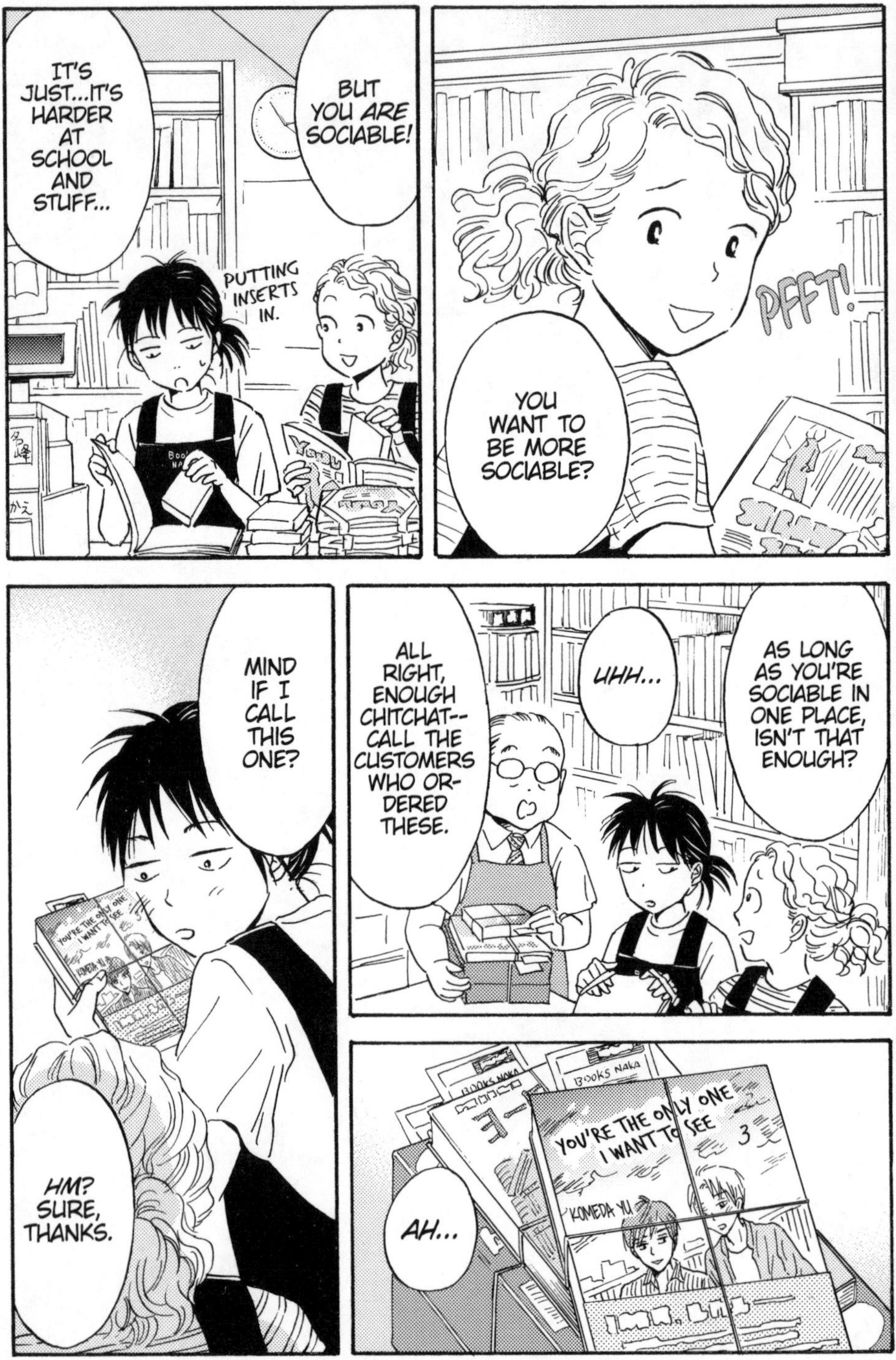
PFFT!
YOU WANT TO BE MORE SOCIABLE?
BUT YOU ARE SOCIABLE!
IT'S JUST...IT'S HARDER AT SCHOOL AND STUFF...
PUTTING INSERTS IN.
AS LONG AS YOU'RE SOCIABLE IN ONE PLACE, ISN'T THAT ENOUGH?
UHH...
ALL RIGHT, ENOUGH CHITCHAT--CALL THE CUSTOMERS WHO ORDERED THESE.
BOOKS NAKA
YOU'RE THE ONLY ONE I WANT TO SEE 3
KOMEDA YU
AH...
MIND IF I CALL THIS ONE?
HM? SURE, THANKS.

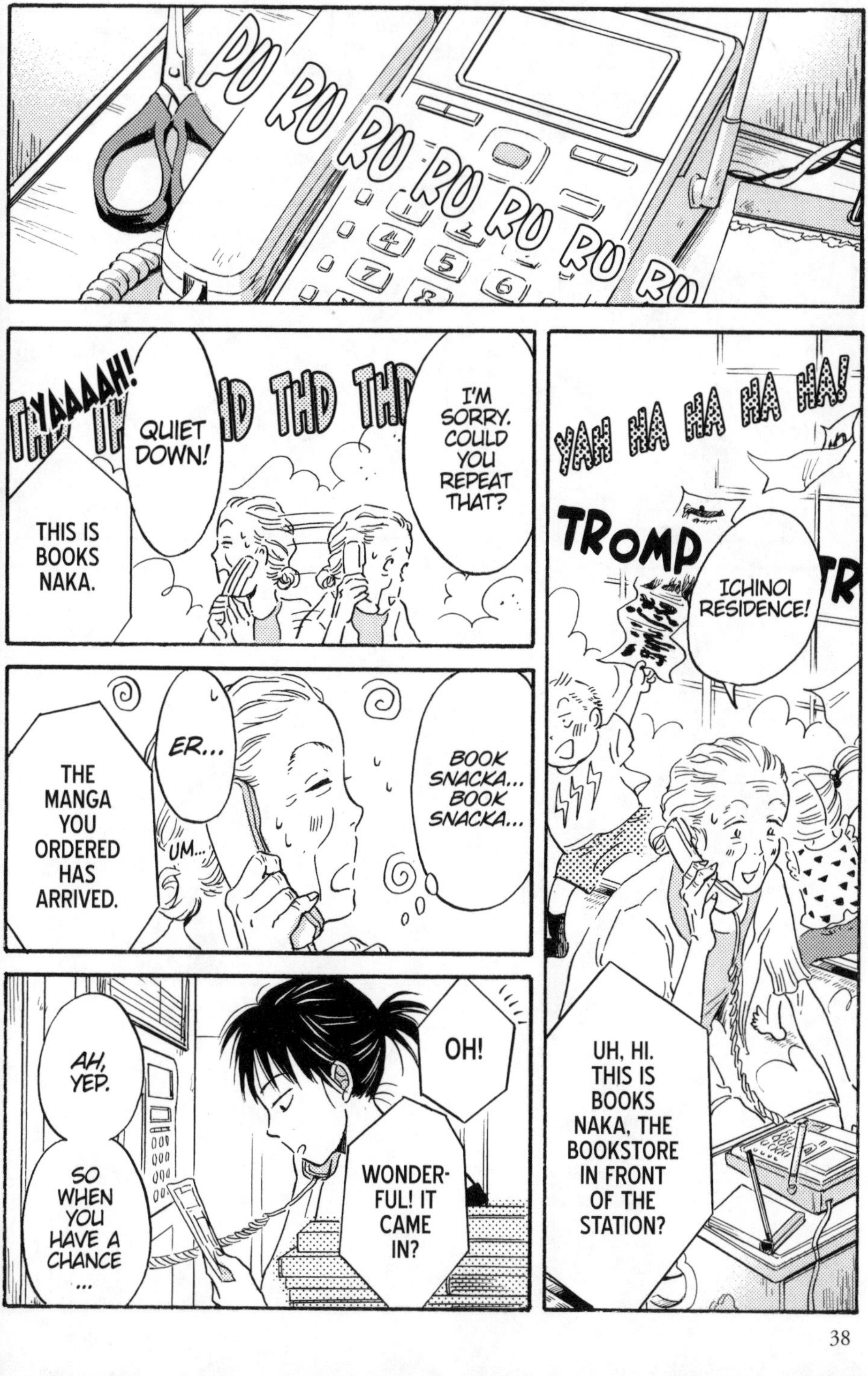
PU RU RU RU RU RU RU RU
YAH HA HA HA HA!
TROMP TR
ICHINOI RESIDENCE!
UH, HI. THIS IS BOOKS NAKA, THE BOOKSTORE IN FRONT OF THE STATION?
THD THD THD
TYAAAAH!
I'M SORRY. COULD YOU REPEAT THAT?
QUIET DOWN!
THIS IS BOOKS NAKA.
BOOK SNACKA... BOOK SNACKA...
ER...
UM...
THE MANGA YOU ORDERED HAS ARRIVED.
OH!
WONDER-FUL! IT CAME IN?
AH, YEP.
SO WHEN YOU HAVE A CHANCE ...

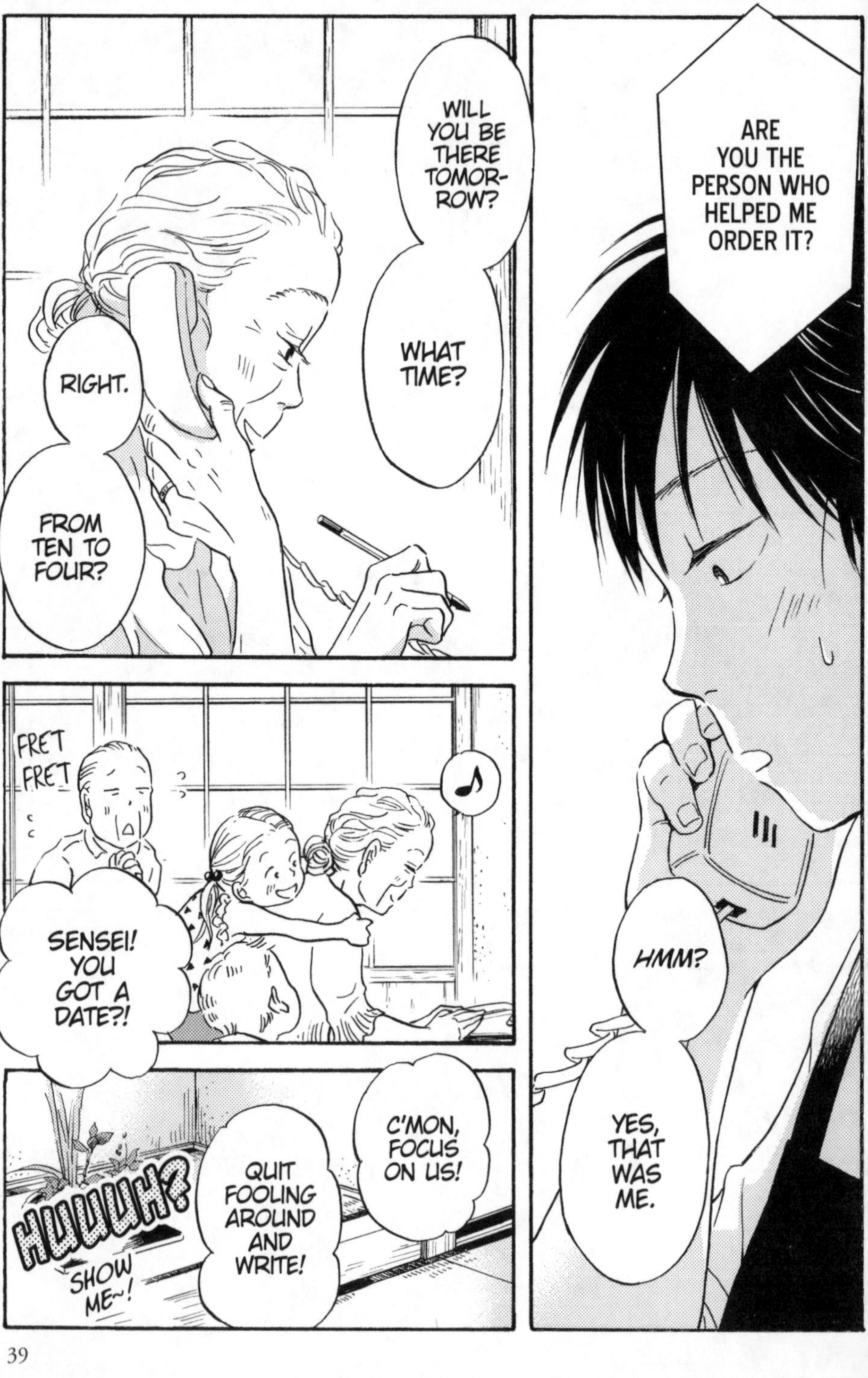
ARE YOU THE PERSON WHO HELPED ME ORDER IT?
HMM?
YES, THAT WAS ME.
WILL YOU BE THERE TOMOR-ROW?
WHAT TIME?
RIGHT.
FROM TEN TO FOUR?
FRET FRET
♪
SENSEI! YOU GOT A DATE?!
C'MON, FOCUS ON US!
QUIT FOOLING AROUND AND WRITE!
HUUUH?
SHOW ME~!

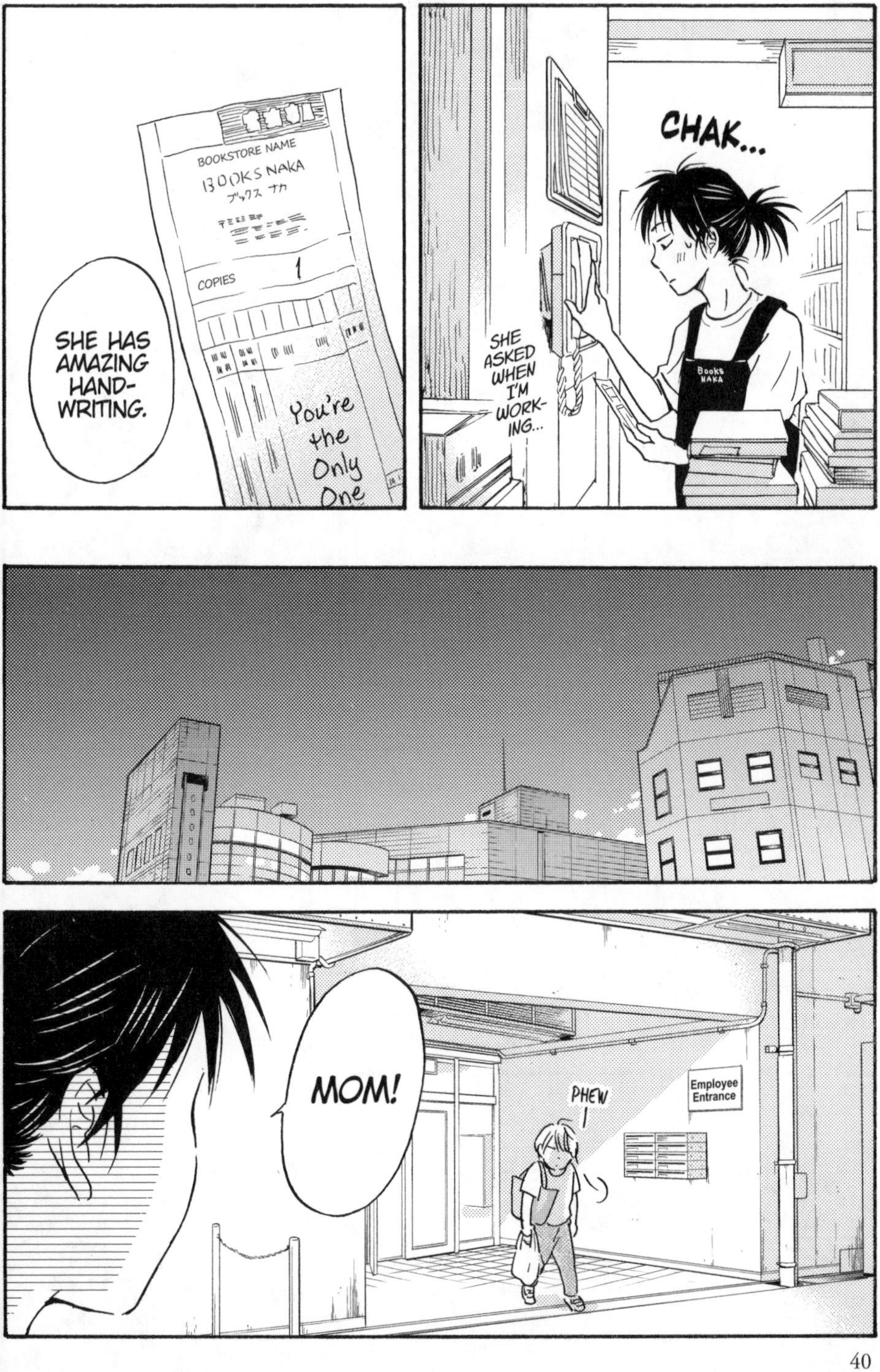
CHAK...
Books NAKA
SHE ASKED WHEN I'M WORKING...
BOOKSTORE NAME
BOOKS NAKA
ブックス ナカ
COPIES
1
You're the Only One
SHE HAS AMAZING HANDWRITING.
Employee Entrance
PHEW
MOM!

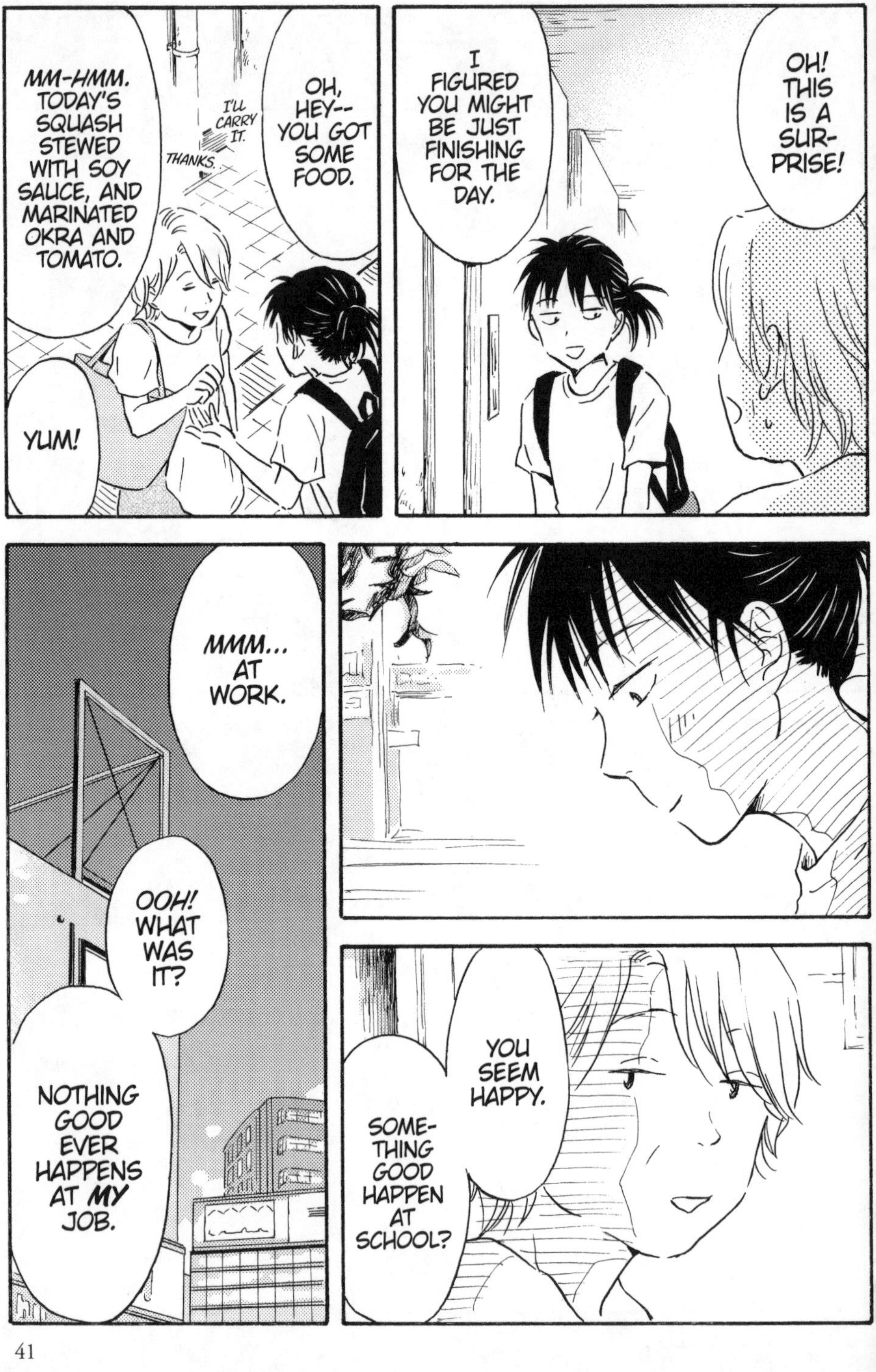
OH! THIS IS A SUR-PRISE!
I FIGURED YOU MIGHT BE JUST FINISHING FOR THE DAY.
OH, HEY-- YOU GOT SOME FOOD.
I'LL CARRY IT.
THANKS.
MM-HMM. TODAY'S SQUASH STEWED WITH SOY SAUCE, AND MARINATED OKRA AND TOMATO.
YUM!
YOU SEEM HAPPY.
SOME-THING GOOD HAPPEN AT SCHOOL?
MMM... AT WORK.
OOH! WHAT WAS IT?
NOTHING GOOD EVER HAPPENS AT MY JOB.

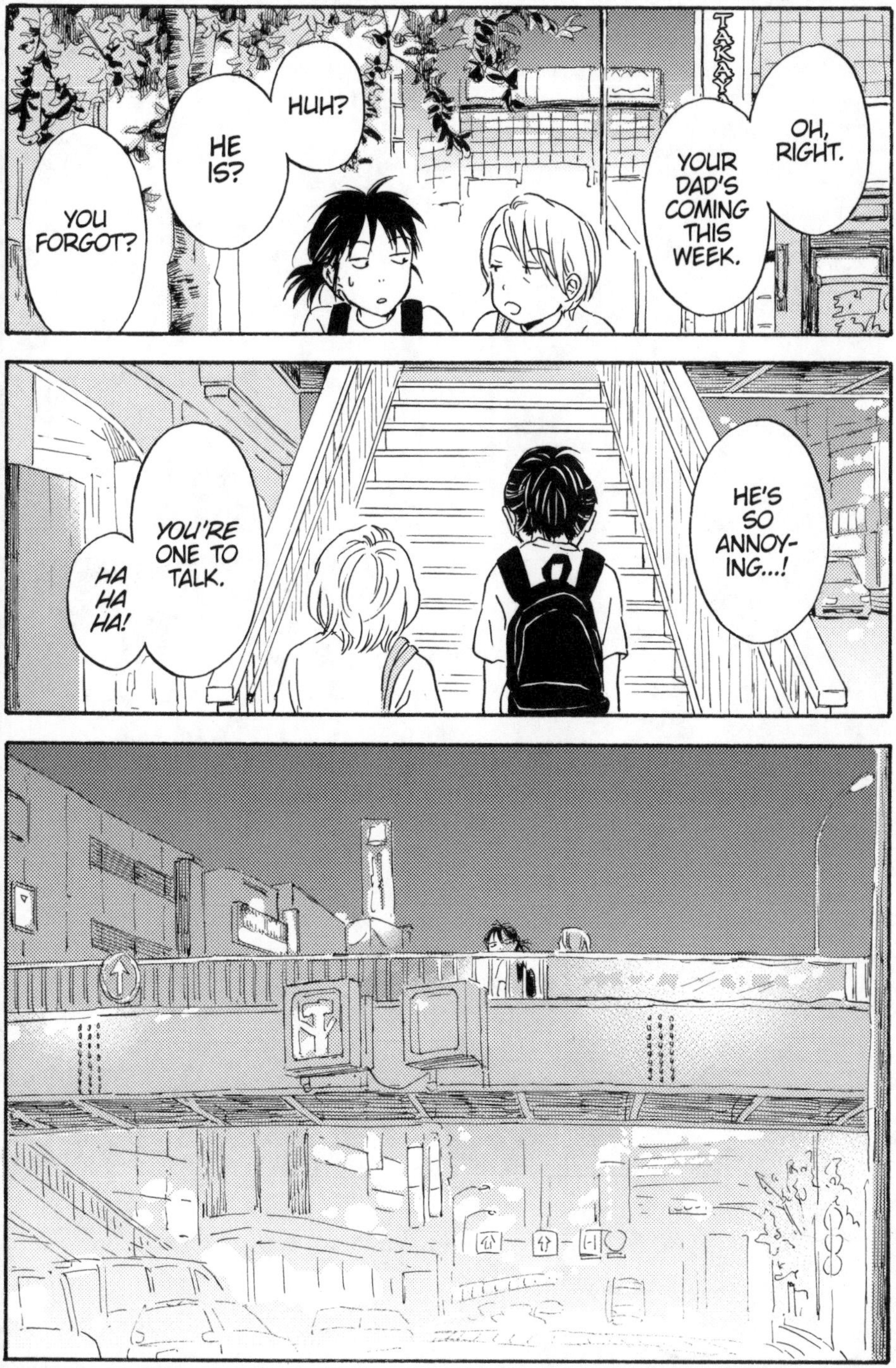
OH, RIGHT.
YOUR DAD'S COMING THIS WEEK.
HUH?
HE IS?
YOU FORGOT?
HE'S SO ANNOY-ING...!
YOU'RE ONE TO TALK.
HA HA HA!

Chapter 3/END

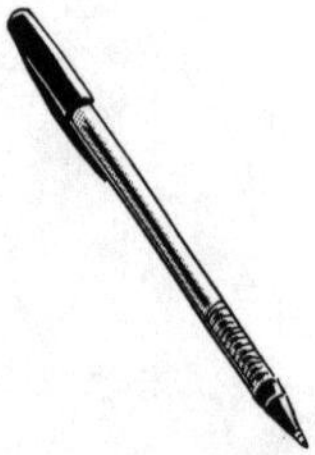

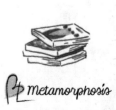
metamorphosis

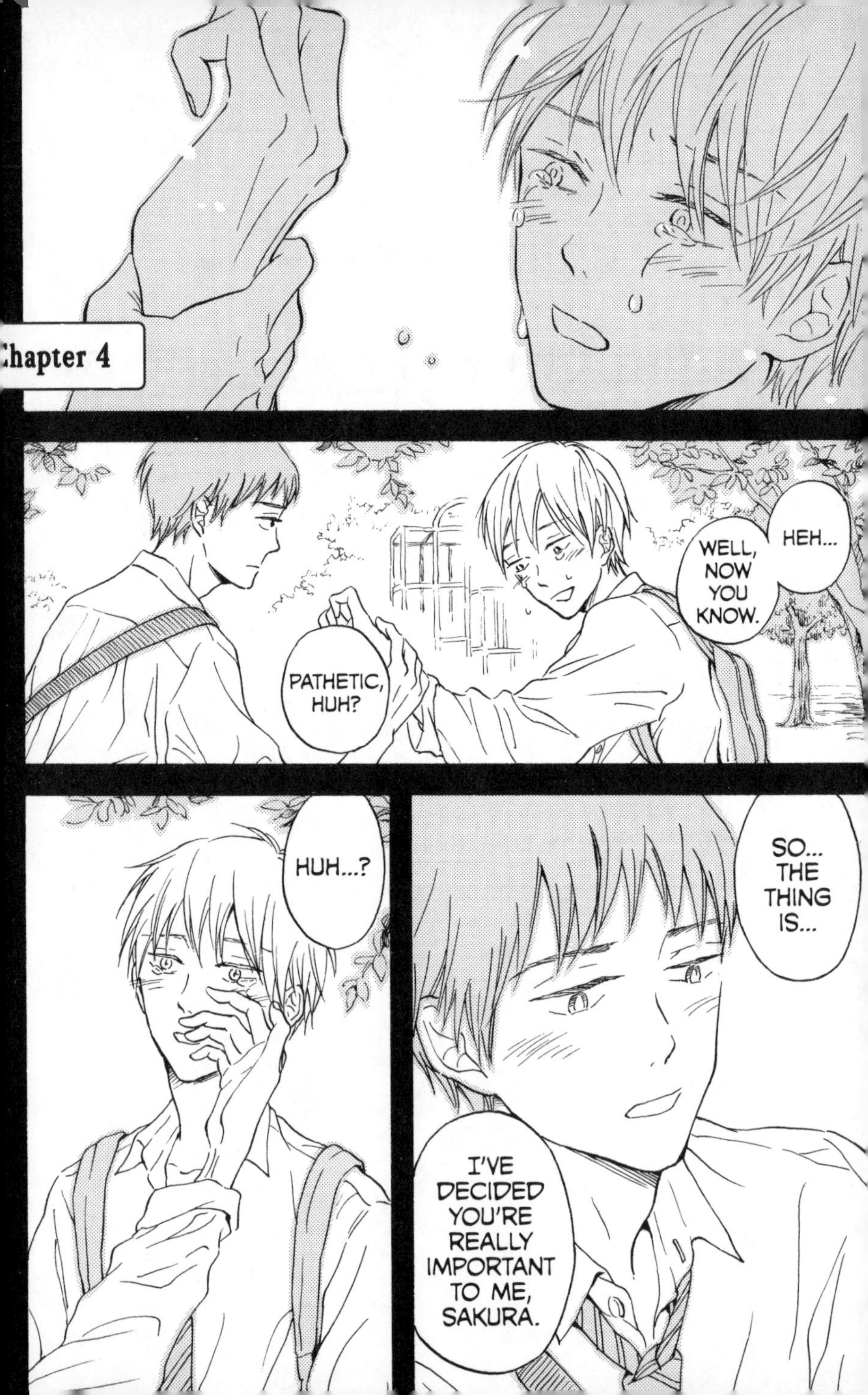
Chapter 4
HEH...
WELL, NOW YOU KNOW.
PATHETIC, HUH?
SO... THE THING IS...
I'VE DECIDED YOU'RE REALLY IMPORTANT TO ME, SAKURA.
HUH...?

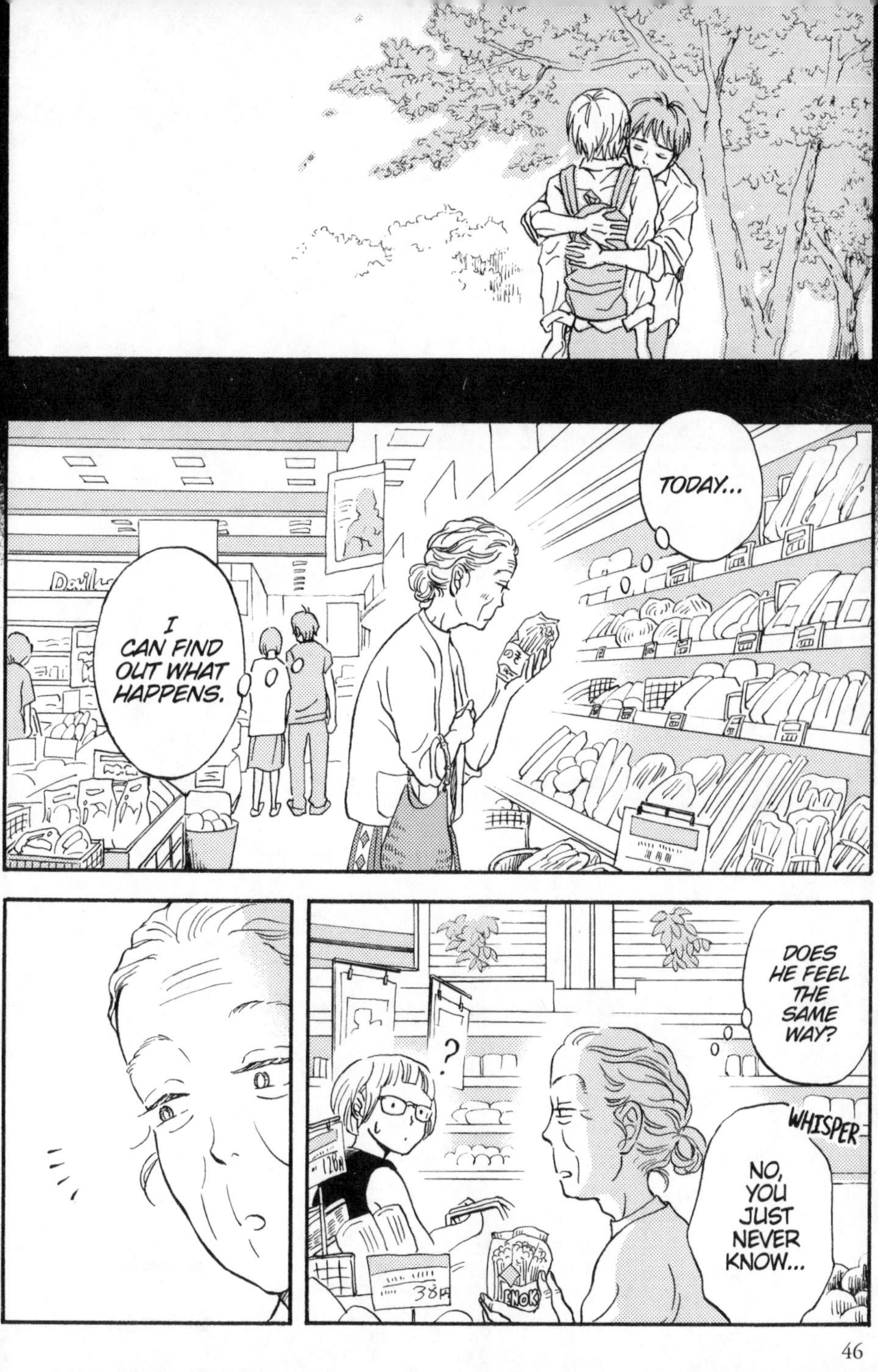
TODAY...
I CAN FIND OUT WHAT HAPPENS.
DOES HE FEEL THE SAME WAY?
WHISPER
NO, YOU JUST NEVER KNOW...

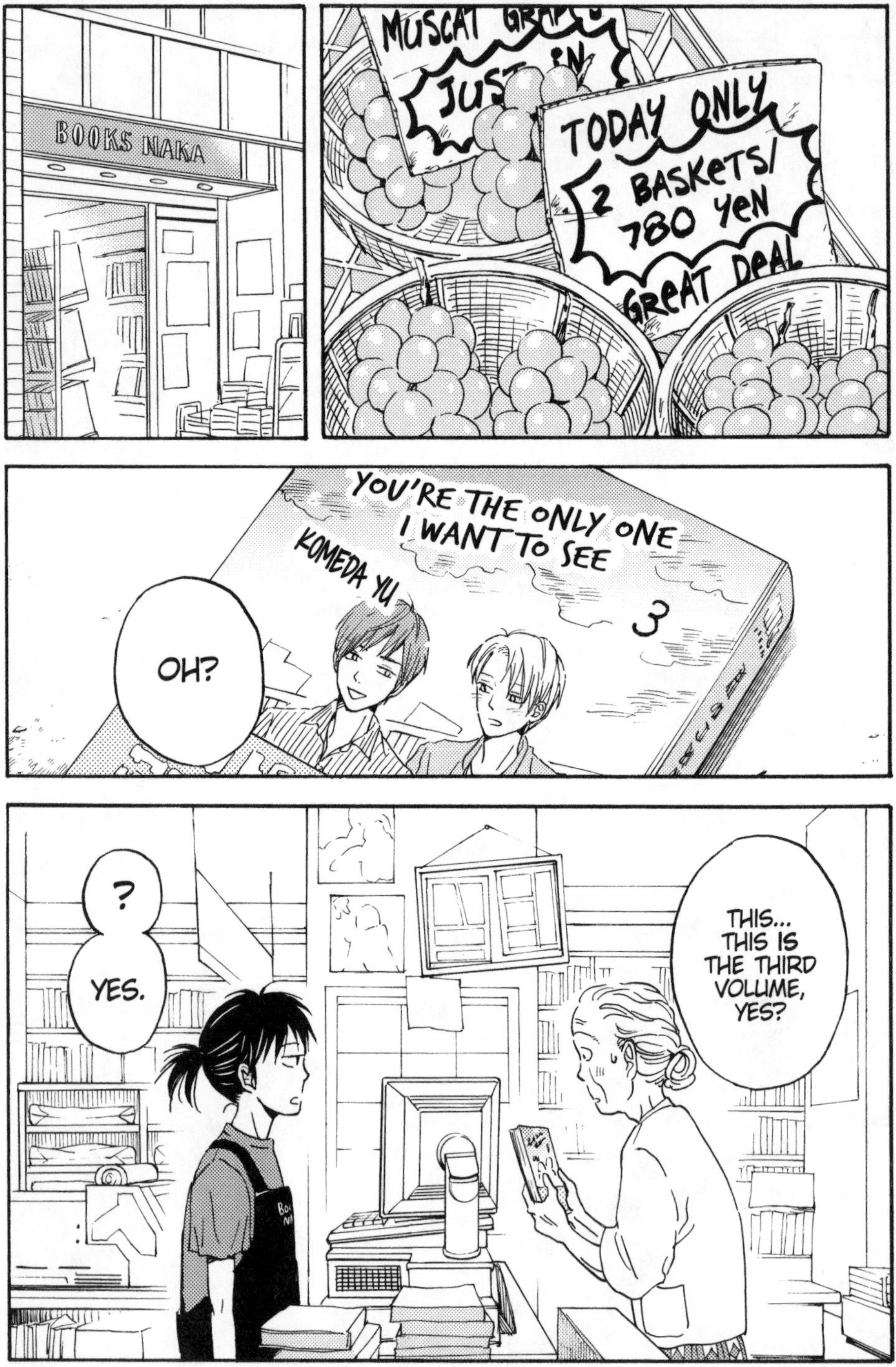
MUSCAT
TODAY ONLY
2 BASKETS/
780 YEN
GREAT DEAL
BOOKS NAKA
YOU'RE THE ONLY ONE I WANT TO SEE
KOMEDA YU
3
OH?
THIS... THIS IS THE THIRD VOLUME, YES?
?
YES.

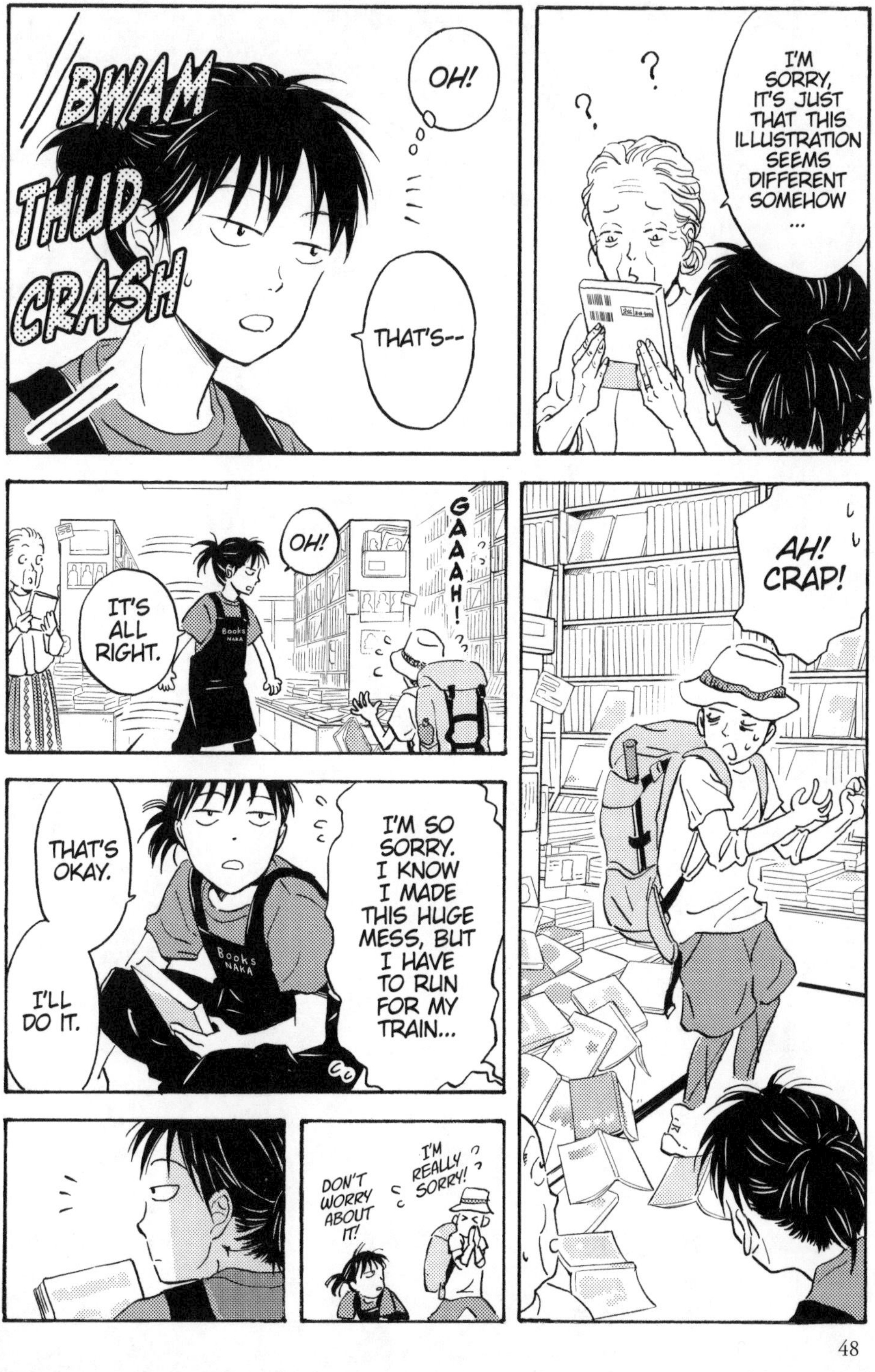
I'M SORRY, IT'S JUST THAT THIS ILLUSTRATION SEEMS DIFFERENT SOMEHOW ...
?
?
BWAM
THUD
CRASH
OH!
THAT'S--
AH! CRAP!
GAAAAH!
OH!
IT'S ALL RIGHT.
I'M SO SORRY. I KNOW I MADE THIS HUGE MESS, BUT I HAVE TO RUN FOR MY TRAIN...
THAT'S OKAY.
I'LL DO IT.
I'M REALLY SORRY!
DON'T WORRY ABOUT IT!

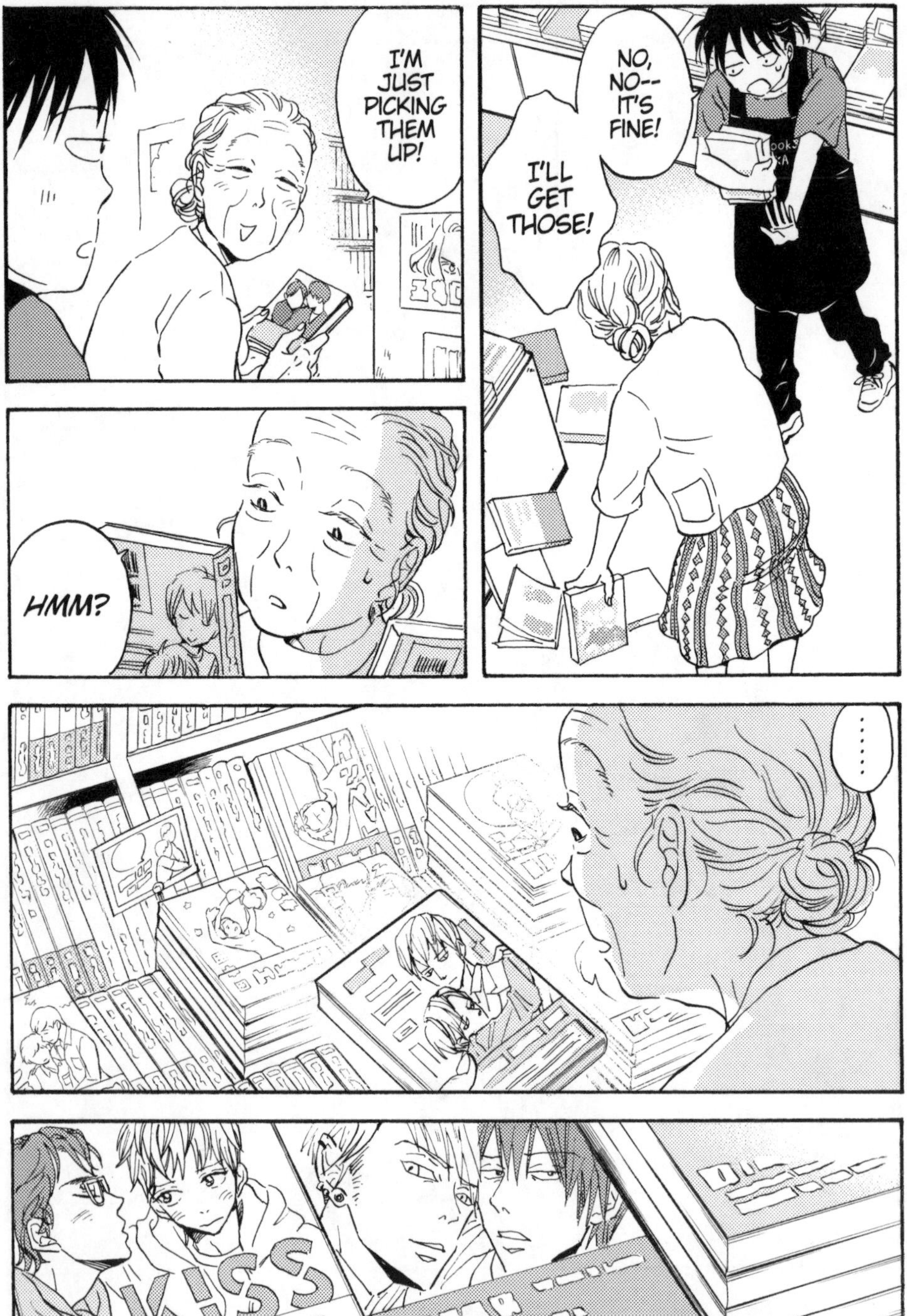
NO, NO-- IT'S FINE!
I'LL GET THOSE!
I'M JUST PICKING THEM UP!
HMM?
......
KISS

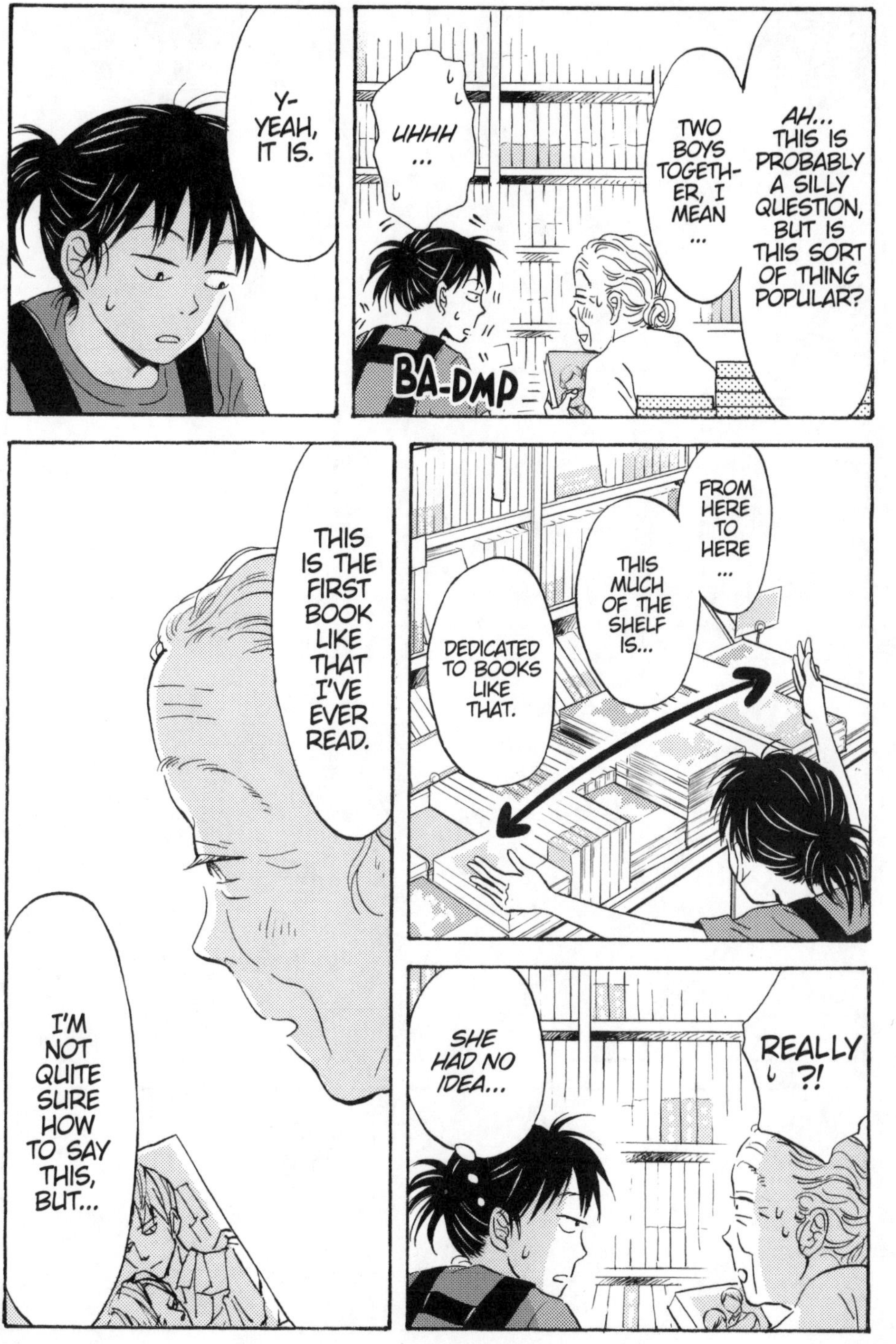
AH... THIS IS PROBABLY A SILLY QUESTION, BUT IS THIS SORT OF THING POPULAR?
TWO BOYS TOGETH-ER, I MEAN ...
UHHH ...
BA-DMP
Y-YEAH, IT IS.
FROM HERE TO HERE ...
THIS MUCH OF THE SHELF IS...
DEDICATED TO BOOKS LIKE THAT.
REALLY ?!
SHE HAD NO IDEA...
THIS IS THE FIRST BOOK LIKE THAT I'VE EVER READ.
I'M NOT QUITE SURE HOW TO SAY THIS, BUT...

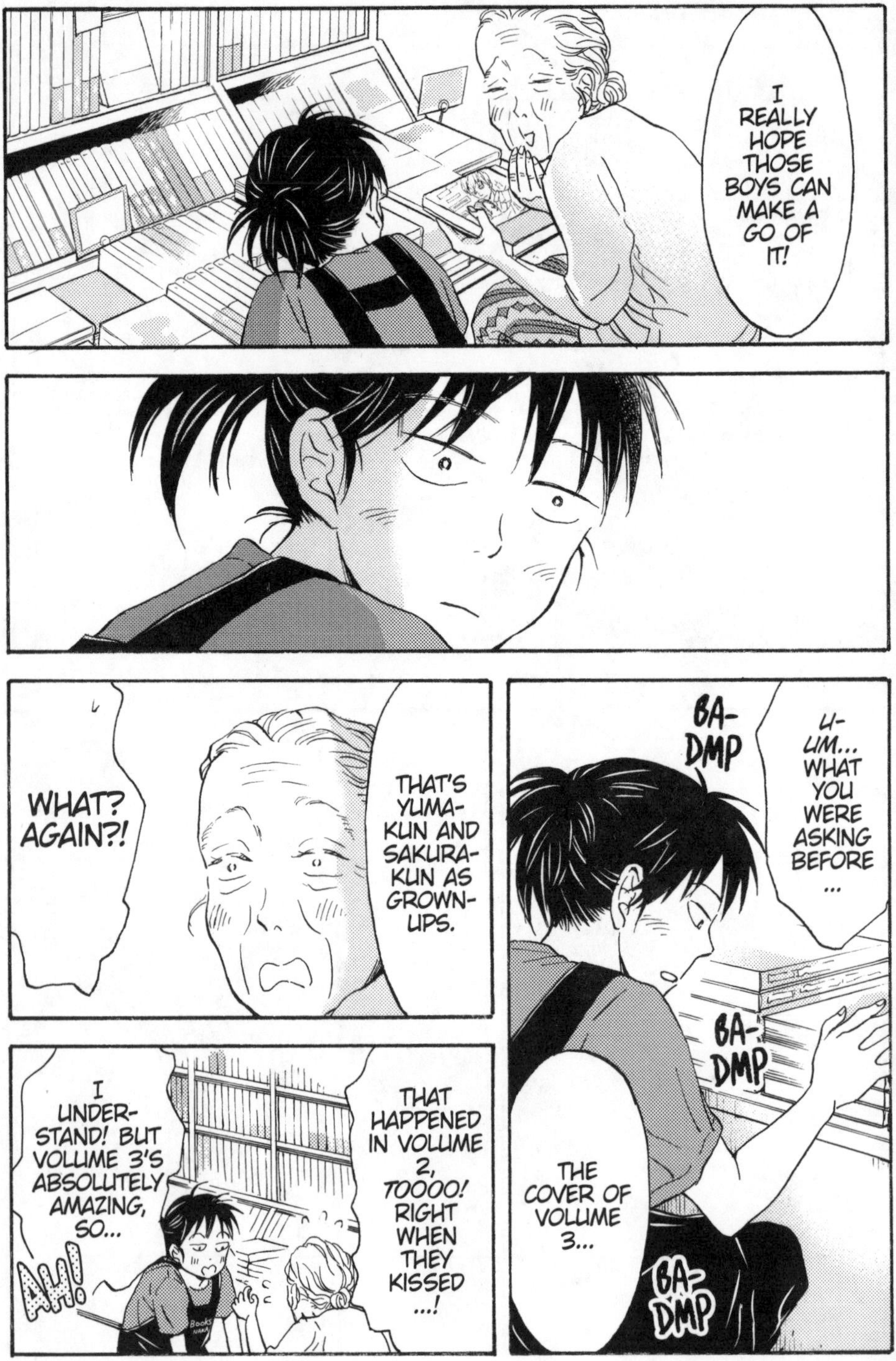
I REALLY HOPE THOSE BOYS CAN MAKE A GO OF IT!
U-UM... WHAT YOU WERE ASKING BEFORE ...
BA-DMP
BA-DMP
THE COVER OF VOLUME 3...
BA-DMP
THAT'S YUMA-KUN AND SAKURA-KUN AS GROWN-UPS.
WHAT? AGAIN?!
THAT HAPPENED IN VOLUME 2, TOOOO! RIGHT WHEN THEY KISSED ...!
I UNDER-STAND! BUT VOLUME 3'S ABSOLUTELY AMAZING, SO...
AH!

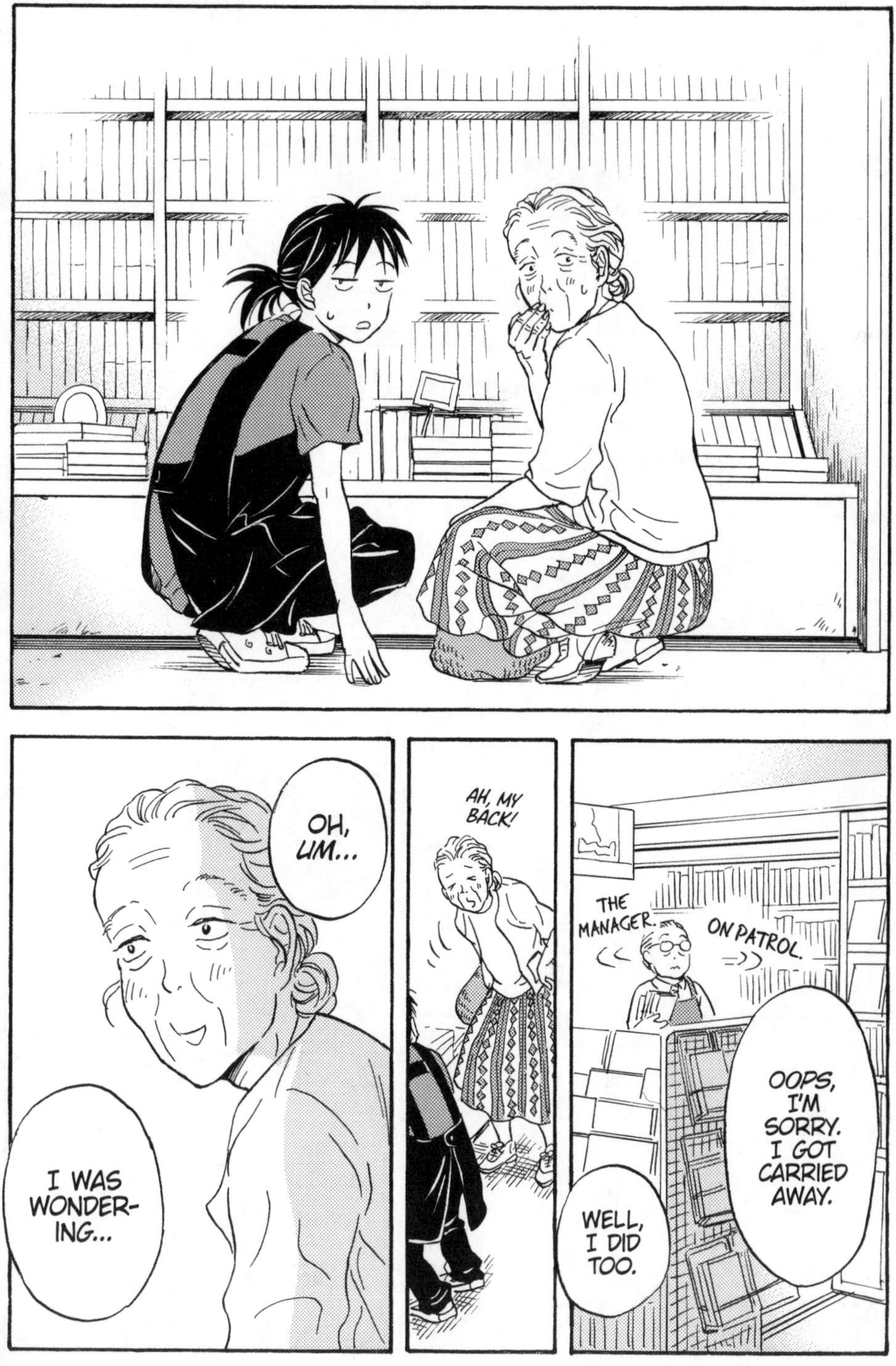
THE MANAGER.
ON PATROL.
OOPS, I'M SORRY. I GOT CARRIED AWAY.
WELL, I DID TOO.
AH, MY BACK!
OH, UM...
I WAS WONDER-ING...

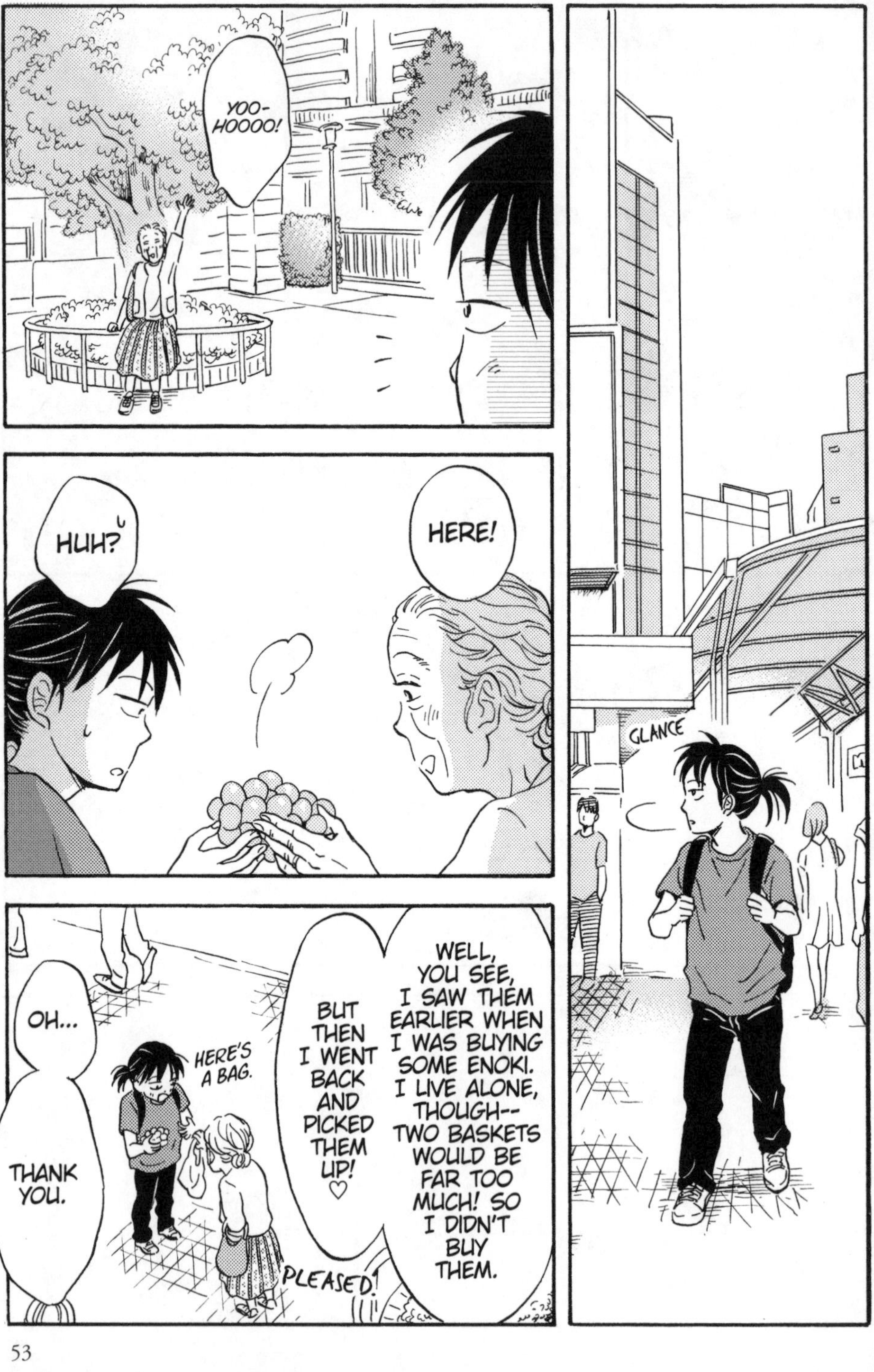
GLANCE
YOO-HOOOO!
HERE!
HUH?
WELL, YOU SEE, I SAW THEM EARLIER WHEN I WAS BUYING SOME ENOKI. I LIVE ALONE, THOUGH-- TWO BASKETS WOULD BE FAR TOO MUCH! SO I DIDN'T BUY THEM.
BUT THEN I WENT BACK AND PICKED THEM UP! ♡
PLEASED
HERE'S A BAG.
OH...
THANK YOU.

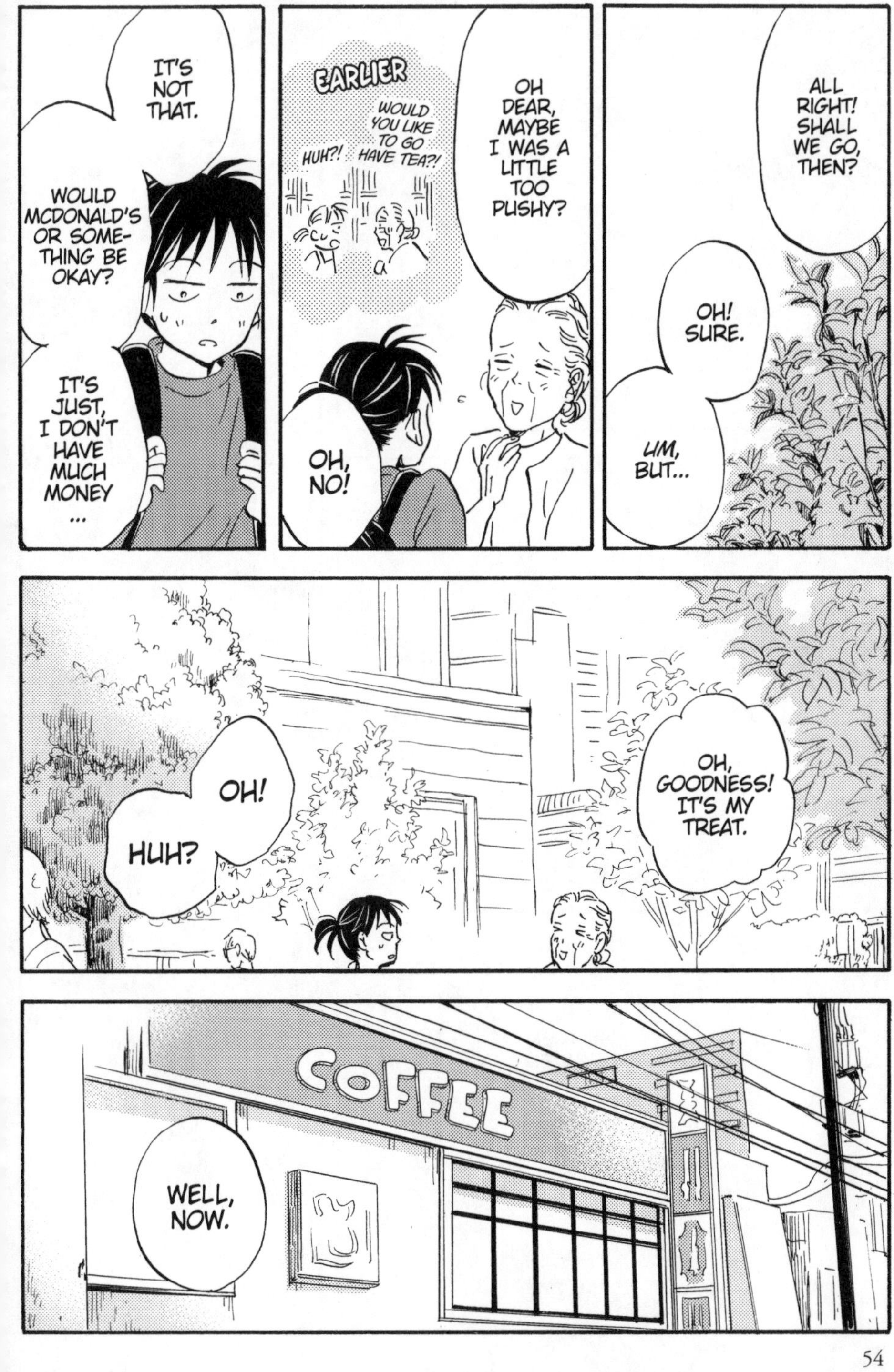
ALL RIGHT! SHALL WE GO, THEN?
OH! SURE.
UM, BUT...
OH DEAR, MAYBE I WAS A LITTLE TOO PUSHY?
OH, NO!
EARLIER
WOULD YOU LIKE TO GO HAVE TEA?!
HUH?!
IT'S NOT THAT.
WOULD MCDONALD'S OR SOMETHING BE OKAY?
IT'S JUST, I DON'T HAVE MUCH MONEY ...
OH, GOODNESS! IT'S MY TREAT.
OH!
HUH?
COFFEE
WELL, NOW.

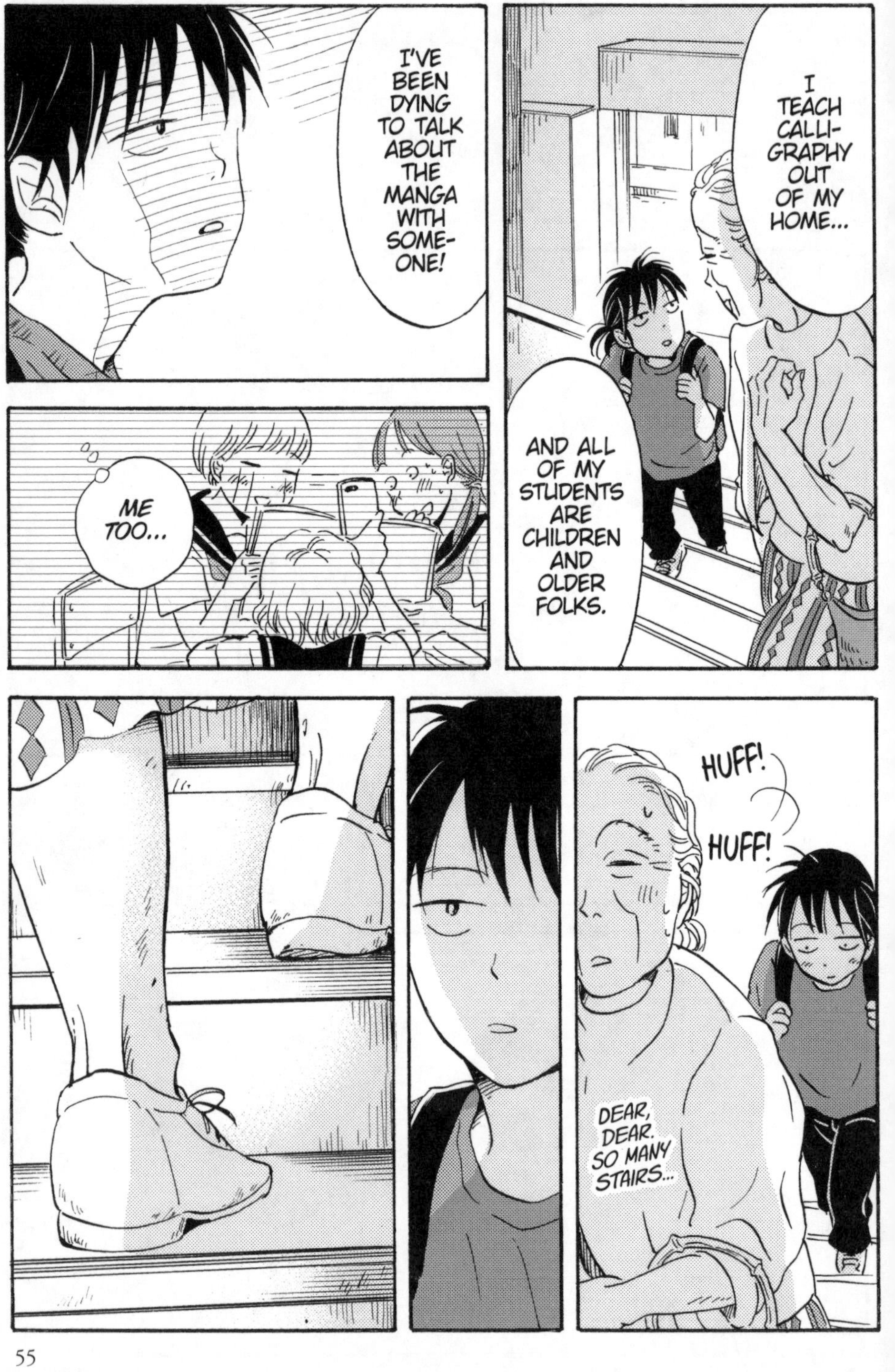
I TEACH CALLI-GRAPHY OUT OF MY HOME...
AND ALL OF MY STUDENTS ARE CHILDREN AND OLDER FOLKS.
I'VE BEEN DYING TO TALK ABOUT THE MANGA WITH SOME-ONE!
ME TOO...
HUFF!
HUFF!
DEAR, DEAR. SO MANY STAIRS...

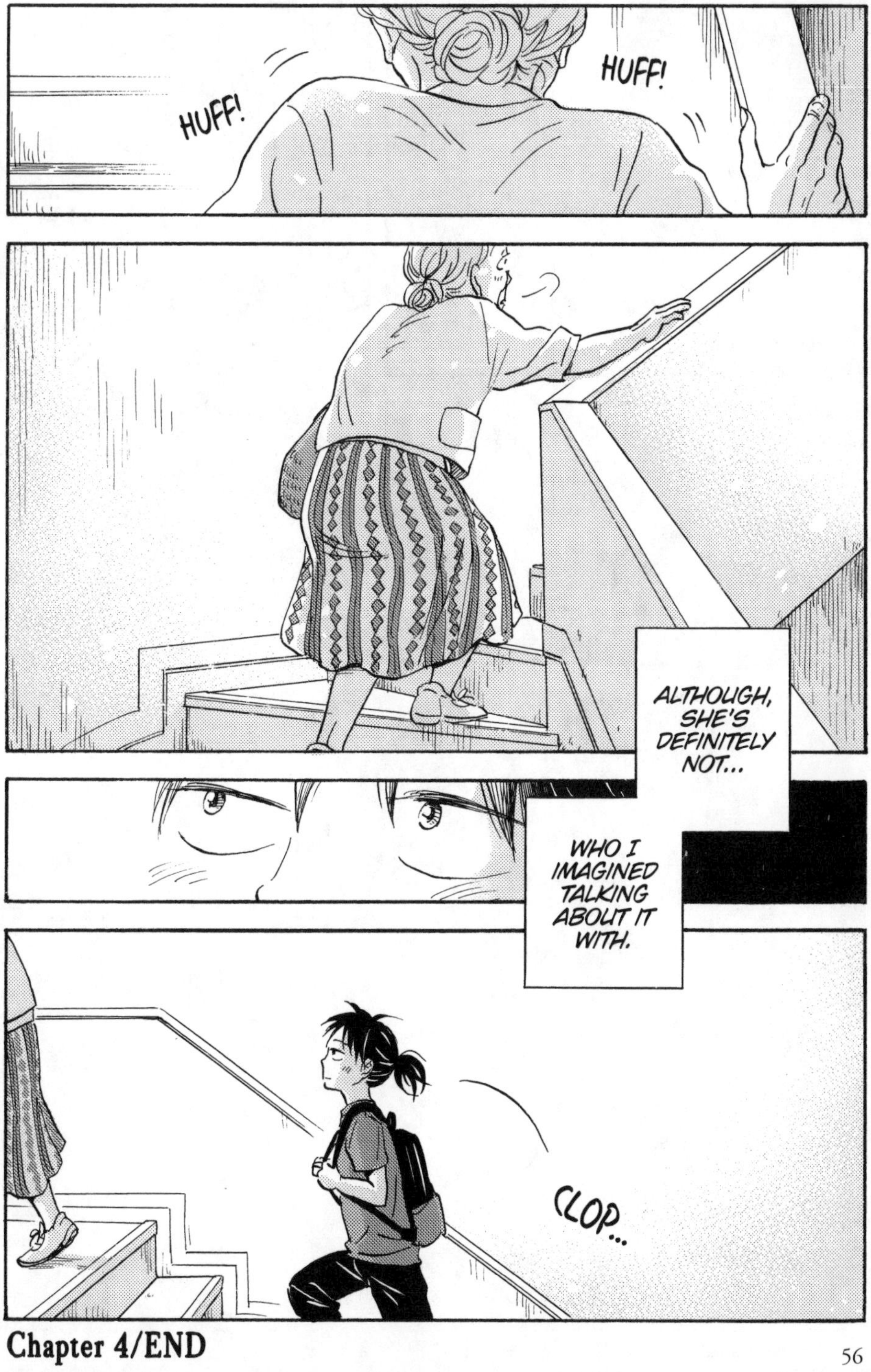
HUFF!
HUFF!
ALTHOUGH, SHE'S DEFINITELY NOT...
WHO I IMAGINED TALKING ABOUT IT WITH.
CLOP...

Chapter 4/END

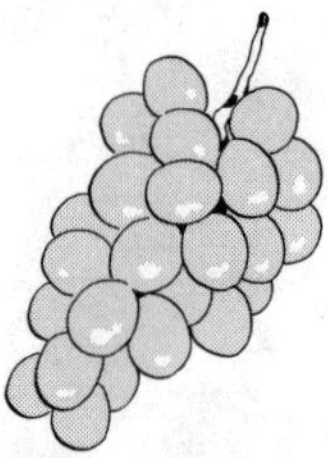

Chapter 5

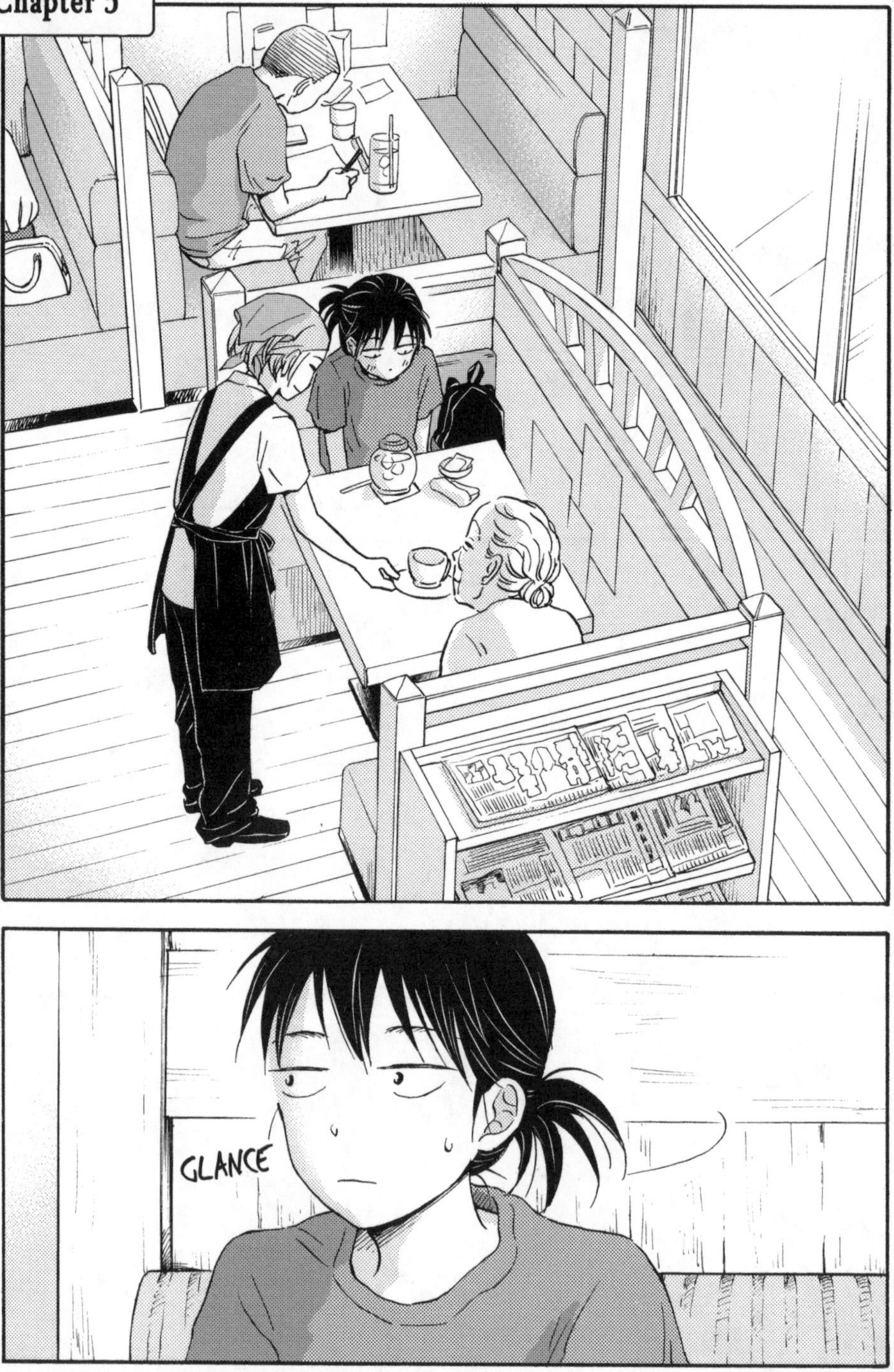
GLANCE

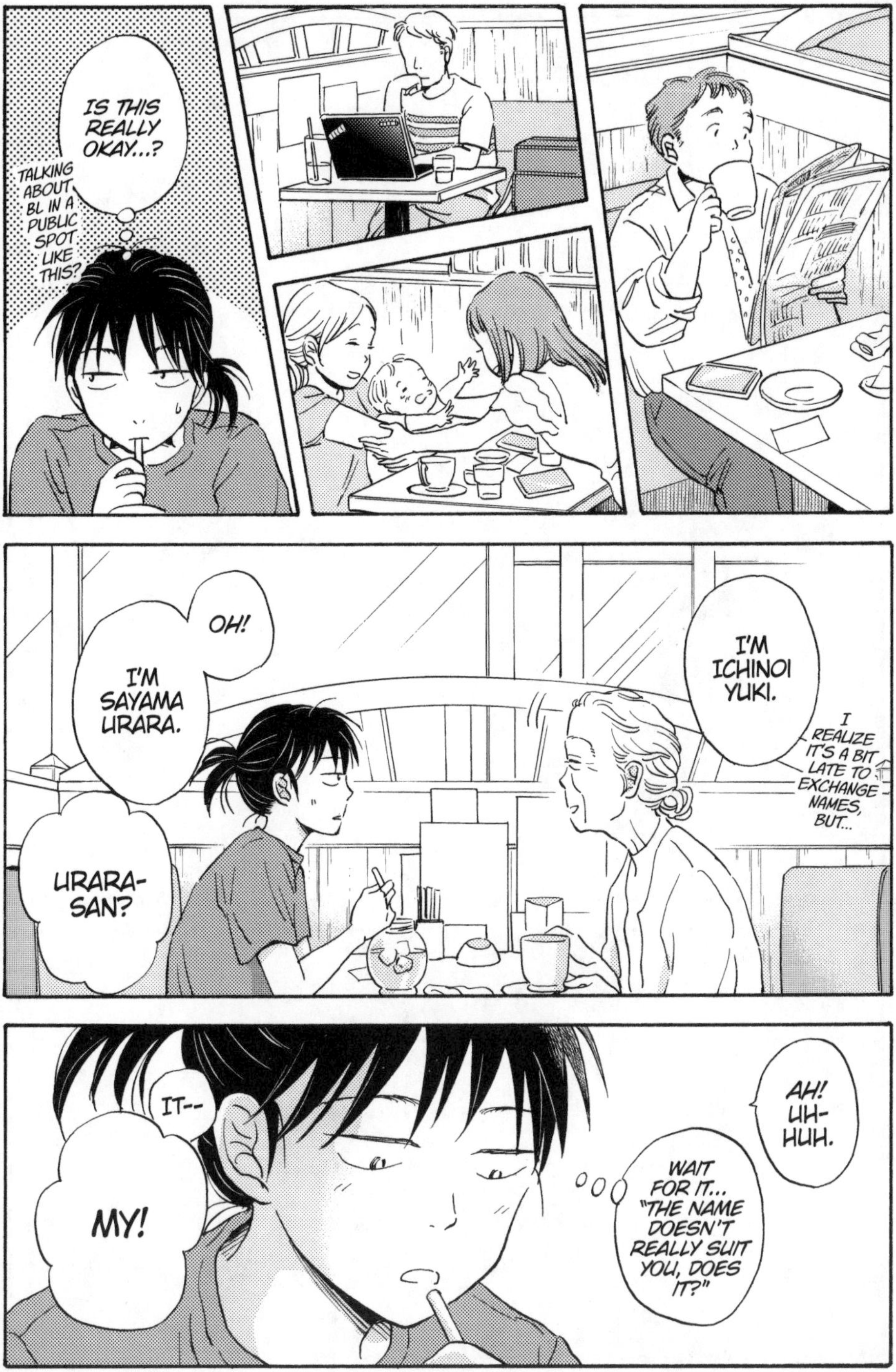
IS THIS REALLY OKAY...?
TALKING ABOUT BL IN A PUBLIC SPOT LIKE THIS?
I'M ICHINOI YUKI.
I REALIZE IT'S A BIT LATE TO EXCHANGE NAMES, BUT...
OH!
I'M SAYAMA URARA.
URARA-SAN?
AH! UH-HUH.
WAIT FOR IT... "THE NAME DOESN'T REALLY SUIT YOU, DOES IT?"
IT--
MY!

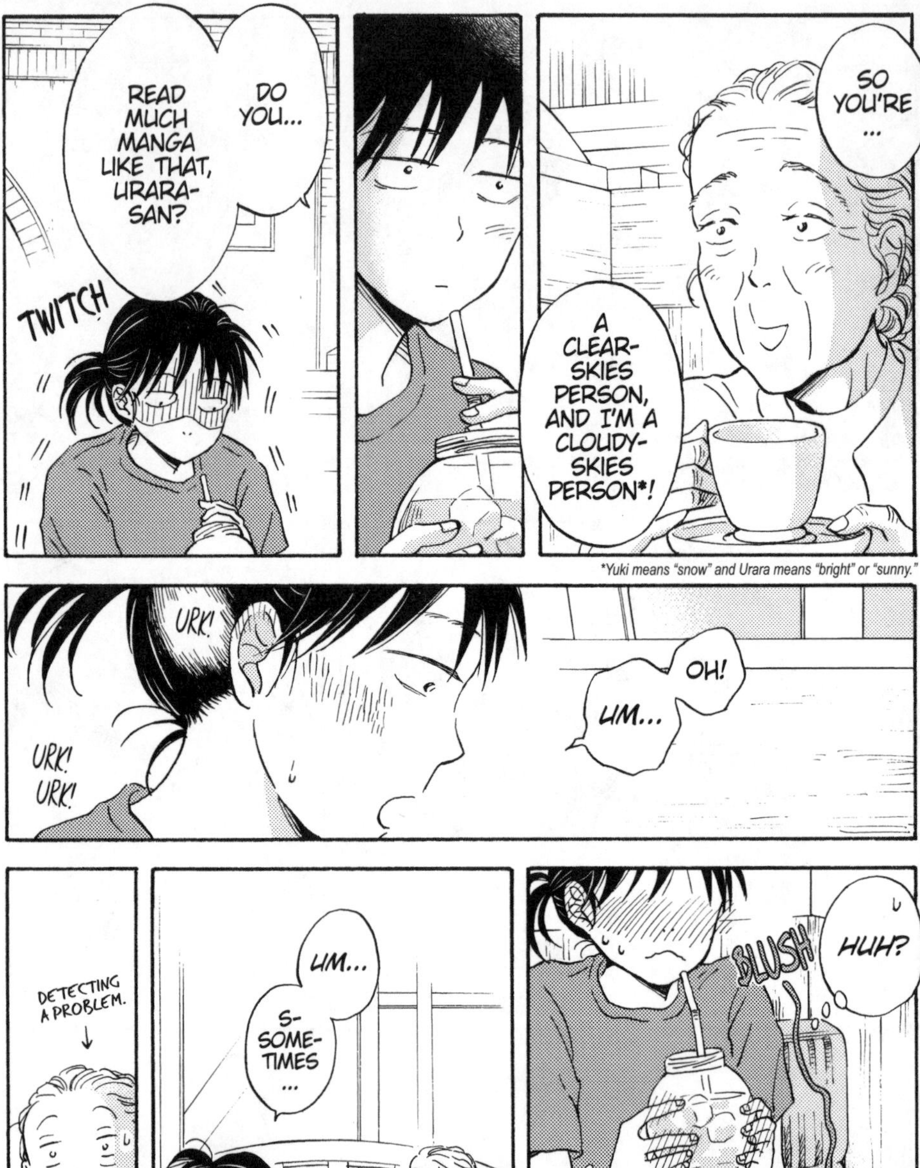
SO YOU'RE ...
A CLEAR-SKIES PERSON, AND I'M A CLOUDY-SKIES PERSON*!
DO YOU...
READ MUCH MANGA LIKE THAT, URARA-SAN?
TWITCH
OH!
UM...
URK!
URK! URK!
HUH?
BLUSH
WHAT THE...
UM...
S-SOMETIMES ...
DETECTING A PROBLEM.
...

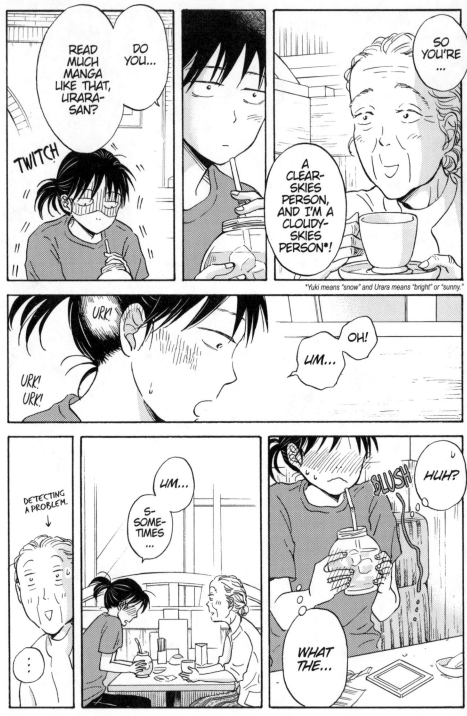

*Yuki means "snow" and Urara means "bright" or "sunny."

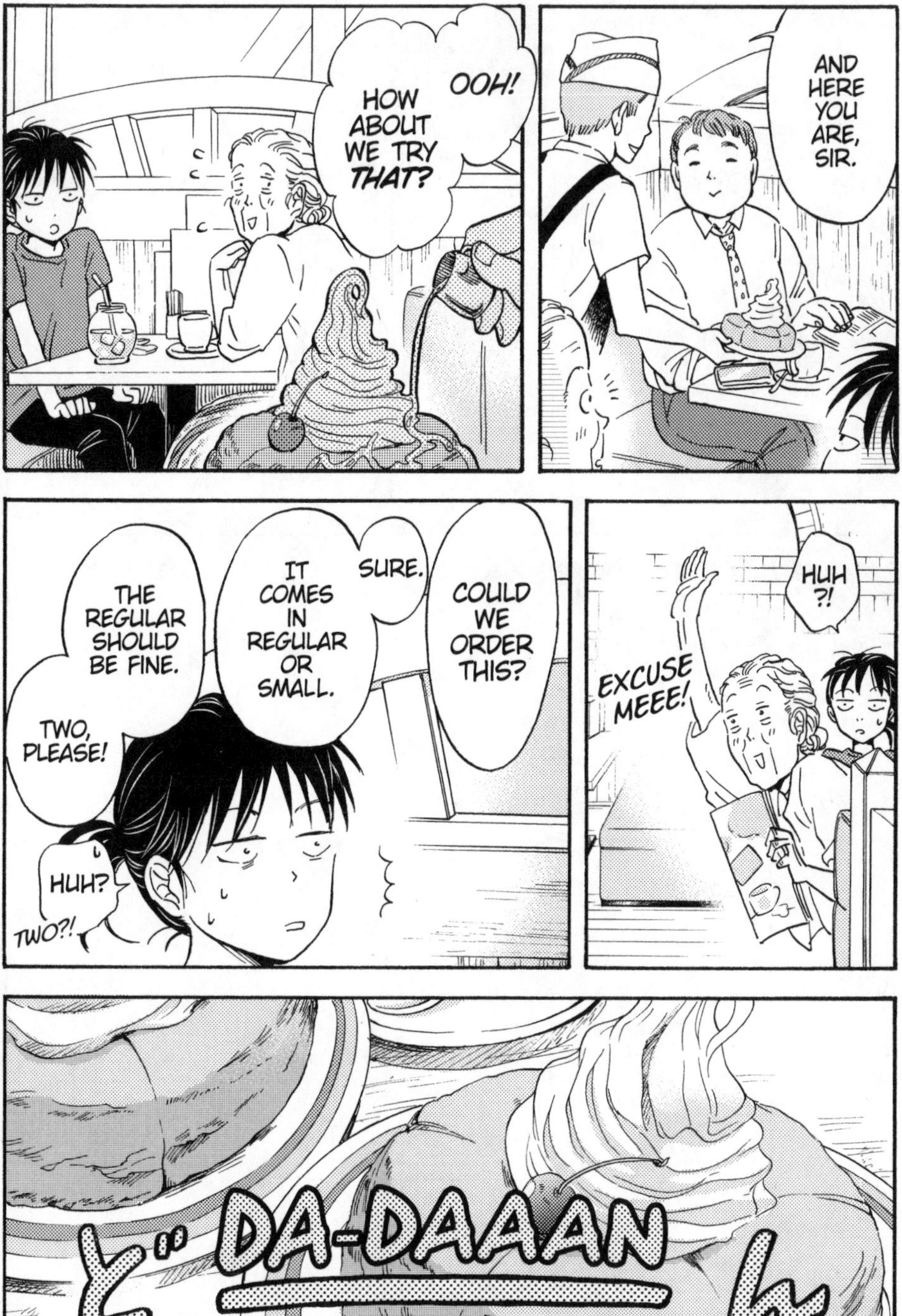
AND HERE YOU ARE, SIR.
OOH!
HOW ABOUT WE TRY THAT?
HUH ?!
EXCUSE MEEE!
COULD WE ORDER THIS?
SURE.
IT COMES IN REGULAR OR SMALL.
THE REGULAR SHOULD BE FINE.
TWO, PLEASE!
HUH?
TWO?!
ど DA-DAAAN ん

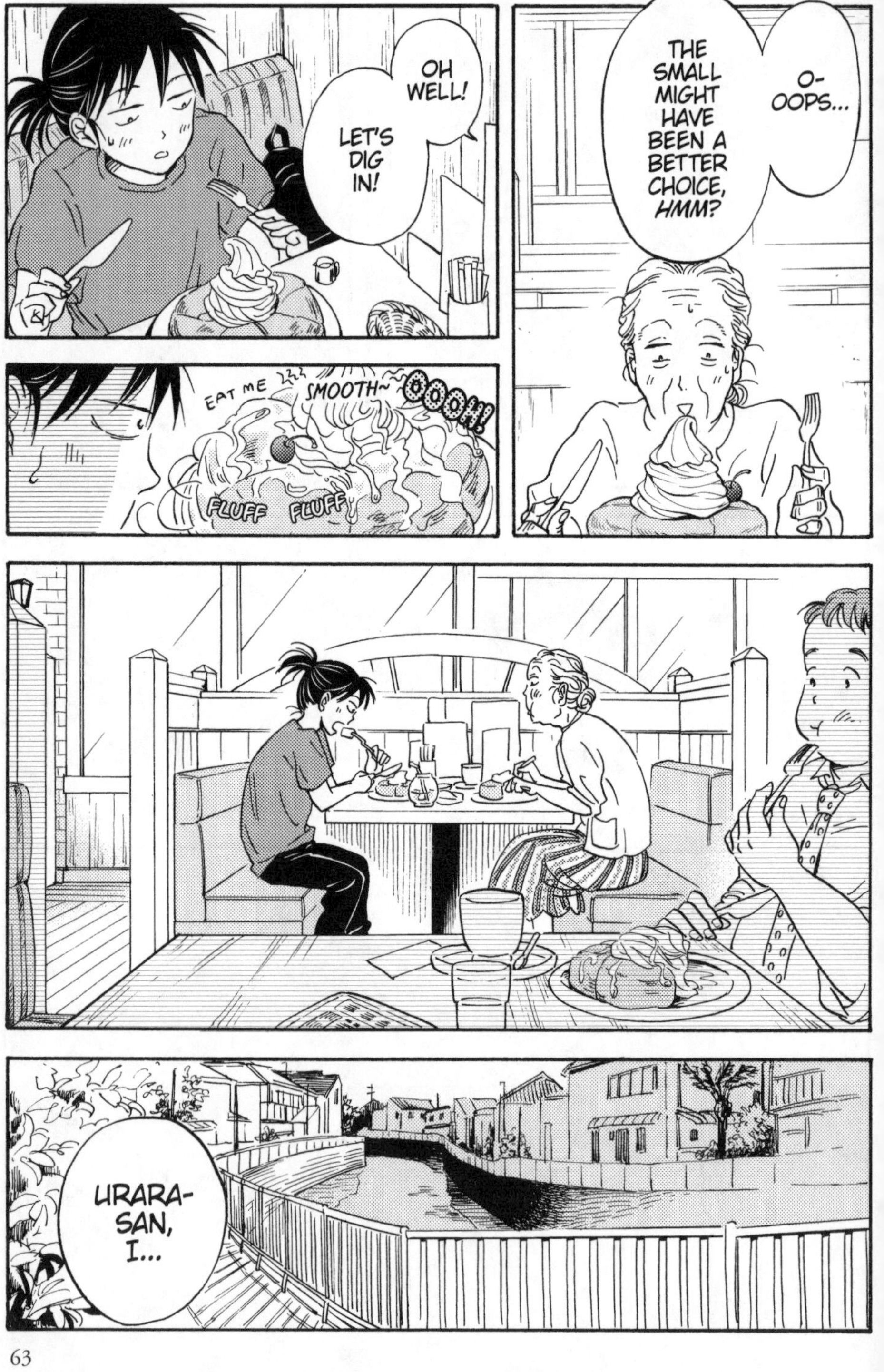
O-OOPS...
THE SMALL MIGHT HAVE BEEN A BETTER CHOICE, HMM?
OH WELL!
LET'S DIG IN!
OOOH!
SMOOTH~
EAT ME
FLUFF FLUFF
URARA-SAN, I...

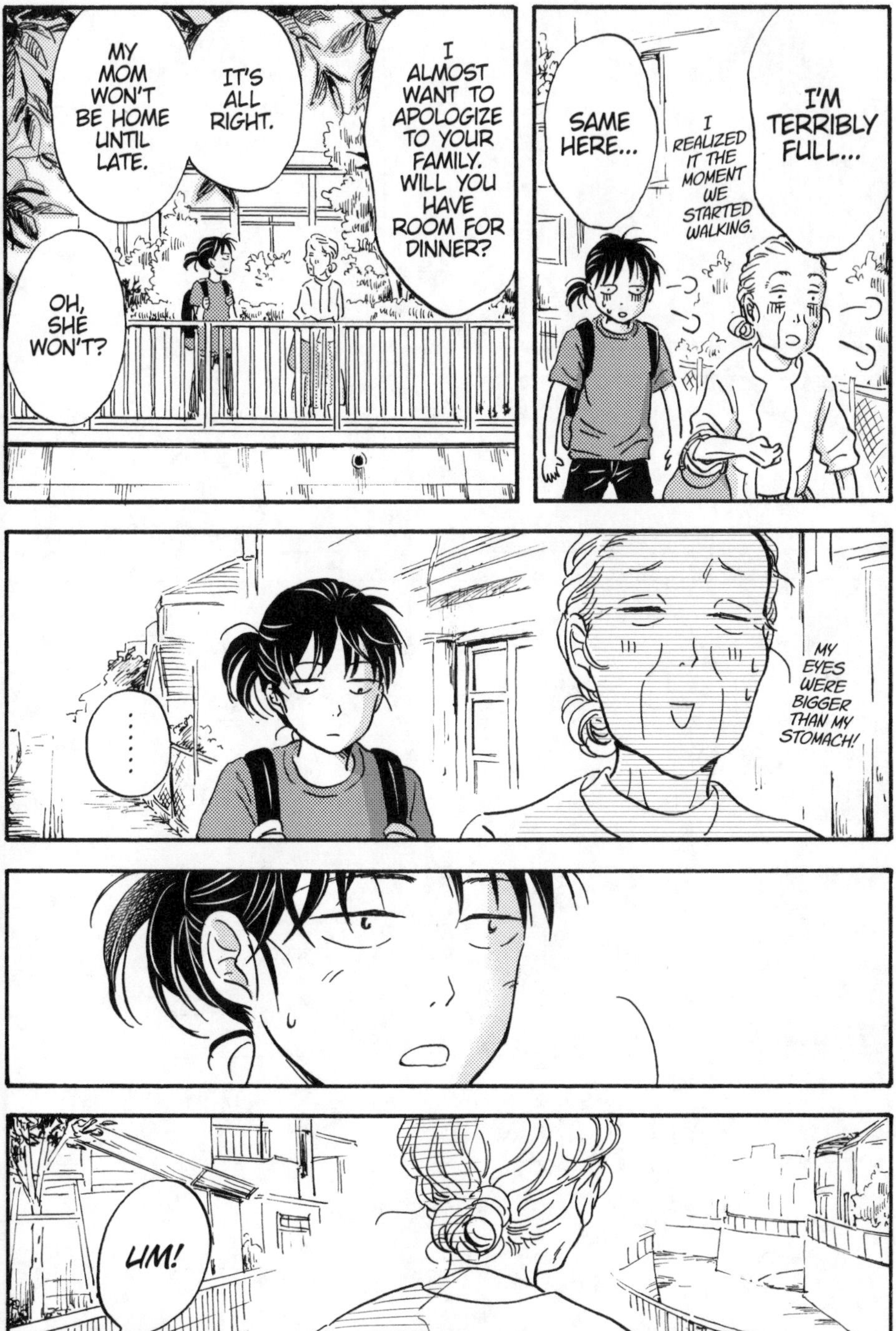
I'M TERRIBLY FULL...
I REALIZED IT THE MOMENT WE STARTED WALKING.
SAME HERE...
I ALMOST WANT TO APOLOGIZE TO YOUR FAMILY. WILL YOU HAVE ROOM FOR DINNER?
IT'S ALL RIGHT.
MY MOM WON'T BE HOME UNTIL LATE.
OH, SHE WON'T?
MY EYES WERE BIGGER THAN MY STOMACH!
......
UM!

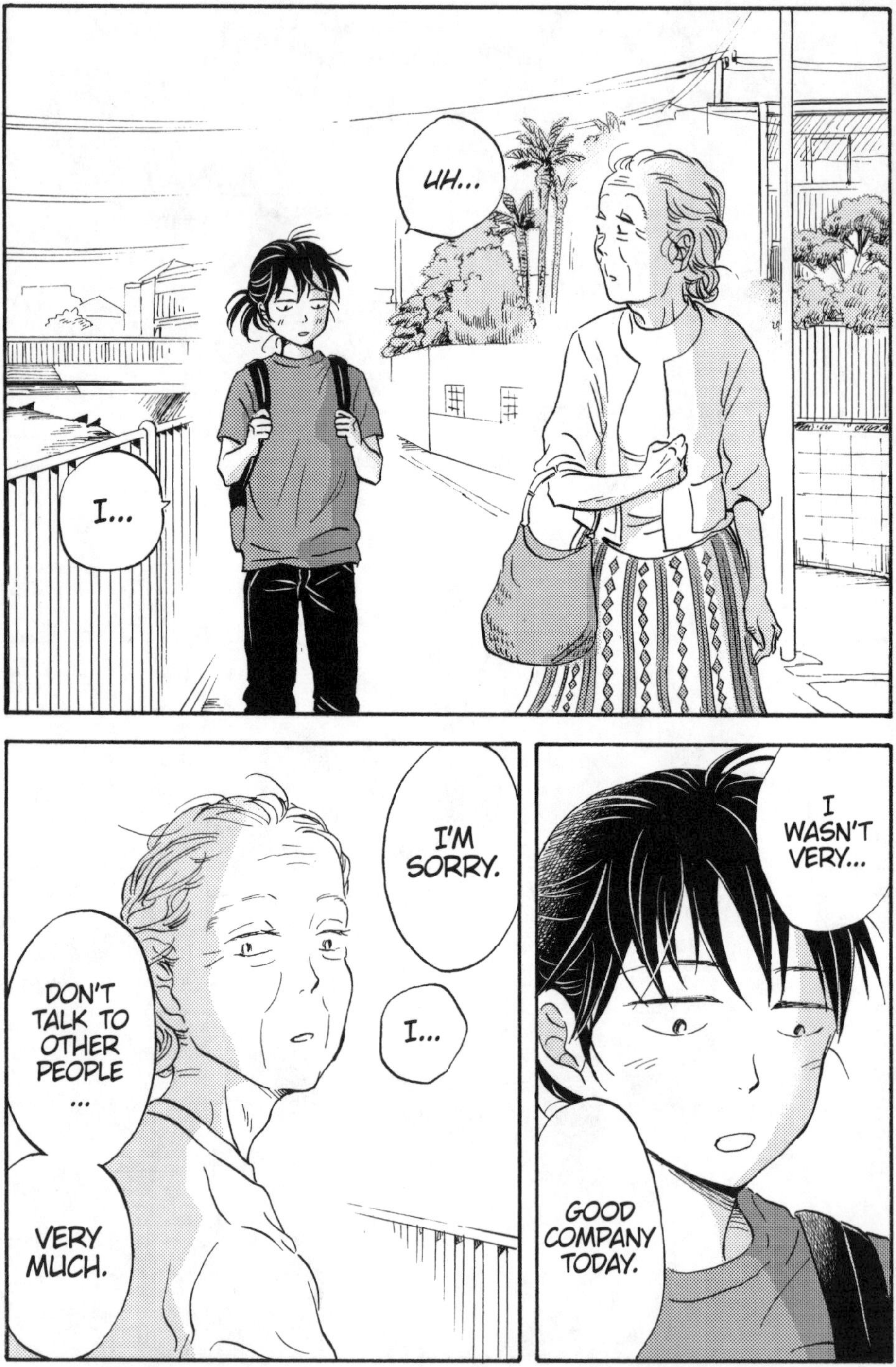
UH...
I...
I WASN'T VERY...
GOOD COMPANY TODAY.
I'M SORRY.
I...
DON'T TALK TO OTHER PEOPLE ...
VERY MUCH.

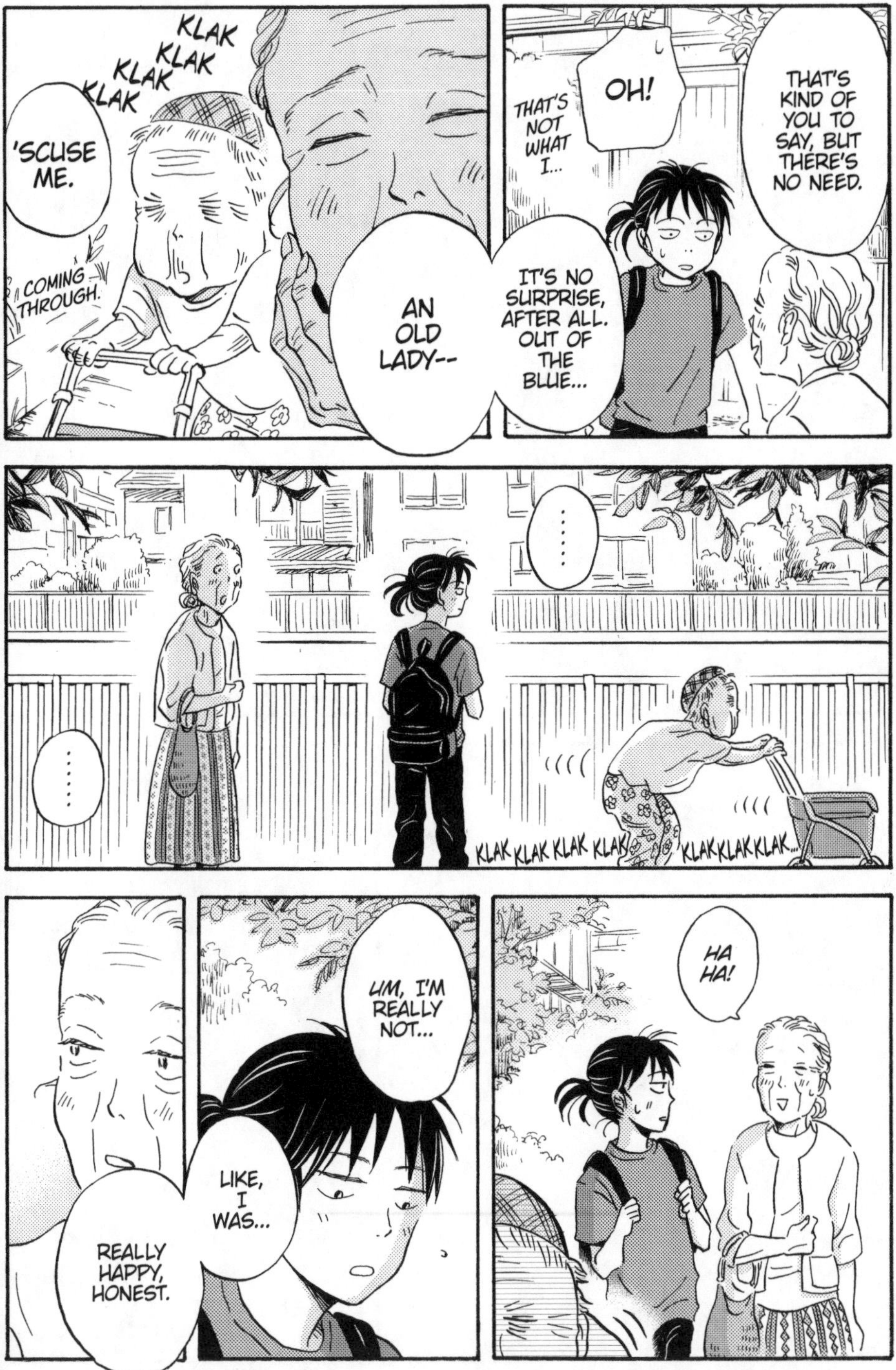
THAT'S KIND OF YOU TO SAY, BUT THERE'S NO NEED.
OH!
THAT'S NOT WHAT I...
IT'S NO SURPRISE, AFTER ALL. OUT OF THE BLUE...
AN OLD LADY--
KLAK KLAK KLAK KLAK
'SCUSE ME.
COMING THROUGH.
......
KLAK KLAK KLAK KLAK KLAK KLAK KLAK...
......
HA HA!
UM, I'M REALLY NOT...
LIKE, I WAS...
REALLY HAPPY, HONEST.

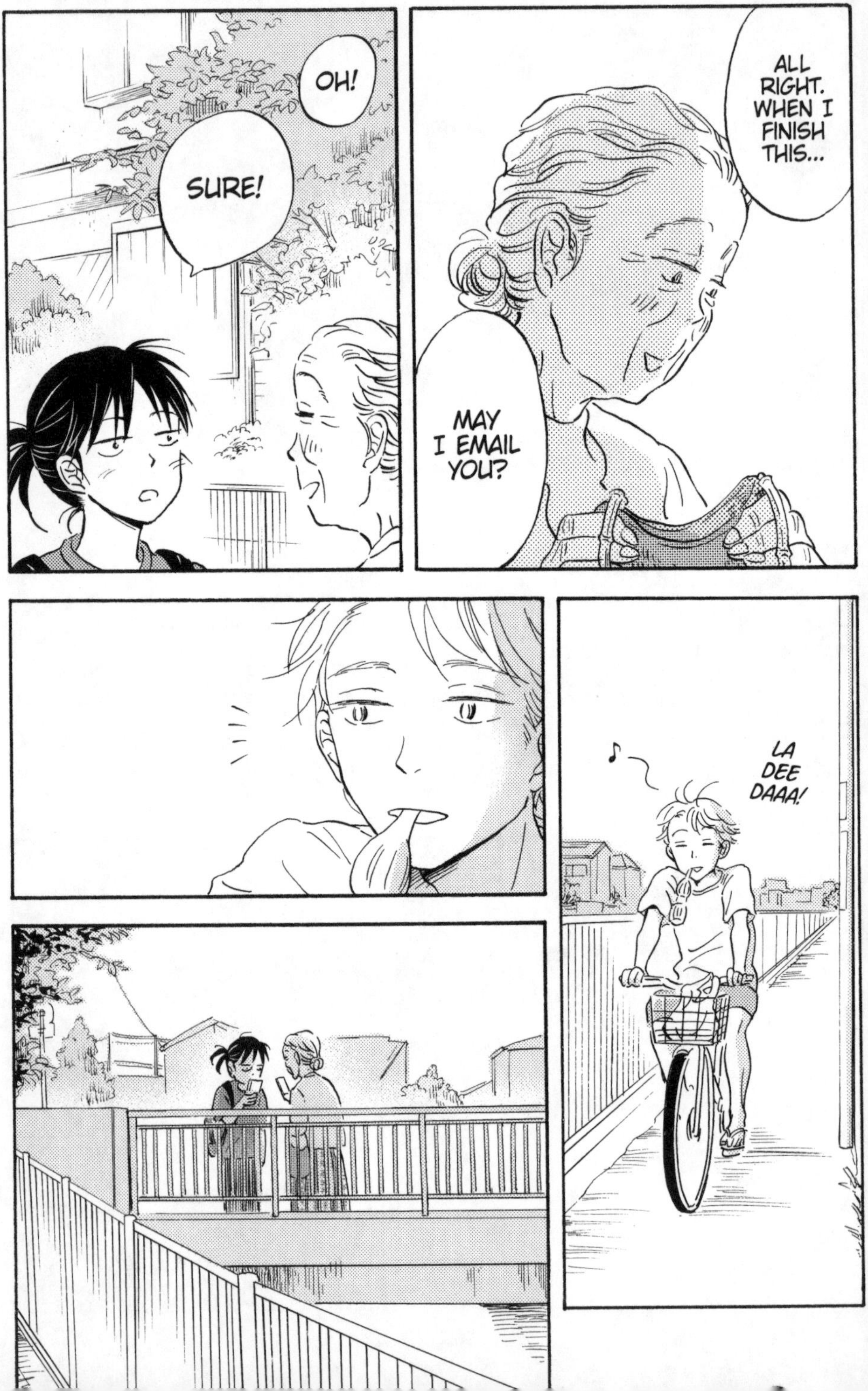
ALL RIGHT. WHEN I FINISH THIS...
MAY I EMAIL YOU?
OH!
SURE!
LA DEE DAAA!

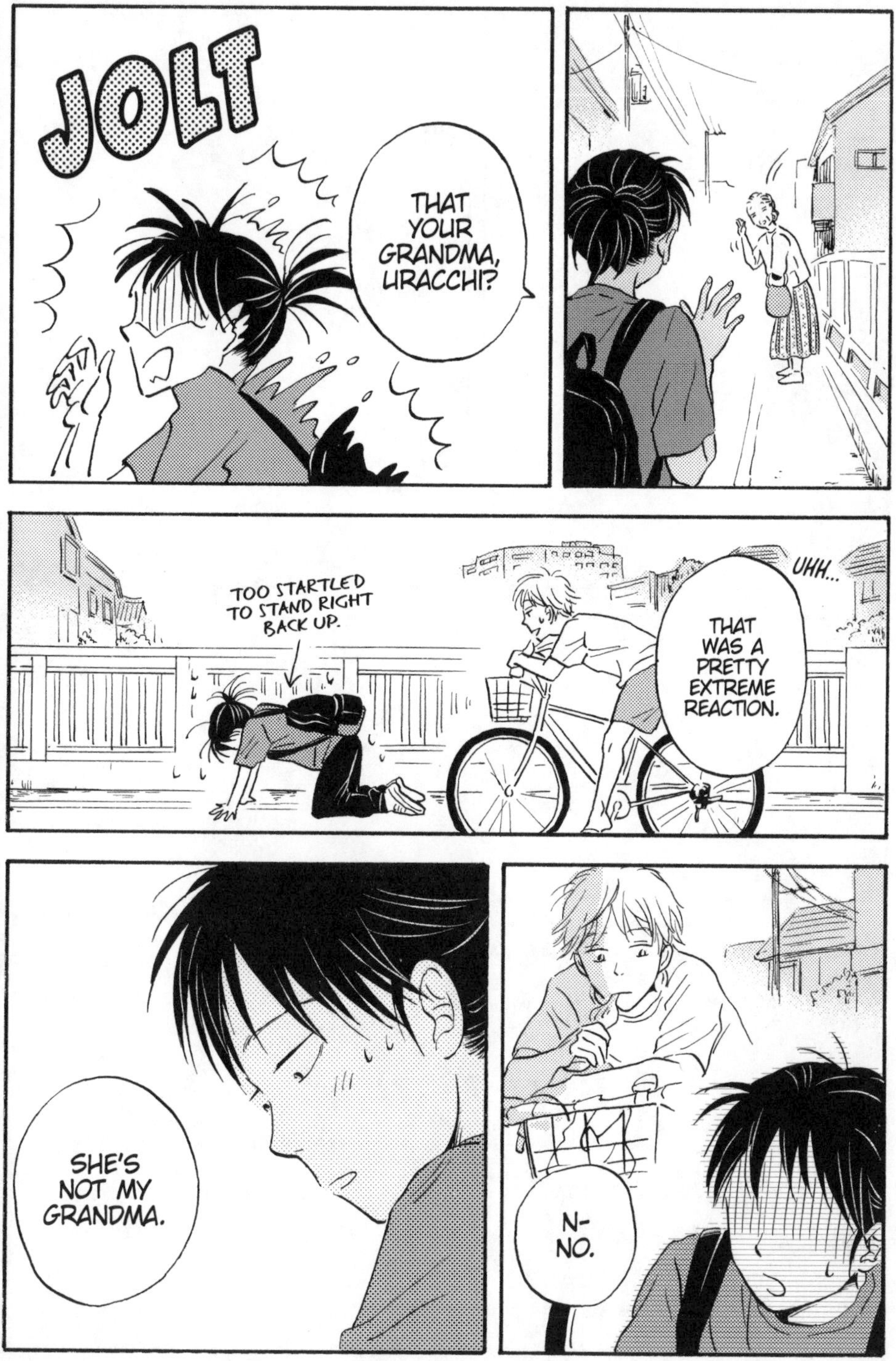
JOLT
THAT YOUR GRANDMA, URACCHI?
UHH...
THAT WAS A PRETTY EXTREME REACTION.
TOO STARTLED TO STAND RIGHT BACK UP.
N-NO.
SHE'S NOT MY GRANDMA.

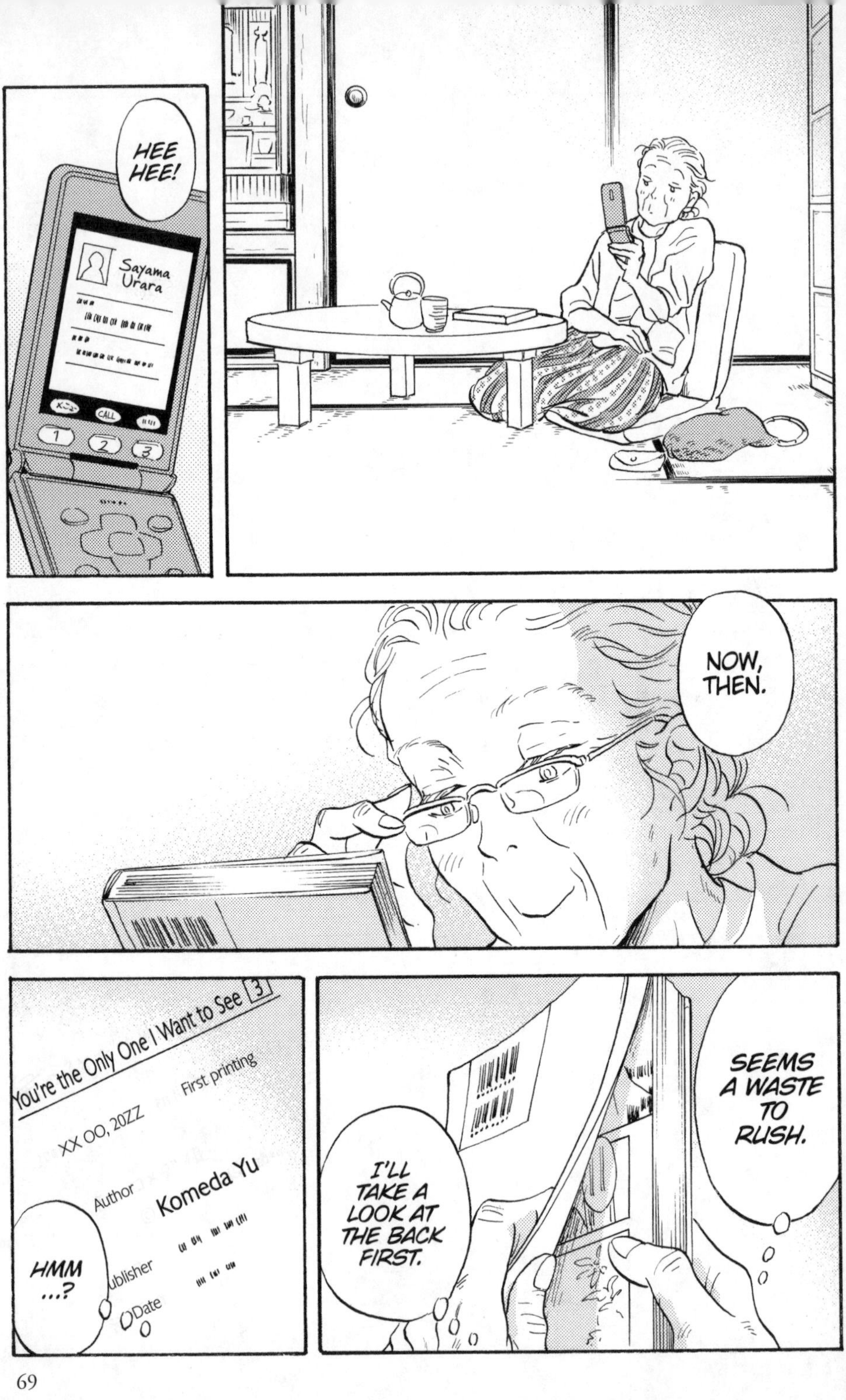
HEE HEE!
Sayama Urara
CALL
1 2 3
NOW, THEN.
SEEMS A WASTE TO RUSH.
I'LL TAKE A LOOK AT THE BACK FIRST.
You're the Only One I Want to See 3
First printing
XX OO, 20ZZ
Author
Komeda Yu
ublisher
Date
HMM ...?

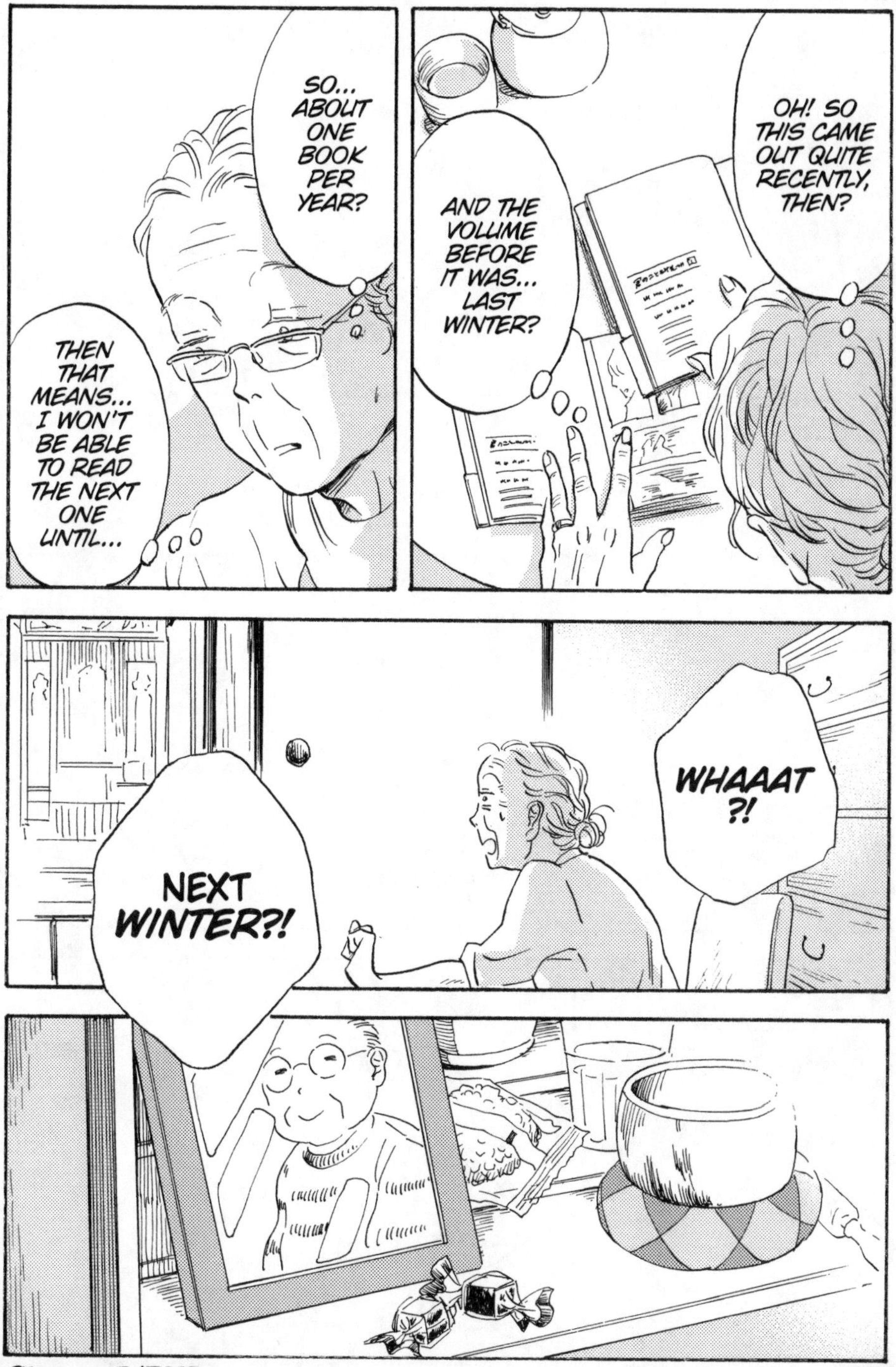
OH! SO THIS CAME OUT QUITE RECENTLY, THEN?
AND THE VOLUME BEFORE IT WAS... LAST WINTER?
SO... ABOUT ONE BOOK PER YEAR?
THEN THAT MEANS... I WON'T BE ABLE TO READ THE NEXT ONE UNTIL...
WHAAAT ?!
NEXT WINTER?!

Chapter 5/END

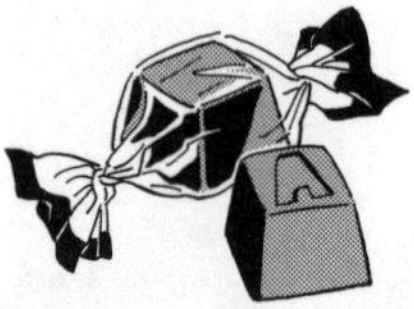

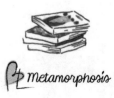
metamorphosis

Chapter 6

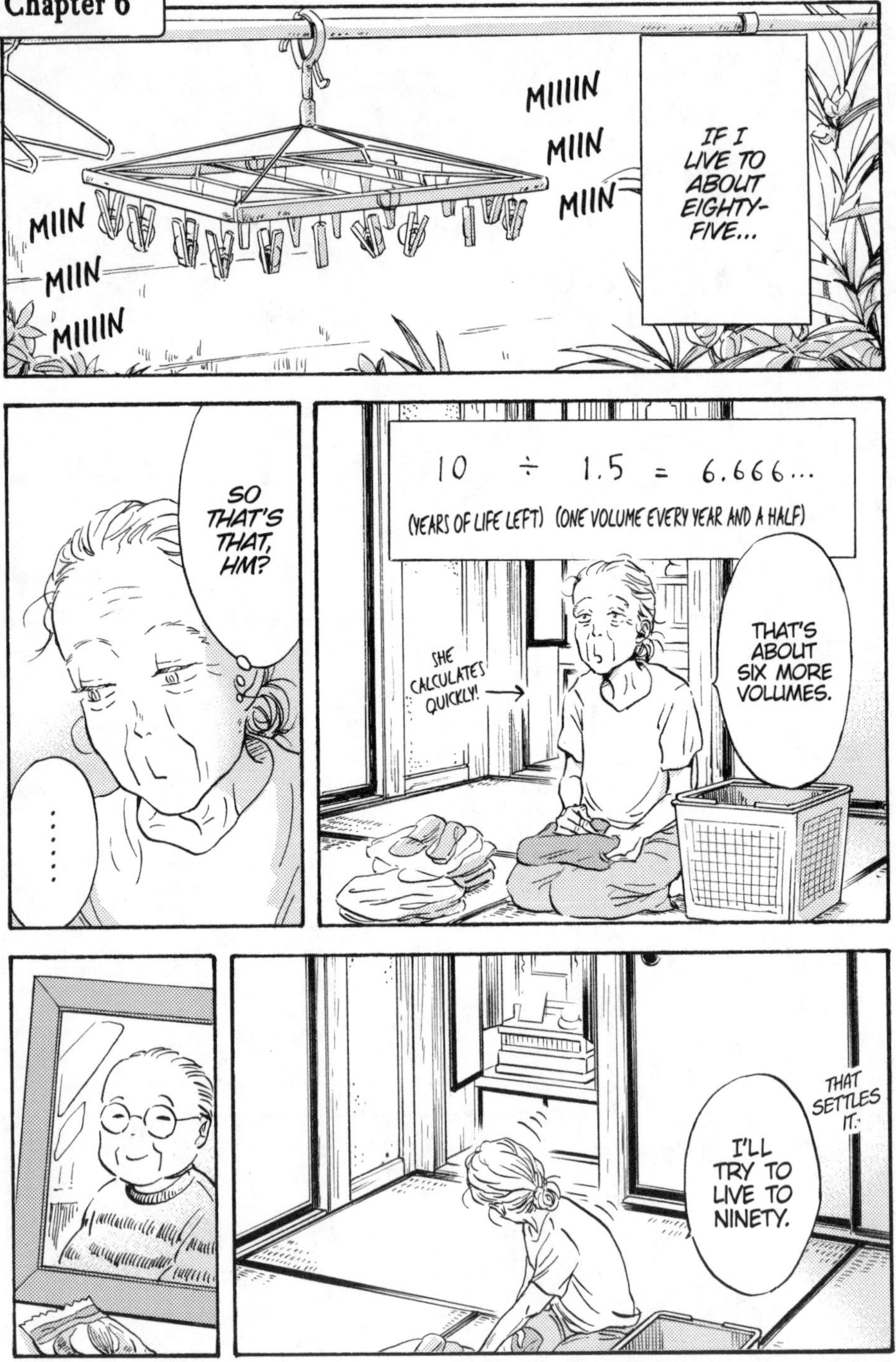
IF I LIVE TO ABOUT EIGHTY-FIVE...
MIIIIN
MIIN
MIIN
MIIN
MIIN
MIIIIN
10 ÷ 1.5 = 6.666...
(YEARS OF LIFE LEFT) (ONE VOLUME EVERY YEAR AND A HALF)
THAT'S ABOUT SIX MORE VOLUMES.
SHE CALCULATES QUICKLY!
SO THAT'S THAT, HM?
......
THAT SETTLES IT.
I'LL TRY TO LIVE TO NINETY.

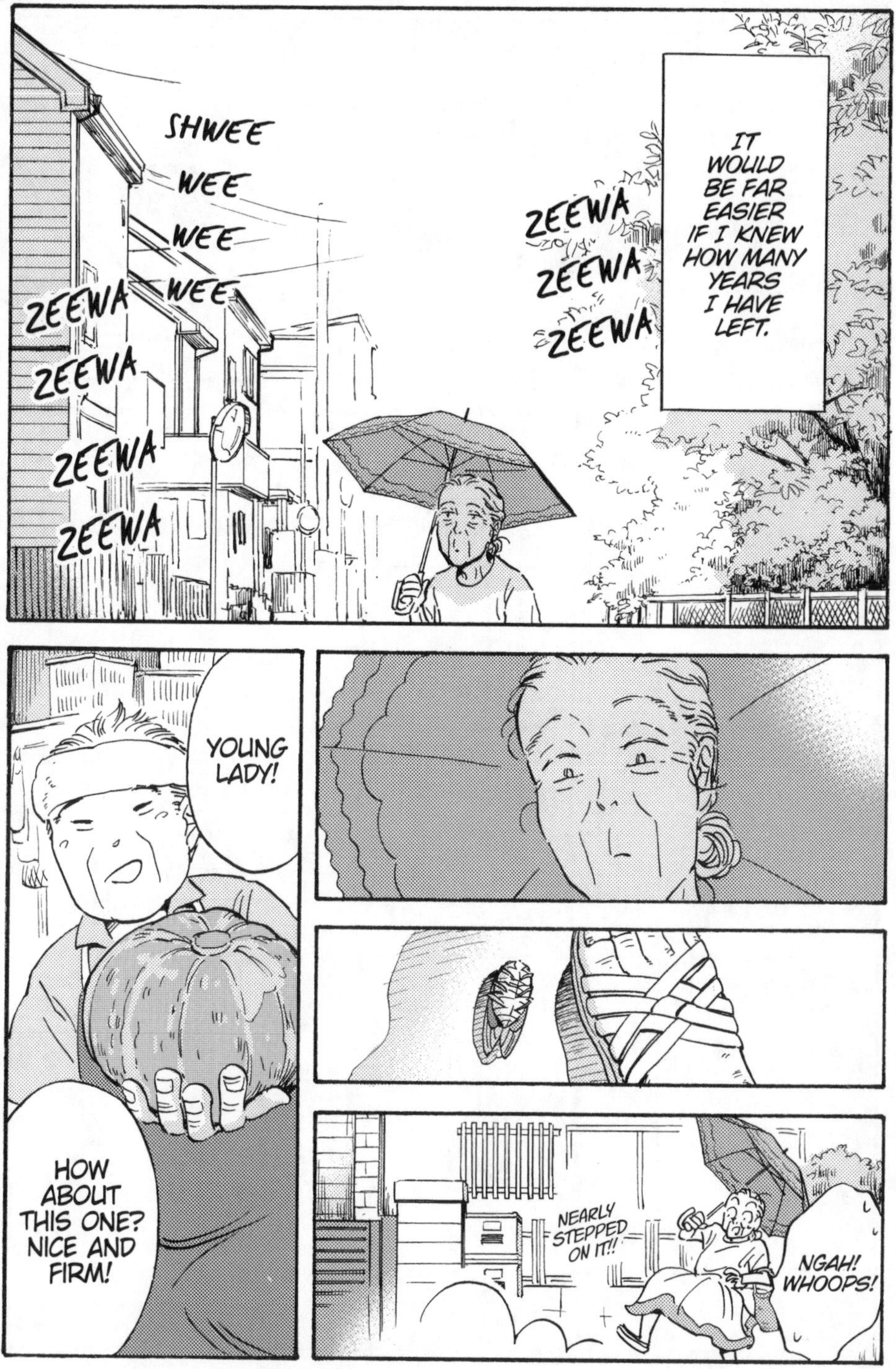
IT WOULD BE FAR EASIER IF I KNEW HOW MANY YEARS I HAVE LEFT.
ZEEWA
ZEEWA
ZEEWA
SHWEE
WEE
WEE
WEE
ZEEWA
ZEEWA
ZEEWA
ZEEWA
NGAH! WHOOPS!
NEARLY STEPPED ON IT!!
YOUNG LADY!
HOW ABOUT THIS ONE? NICE AND FIRM!

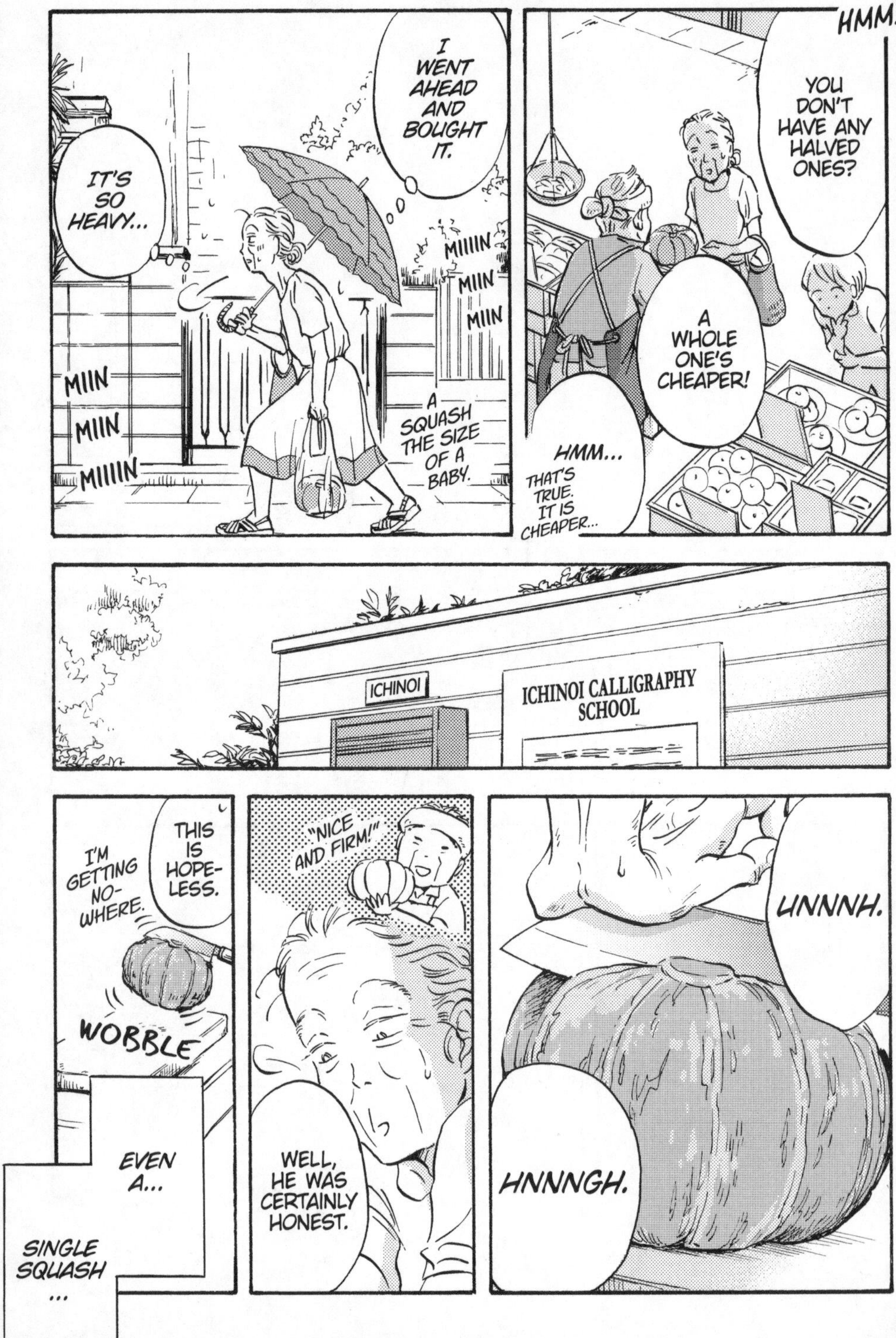
HMM..
YOU DON'T HAVE ANY HALVED ONES?
A WHOLE ONE'S CHEAPER!
HMM...
THAT'S TRUE. IT IS CHEAPER...
I WENT AHEAD AND BOUGHT IT.
IT'S SO HEAVY...
MIIIN
MIIN
MIIN
MIIN
MIIN
MIIIN
A SQUASH THE SIZE OF A BABY.
ICHINOI
ICHINOI CALLIGRAPHY SCHOOL
UNNNH.
HNNNGH.
"NICE AND FIRM!"
WELL, HE WAS CERTAINLY HONEST.
THIS IS HOPE-LESS.
I'M GETTING NO-WHERE.
WOBBLE
EVEN A...
SINGLE SQUASH...

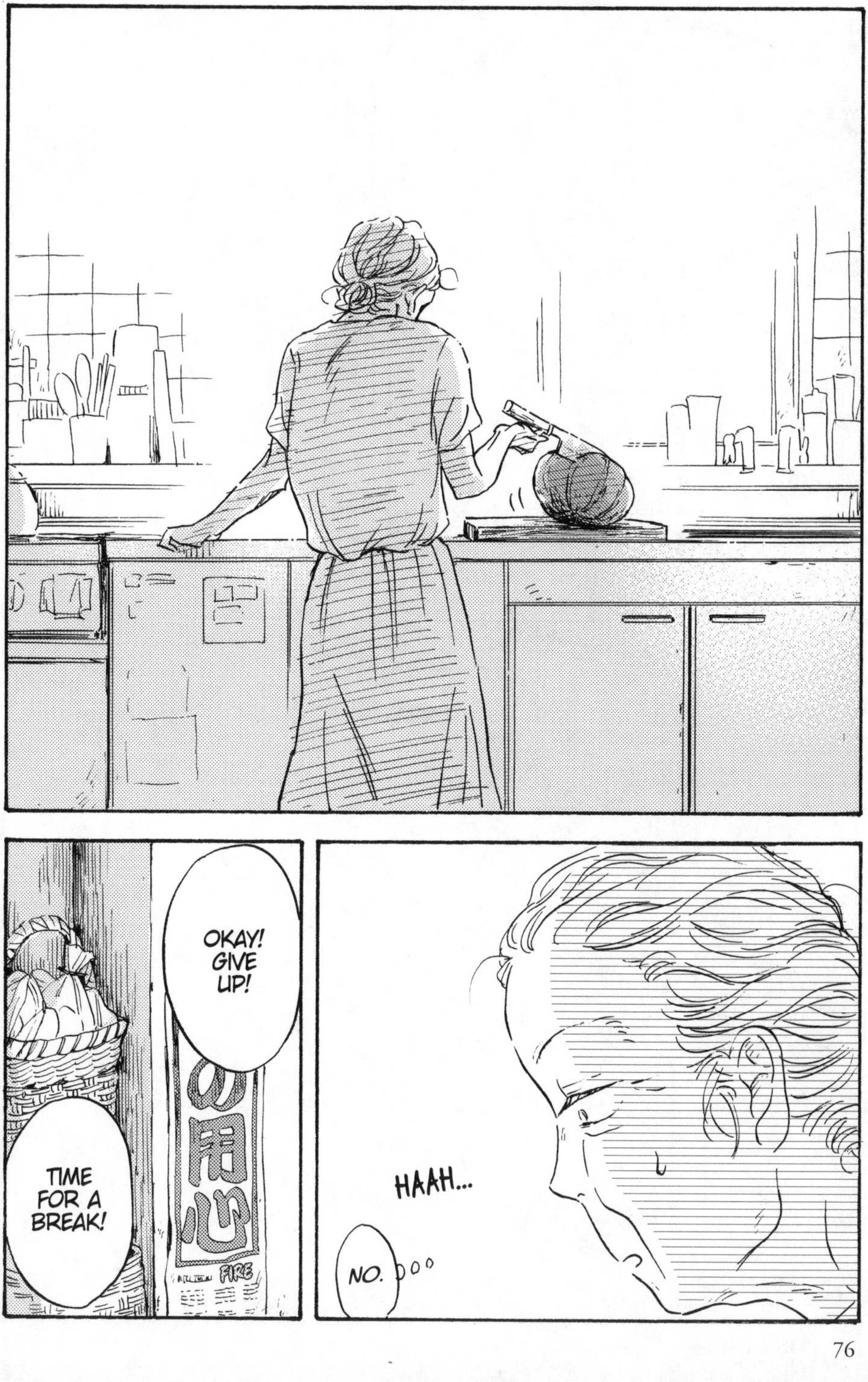
HAAH...
NO.
OKAY! GIVE UP!
の用心
FIRE
TIME FOR A BREAK!

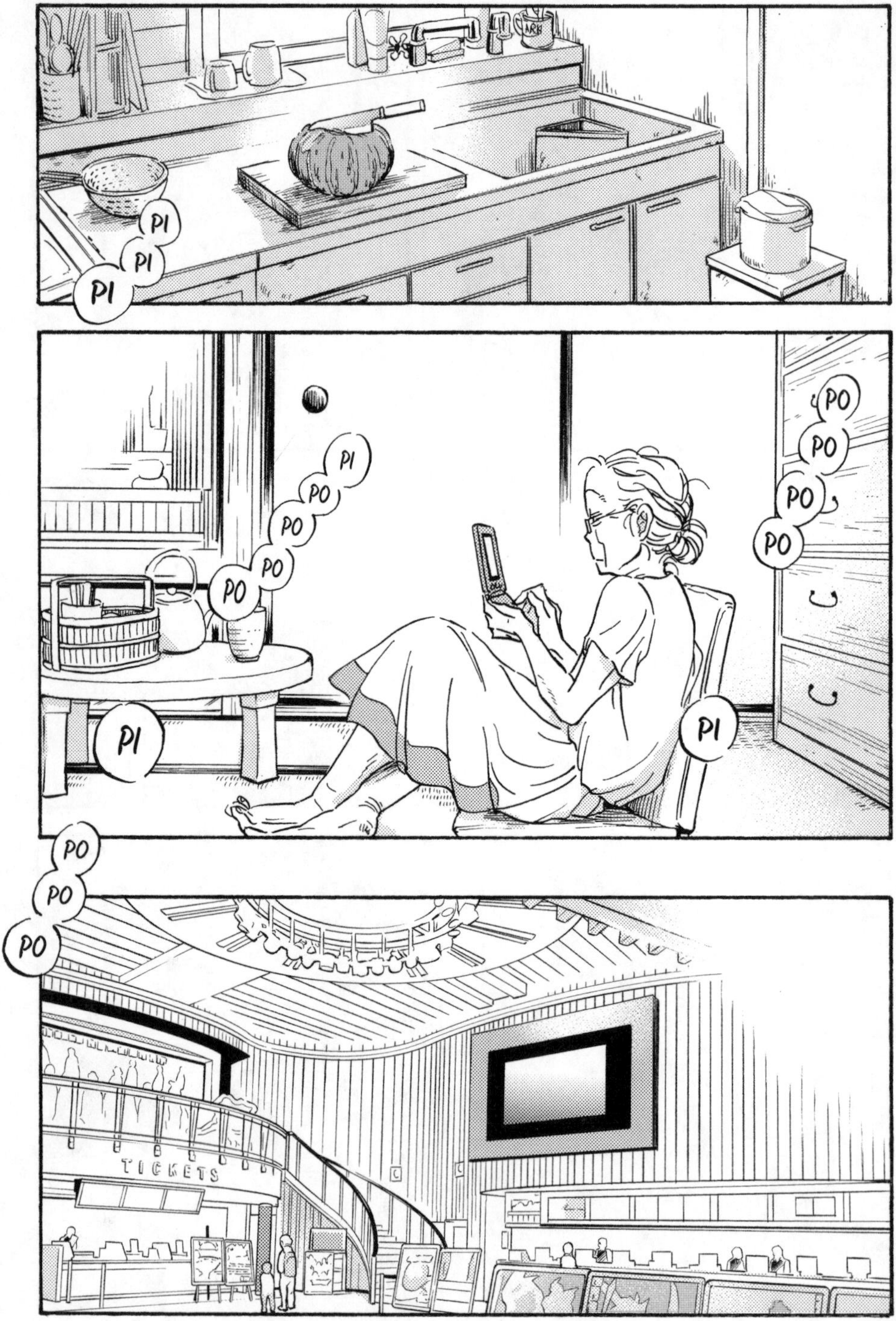
PI
PI
PI
PO
PO
PO
PO
PI
PO
PO
PO
PO
PI
PI
PO
PO
PO
TICKETS

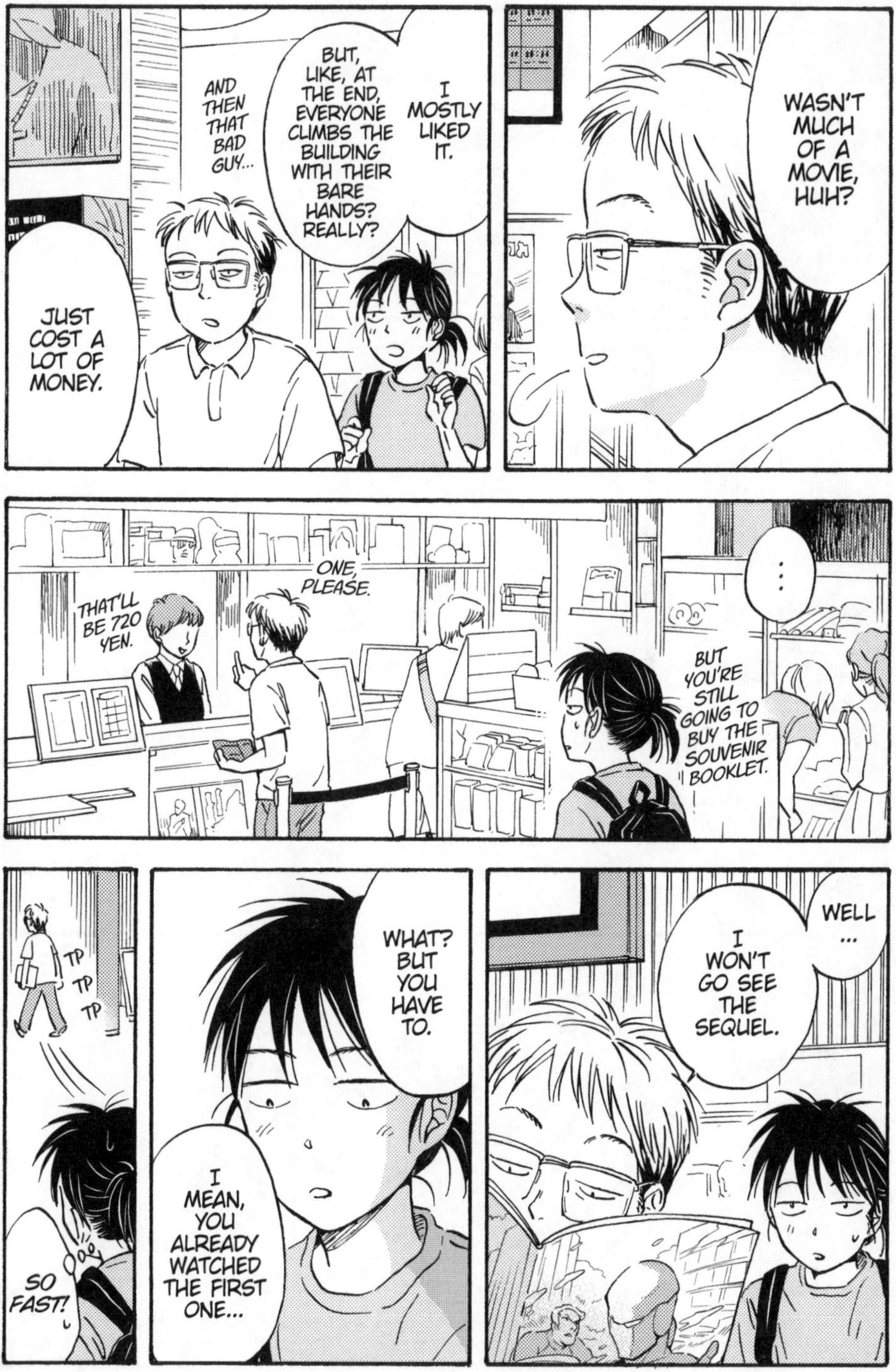
WASN'T MUCH OF A MOVIE, HUH?
I MOSTLY LIKED IT.
BUT, LIKE, AT THE END, EVERYONE CLIMBS THE BUILDING WITH THEIR BARE HANDS? REALLY?
AND THEN THAT BAD GUY...
JUST COST A LOT OF MONEY.
...
BUT YOU'RE STILL GOING TO BUY THE SOUVENIR BOOKLET.
ONE, PLEASE.
THAT'LL BE 720 YEN.
WELL ...
I WON'T GO SEE THE SEQUEL.
WHAT? BUT YOU HAVE TO.
I MEAN, YOU ALREADY WATCHED THE FIRST ONE...
TP
TP
TP
SO FAST!

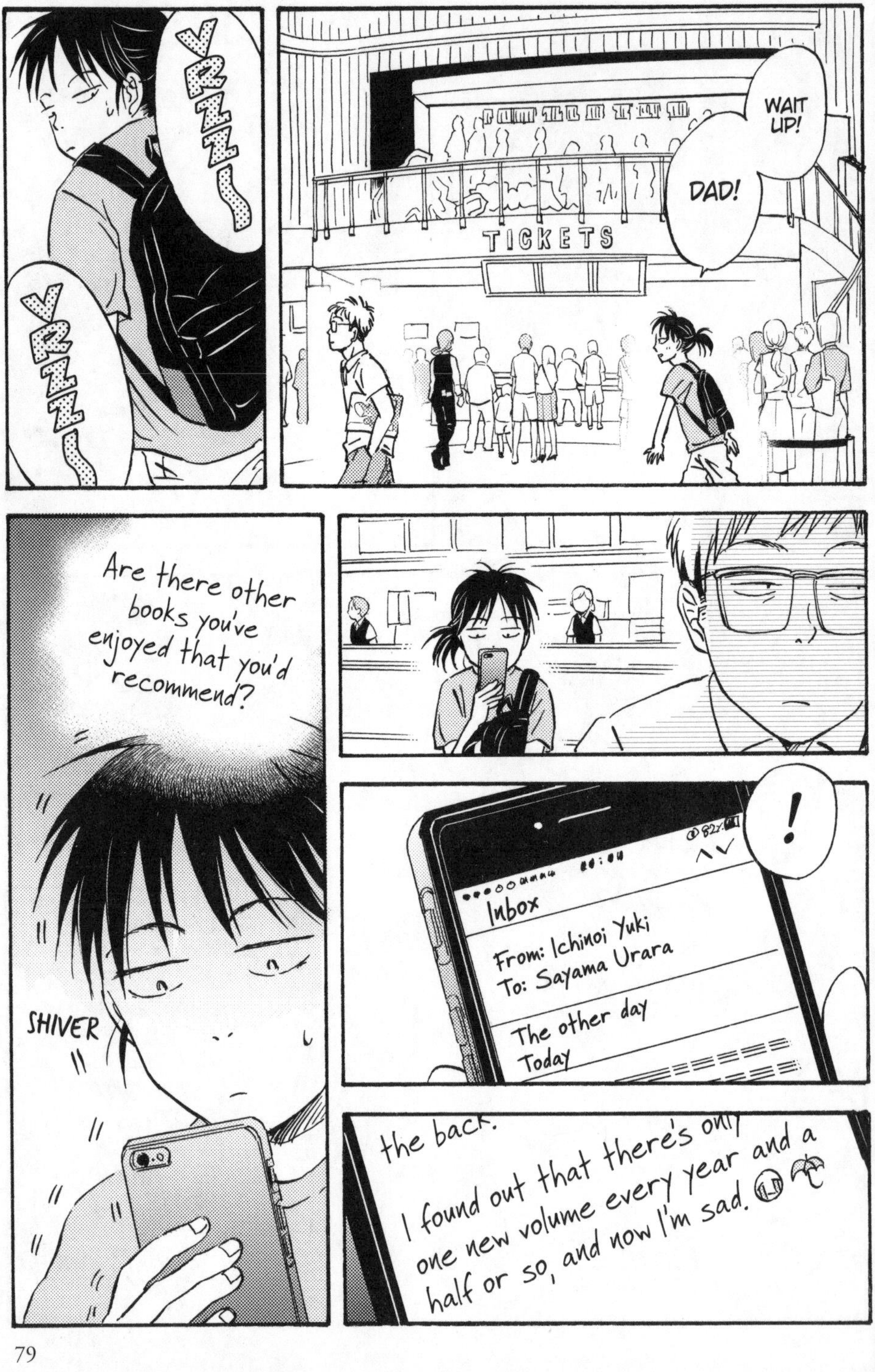

WAIT UP!
DAD!
TICKETS
VRZZ!
VRZZ!
!
Inbox
From: Ichinoi Yuki
To: Sayama Urara
The other day
Today
the back.
I found out that there's only one new volume every year and a half or so, and now I'm sad.
Are there other books you've enjoyed that you'd recommend?
SHIVER

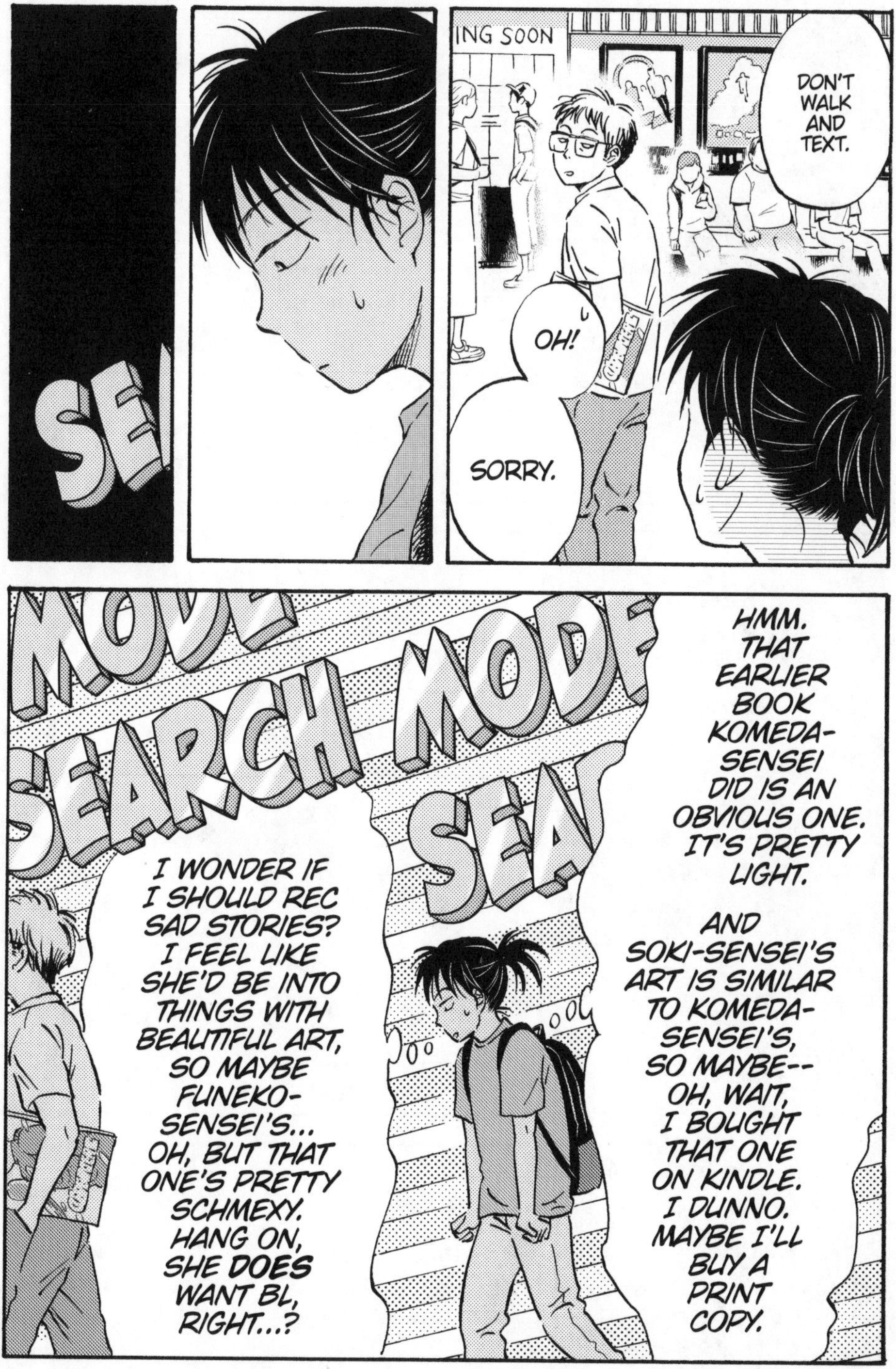
DON'T WALK AND TEXT.
OH!
SORRY.
SEARCH MODE
HMM. THAT EARLIER BOOK KOMEDA-SENSEI DID IS AN OBVIOUS ONE. IT'S PRETTY LIGHT.
AND SOKI-SENSEI'S ART IS SIMILAR TO KOMEDA-SENSEI'S, SO MAYBE-- OH, WAIT, I BOUGHT THAT ONE ON KINDLE. I DUNNO. MAYBE I'LL BUY A PRINT COPY.
I WONDER IF I SHOULD REC SAD STORIES? I FEEL LIKE SHE'D BE INTO THINGS WITH BEAUTIFUL ART, SO MAYBE FUNEKO-SENSEI'S... OH, BUT THAT ONE'S PRETTY SCHMEXY. HANG ON, SHE **DOES** WANT BL, RIGHT...?

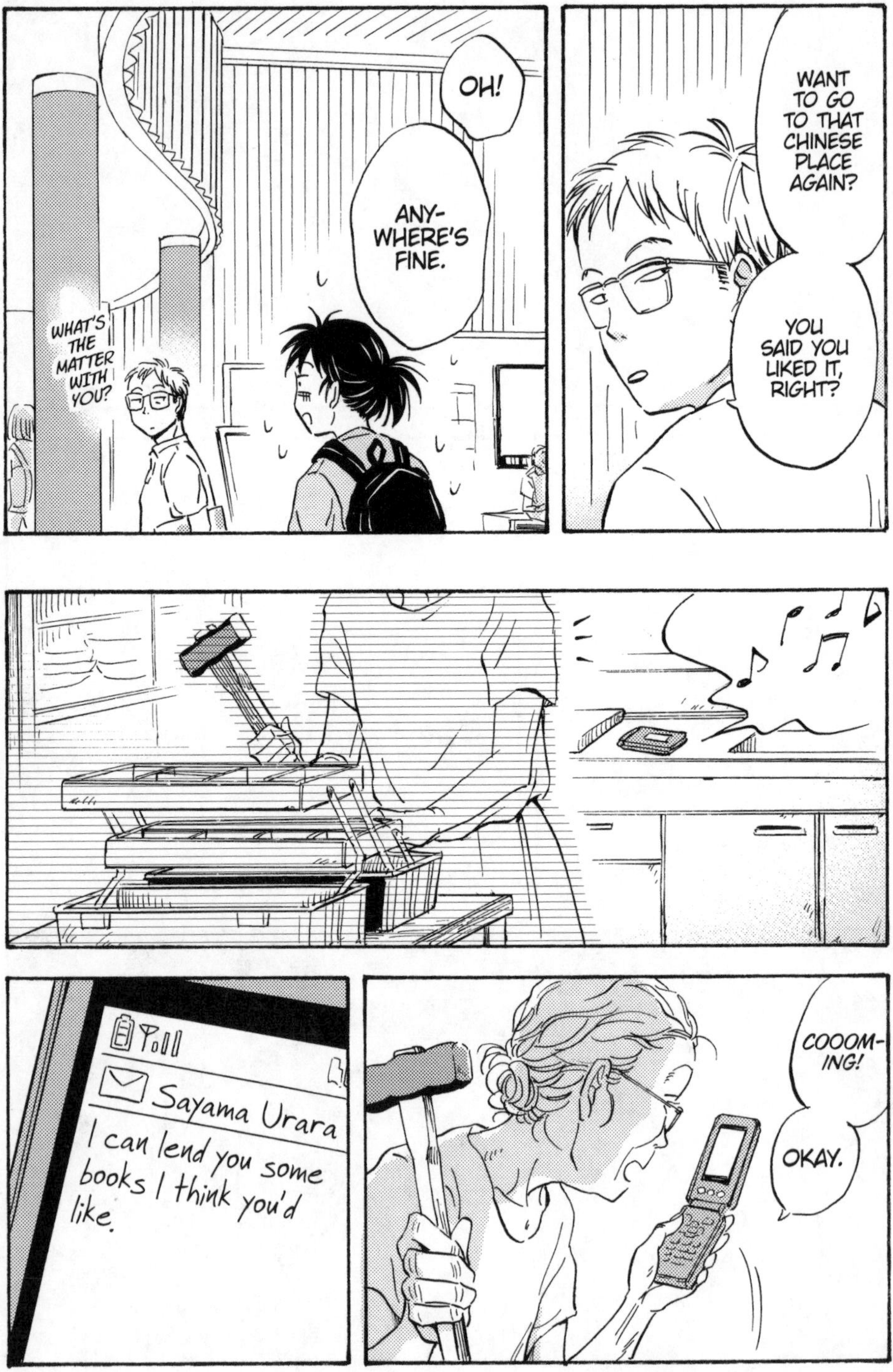
WANT TO GO TO THAT CHINESE PLACE AGAIN?
YOU SAID YOU LIKED IT, RIGHT?
OH!
ANY-WHERE'S FINE.
WHAT'S THE MATTER WITH YOU?
COOOM-ING!
OKAY.
Sayama Urara
I can lend you some books I think you'd like.

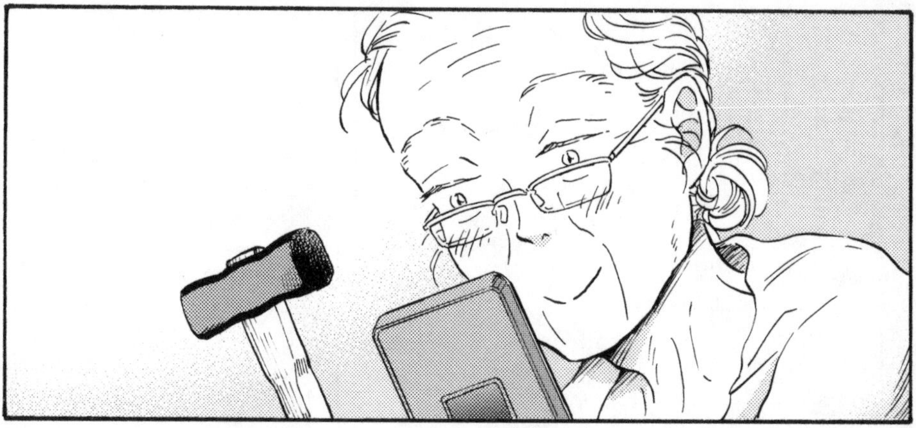

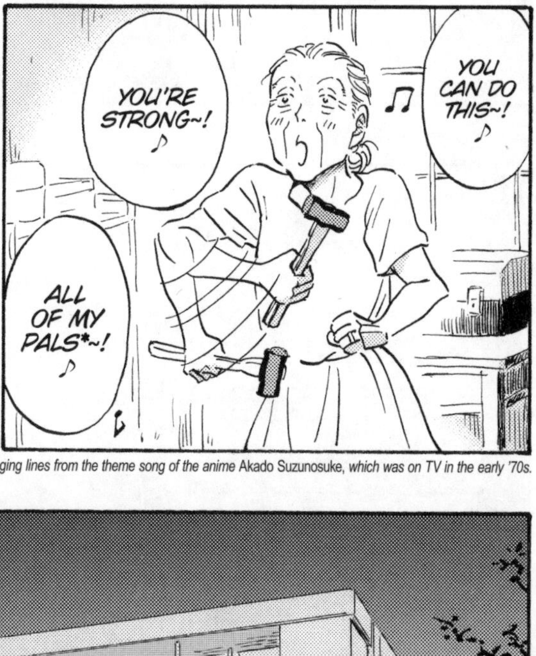
YOU CAN DO THIS~! ♪
YOU'RE STRONG~! ♪
ALL OF MY PALS*~! ♪

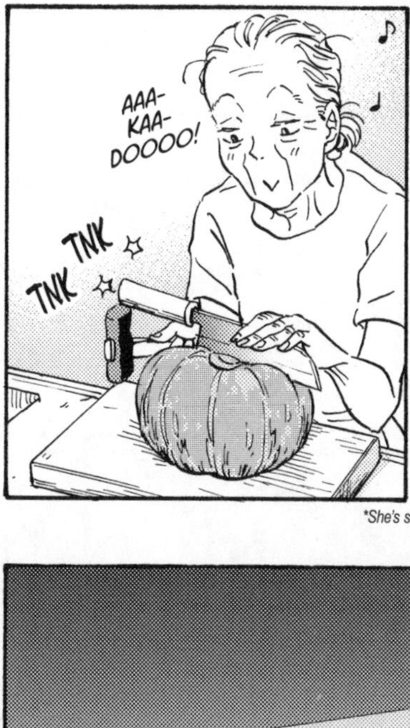
AAA-KAA-DOOOO!
TNK
TNK

*She's singing lines from the theme song of the anime Akado Suzunosuke, which was on TV in the early '70s.

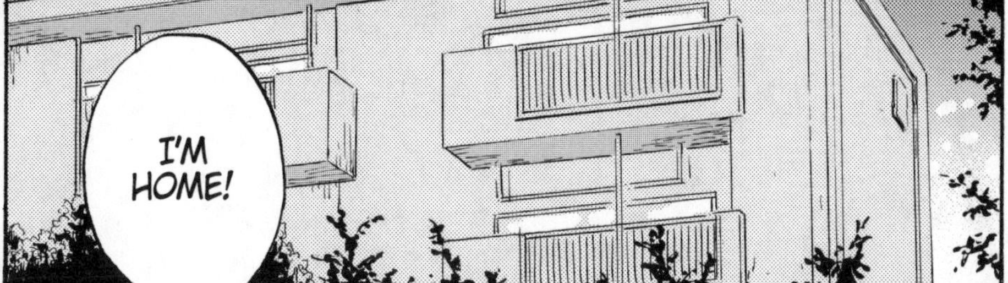
I'M HOME!

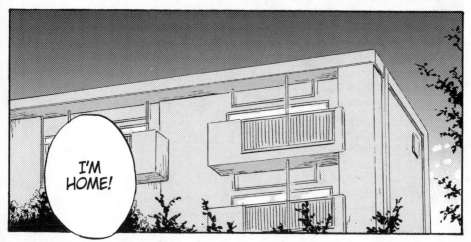

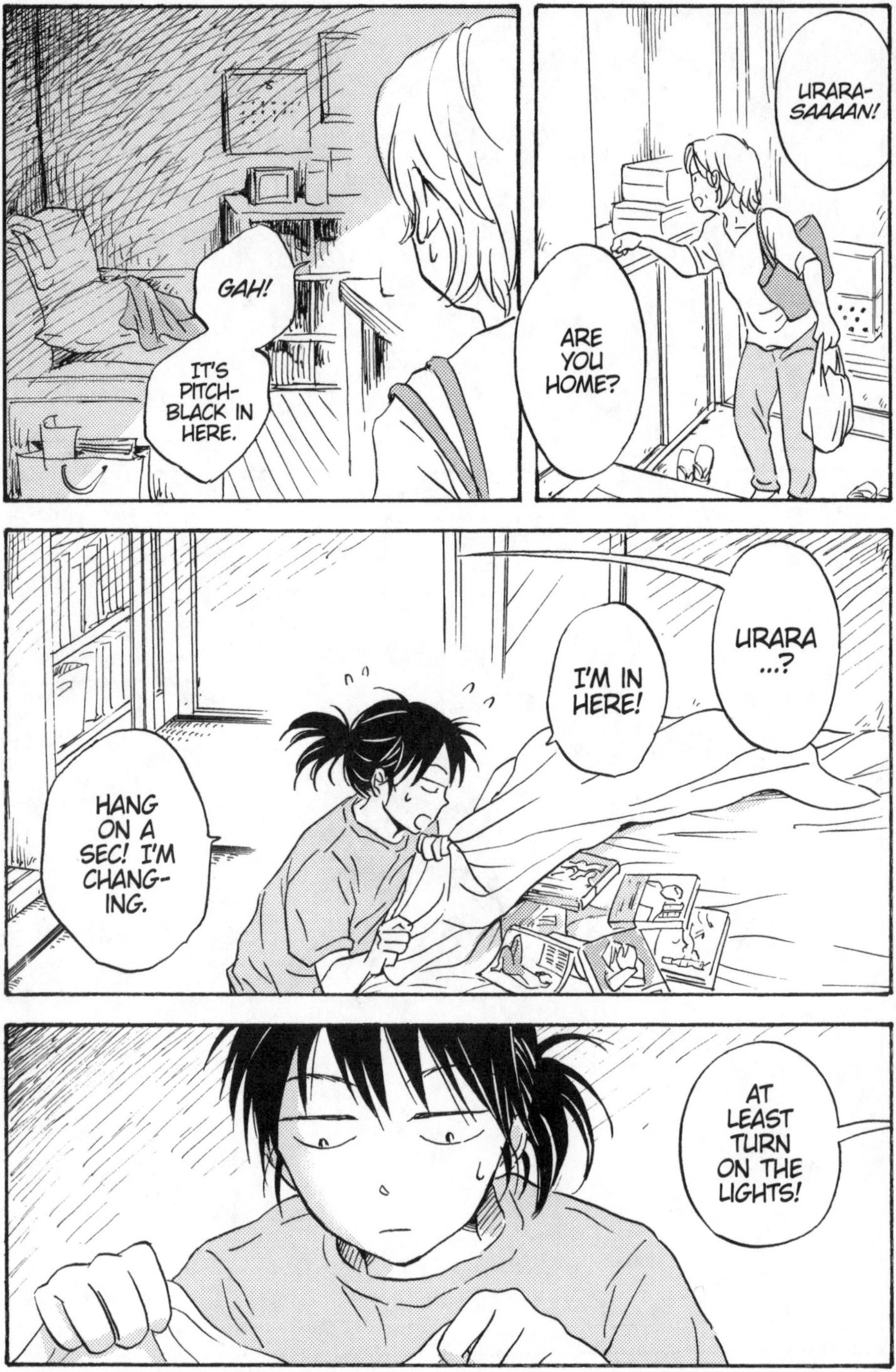
URARA-SAAAAN!
ARE YOU HOME?
GAH!
IT'S PITCH-BLACK IN HERE.
URARA ...?
I'M IN HERE!
HANG ON A SEC! I'M CHANGING.
AT LEAST TURN ON THE LIGHTS!

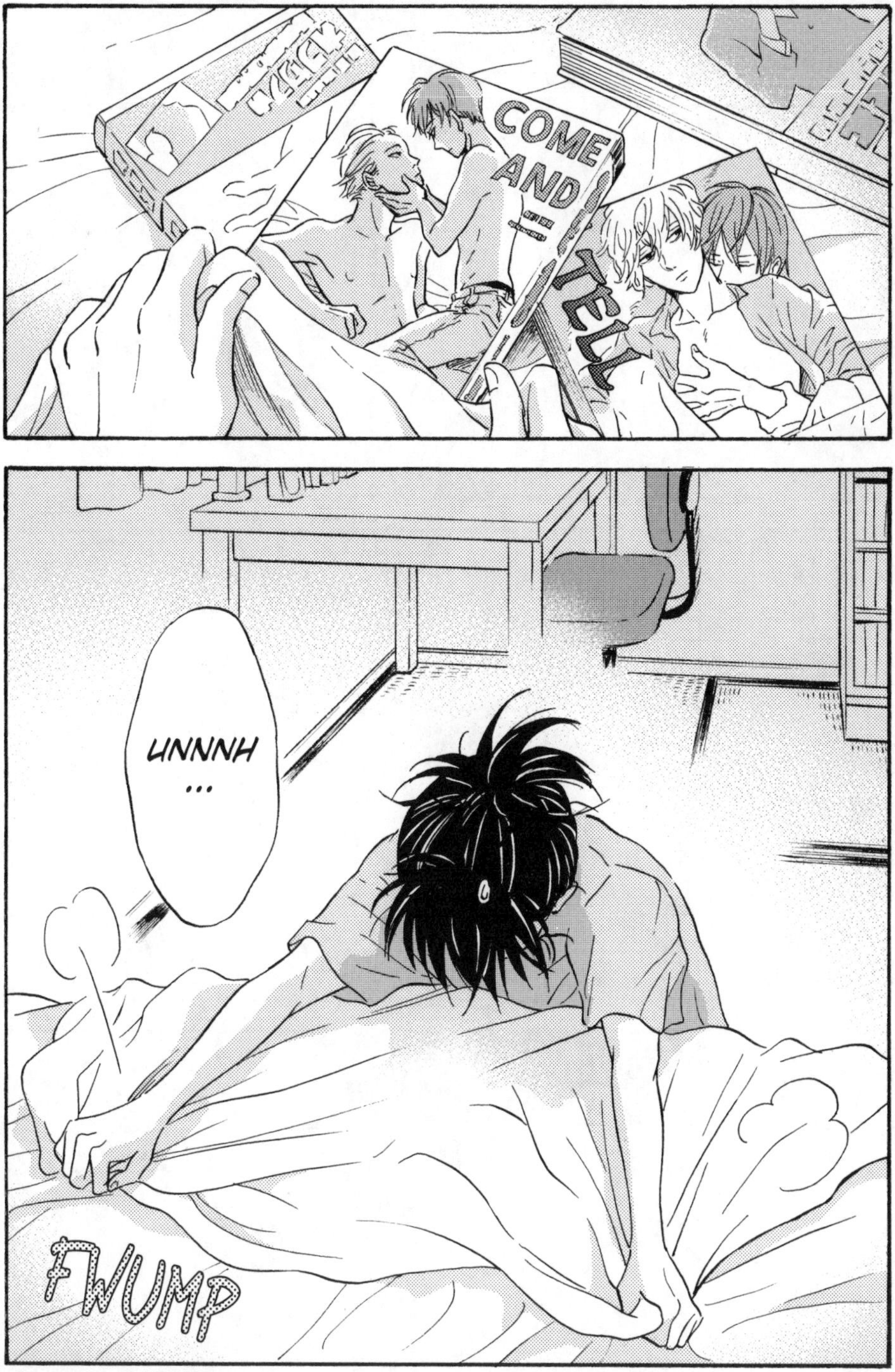
COME AND TELL
UNNNH ...
FWUMP

Chapter 6/END

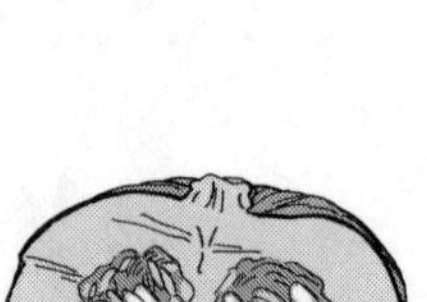

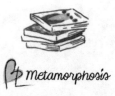

Chapter 7

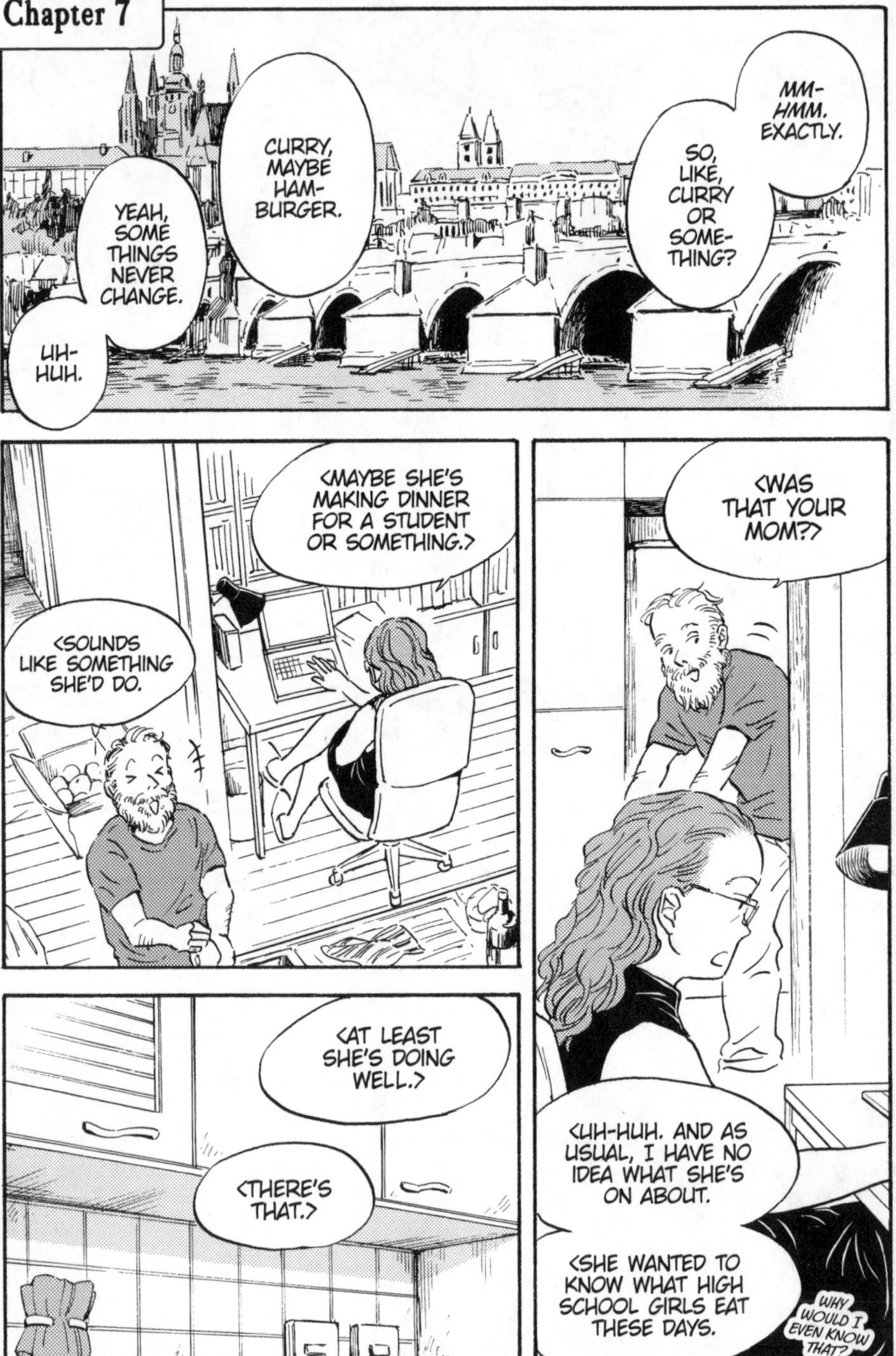

MM-HMM. EXACTLY.
SO, LIKE, CURRY OR SOME-THING?
CURRY, MAYBE HAM-BURGER.
YEAH, SOME THINGS NEVER CHANGE.
UH-HUH.
<WAS THAT YOUR MOM?>
<UH-HUH. AND AS USUAL, I HAVE NO IDEA WHAT SHE'S ON ABOUT.
<SHE WANTED TO KNOW WHAT HIGH SCHOOL GIRLS EAT THESE DAYS.
WHY WOULD I EVEN KNOW THAT?
<MAYBE SHE'S MAKING DINNER FOR A STUDENT OR SOMETHING.>
<SOUNDS LIKE SOMETHING SHE'D DO.
<AT LEAST SHE'S DOING WELL.>
<THERE'S THAT.>

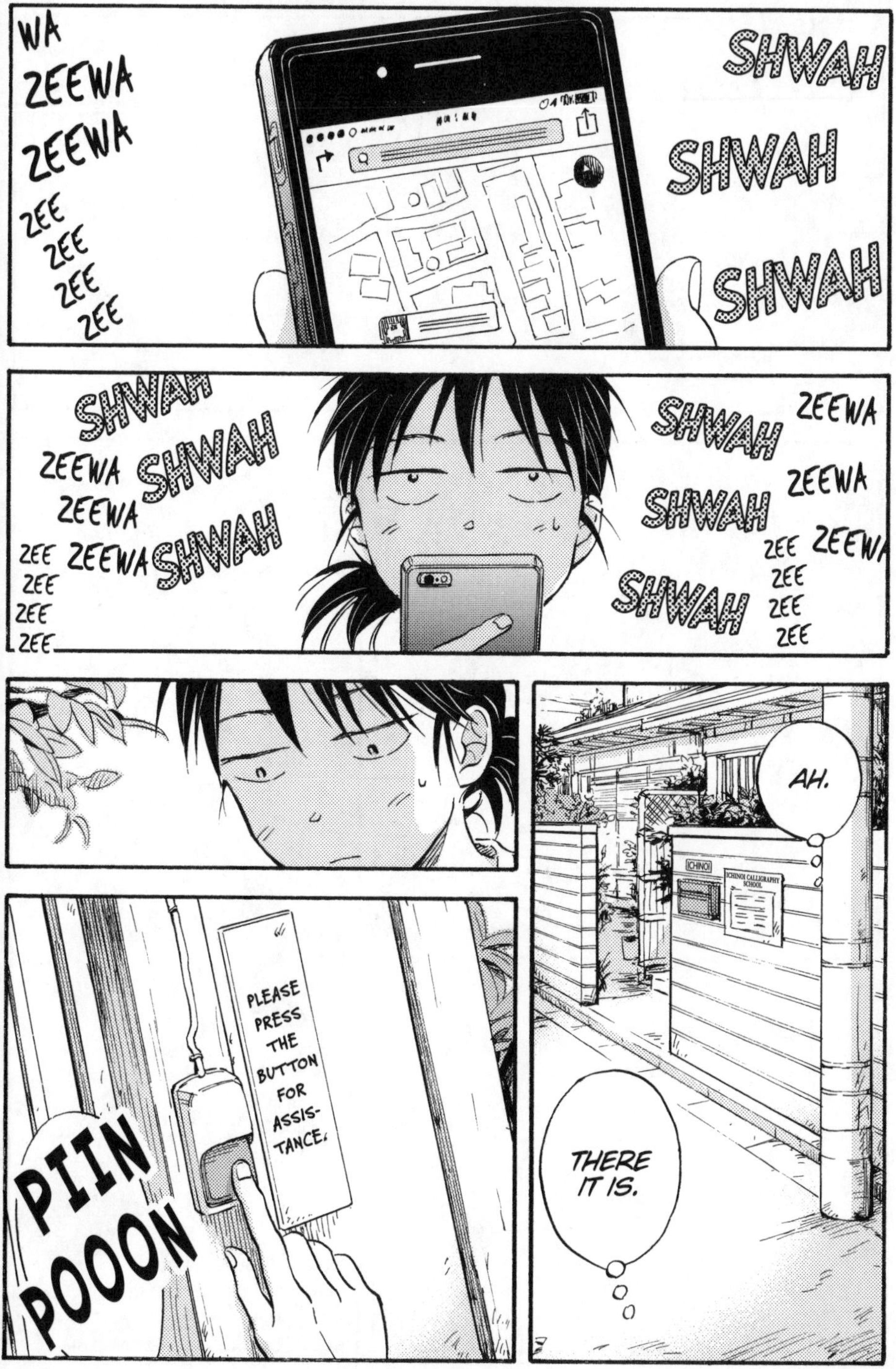
SHWAH
SHWAH
SHWAH
WA
ZEEWA
ZEEWA
ZEE
ZEE
ZEE
ZEE
ZEEWA
SHWAH
ZEEWA
SHWAH
ZEEWA
ZEE
ZEE
ZEE
ZEE
SHWAH
SHWAH
ZEEWA
SHWAH
ZEEWA
ZEEWA
SHWAH
ZEE
ZEE
ZEE
ZEE
AH.
ICHINOI
ICHINOI CALLIGRAPHY SCHOOL
THERE IT IS.
PLEASE PRESS THE BUTTON FOR ASSISTANCE.
PIIN POOON

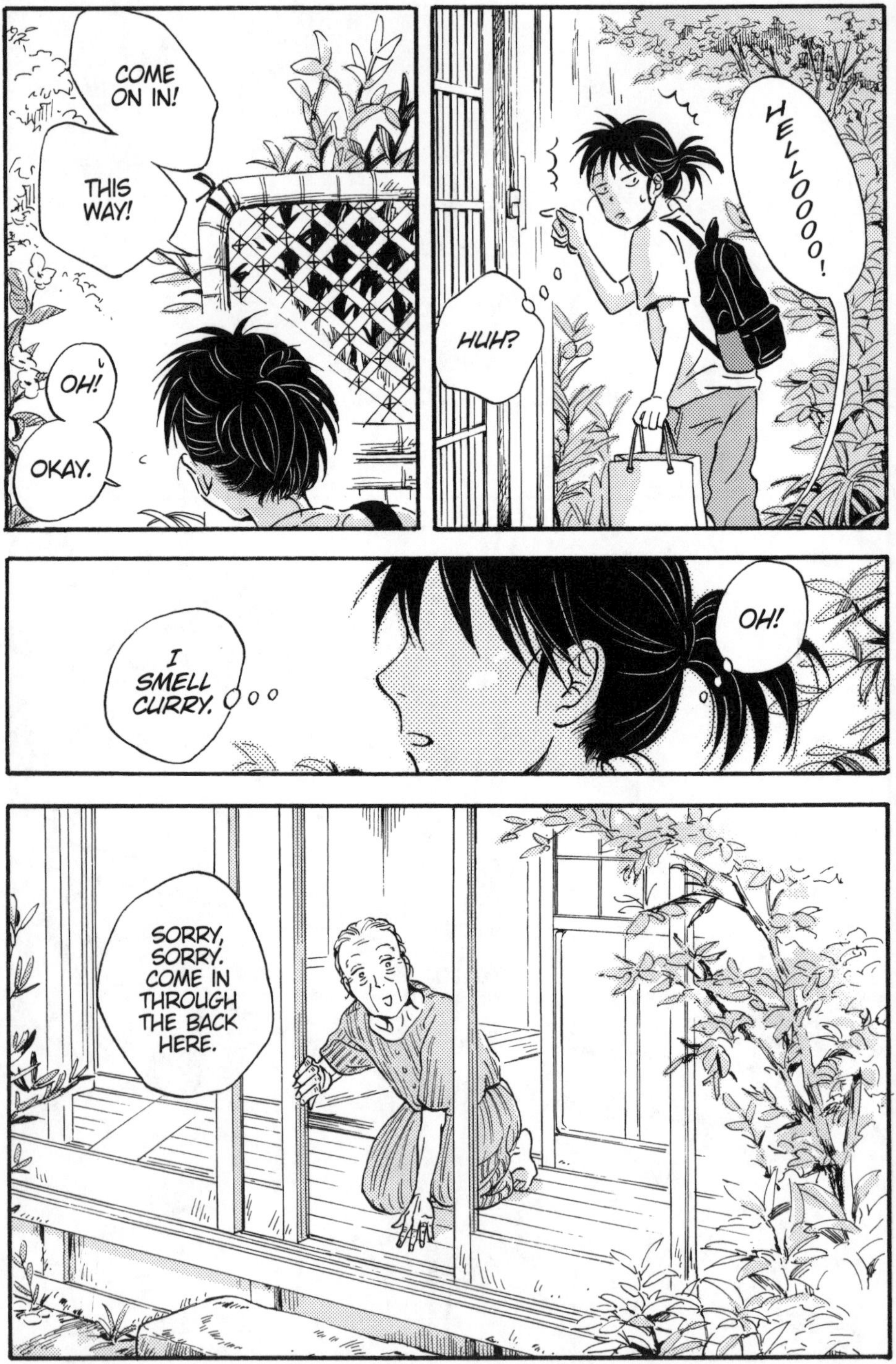
HELLOOOO!
HUH?
COME ON IN!
THIS WAY!
OH!
OKAY.
OH!
I SMELL CURRY.
SORRY, SORRY. COME IN THROUGH THE BACK HERE.

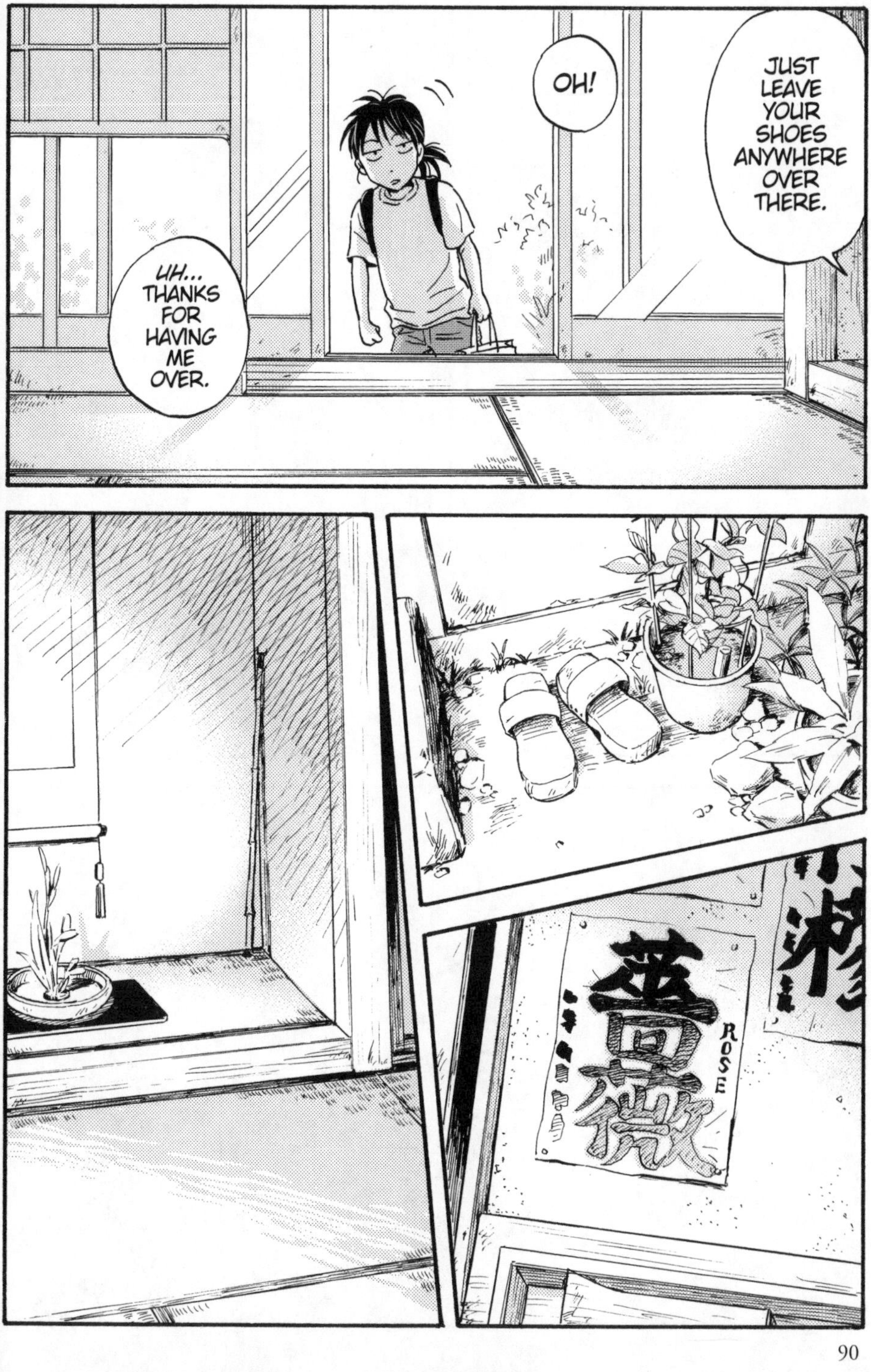
JUST LEAVE YOUR SHOES ANYWHERE OVER THERE.
OH!
UH... THANKS FOR HAVING ME OVER.
薔薇
ROSE

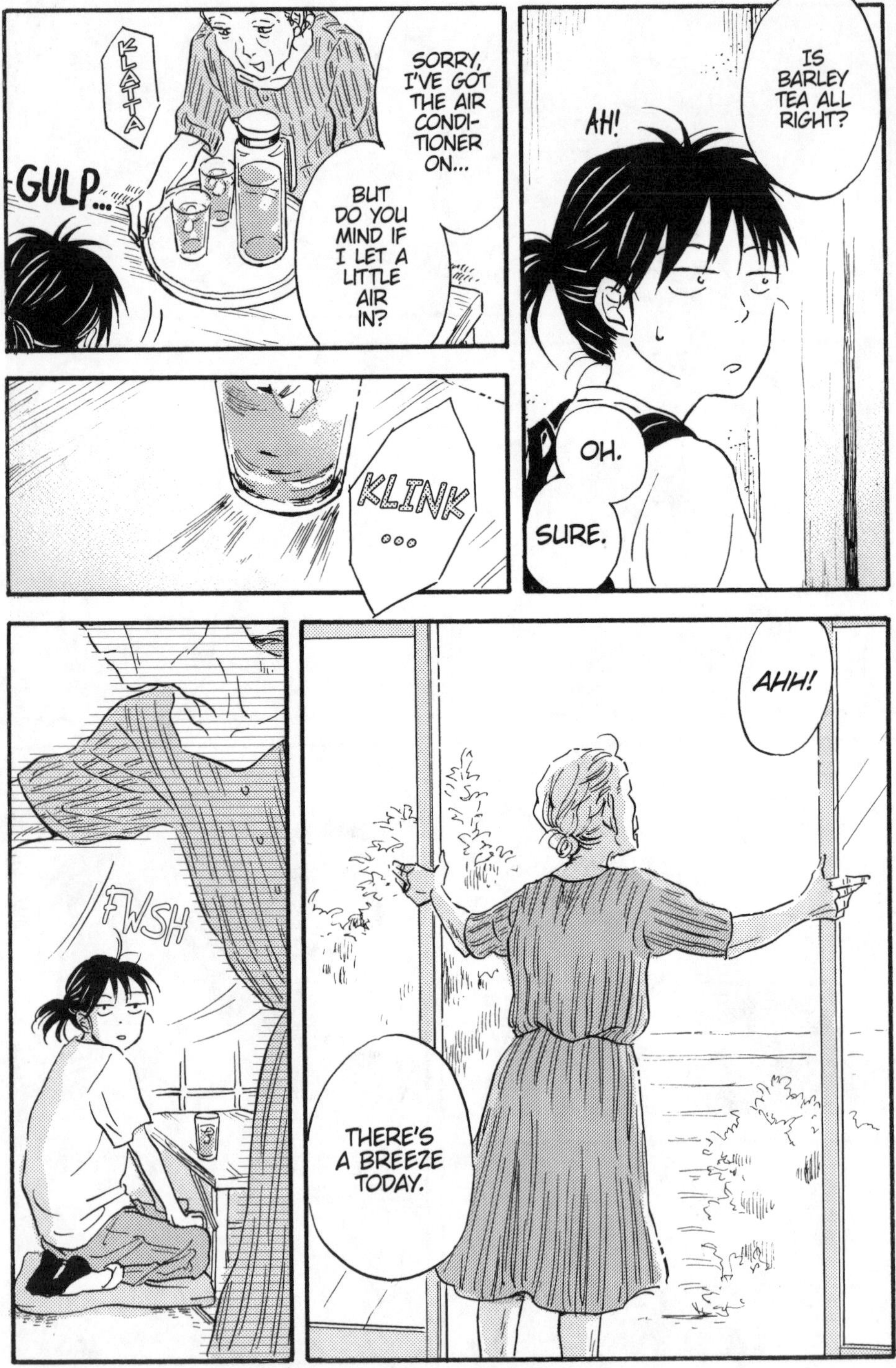
IS BARLEY TEA ALL RIGHT?
AH!
OH.
SURE.
KLATTA
SORRY, I'VE GOT THE AIR CONDITIONER ON...
BUT DO YOU MIND IF I LET A LITTLE AIR IN?
GULP...
KLINK...
AHH!
THERE'S A BREEZE TODAY.
FWSH

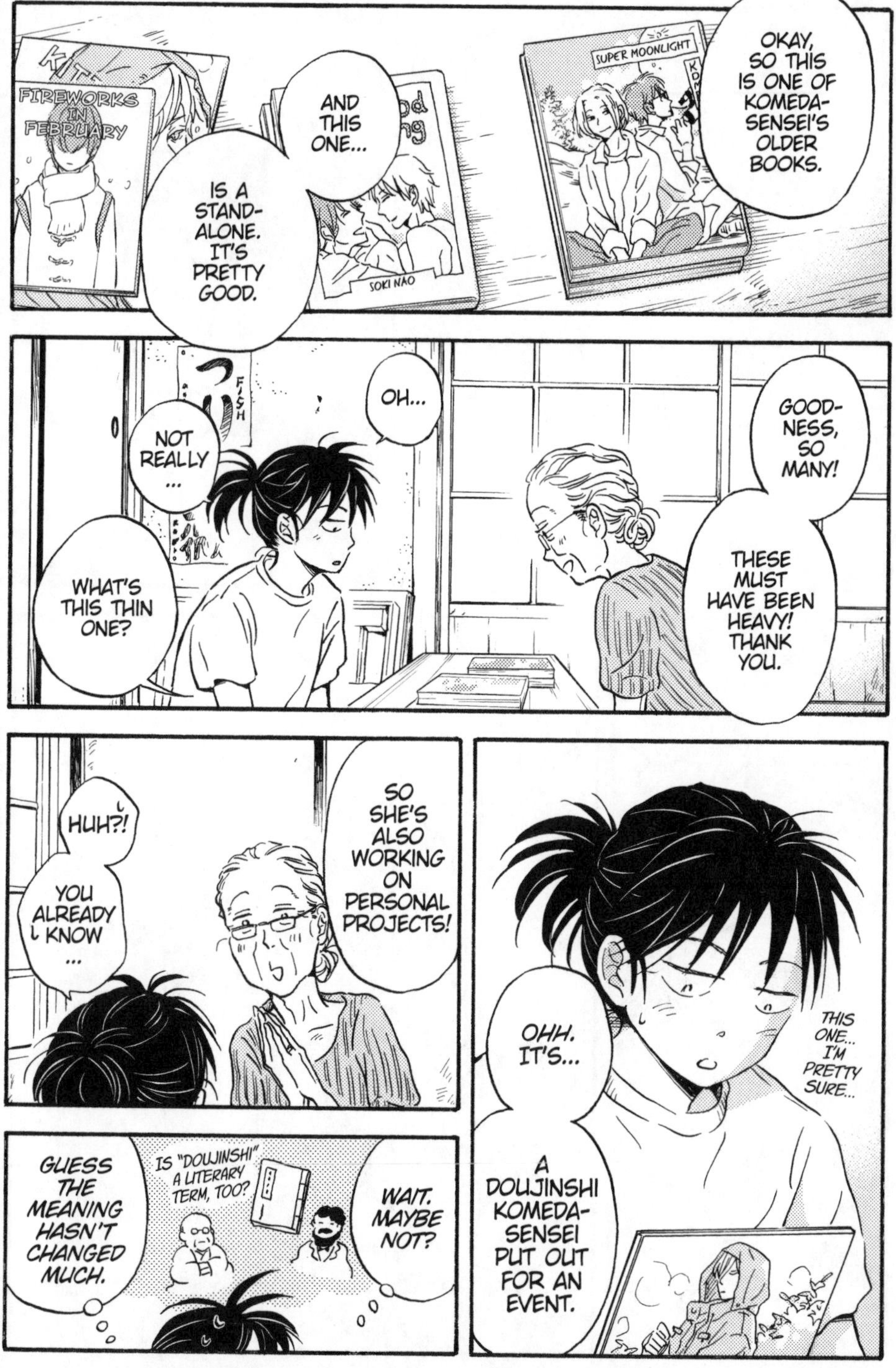
SUPER MOONLIGHT
OKAY, SO THIS IS ONE OF KOMEDA-SENSEI'S OLDER BOOKS.
AND THIS ONE...
IS A STAND-ALONE. IT'S PRETTY GOOD.
SOKI NAO
FIREWORKS IN FEBRUARY
GOODNESS, SO MANY!
THESE MUST HAVE BEEN HEAVY! THANK YOU.
OH...
FISH
NOT REALLY...
WHAT'S THIS THIN ONE?
THIS ONE... I'M PRETTY SURE...
OHH. IT'S...
A DOUJINSHI KOMEDA-SENSEI PUT OUT FOR AN EVENT.
SO SHE'S ALSO WORKING ON PERSONAL PROJECTS!
HUH?!
YOU ALREADY KNOW...
WAIT. MAYBE NOT?
IS "DOUJINSHI" A LITERARY TERM, TOO?
GUESS THE MEANING HASN'T CHANGED MUCH.

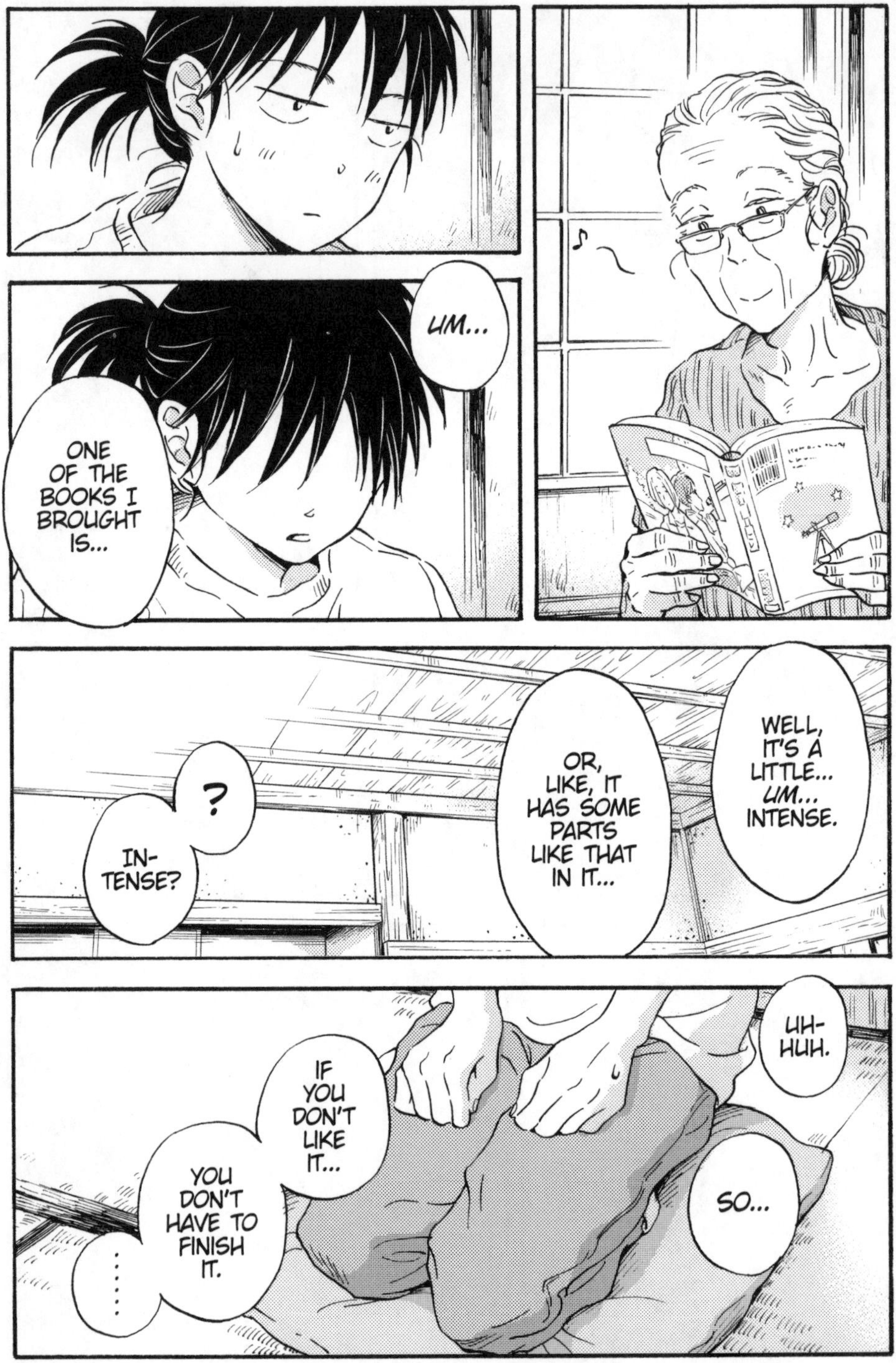
UM...
ONE OF THE BOOKS I BROUGHT IS...
WELL, IT'S A LITTLE... UM... INTENSE.
OR, LIKE, IT HAS SOME PARTS LIKE THAT IN IT...
?
IN-TENSE?
UH-HUH.
SO...
IF YOU DON'T LIKE IT...
YOU DON'T HAVE TO FINISH IT.
......

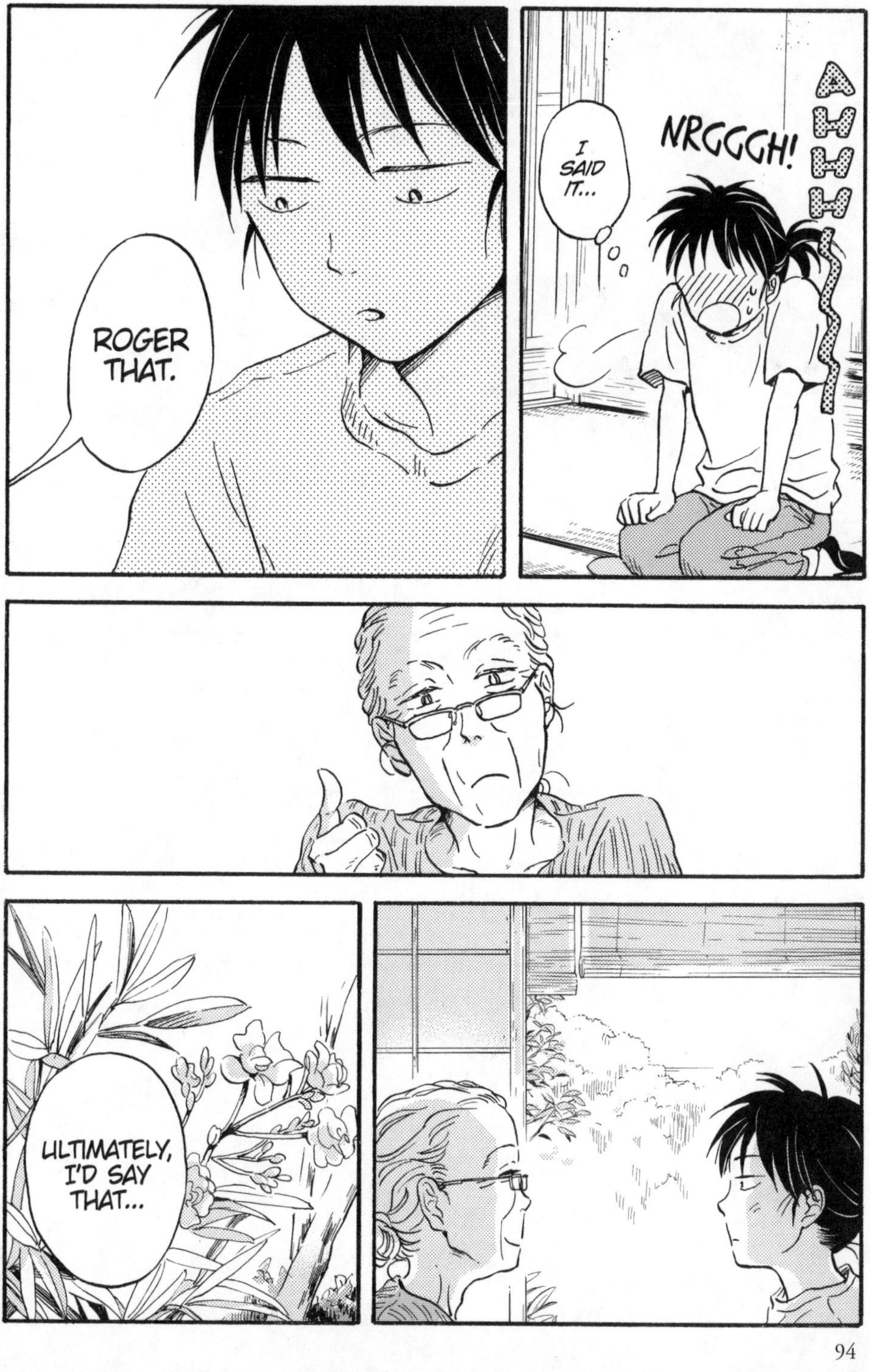
AHHH
NRGGGH!
I SAID IT...
ROGER THAT.
ULTIMATELY, I'D SAY THAT...

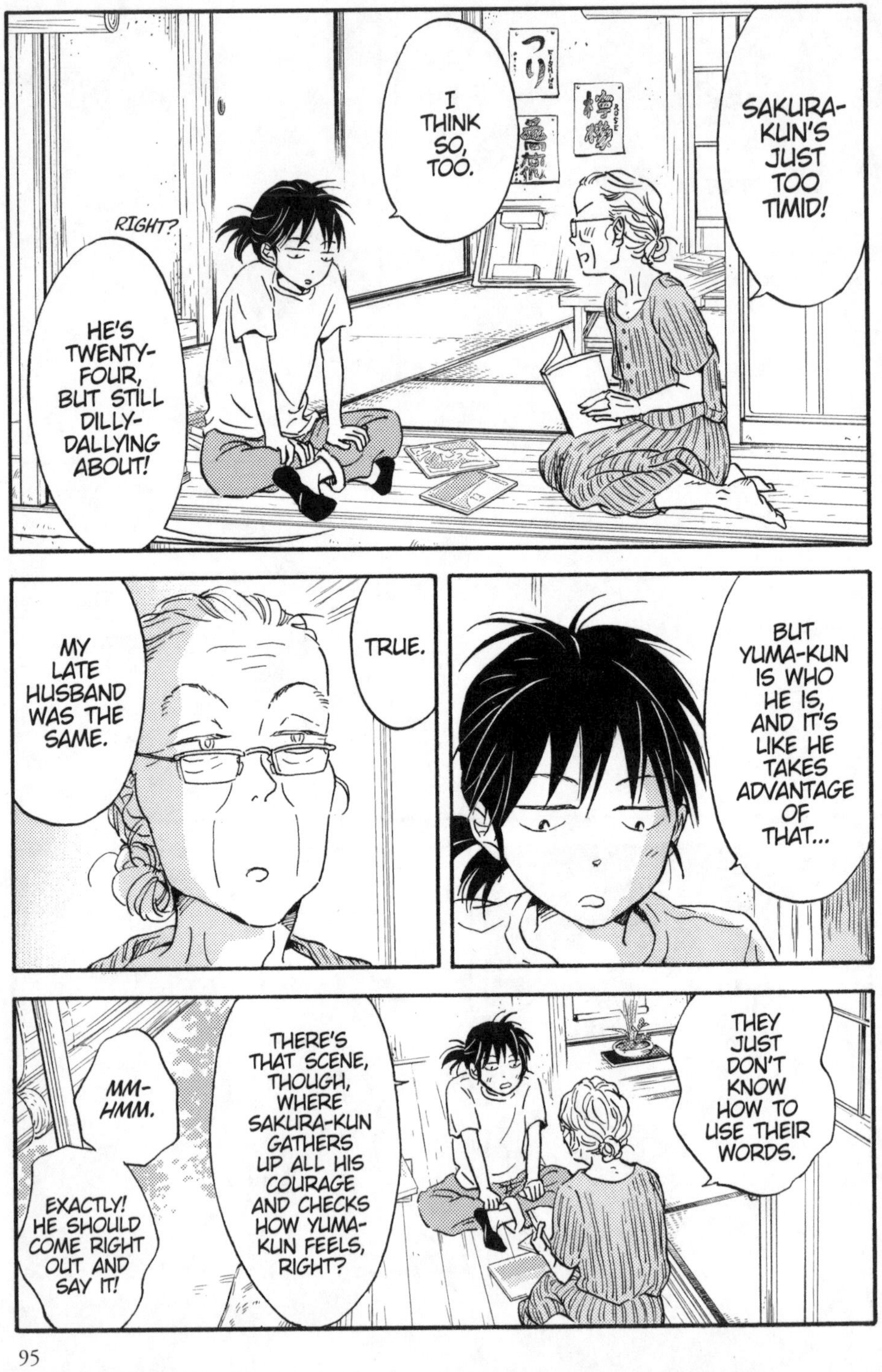
SAKURA-KUN'S JUST TOO TIMID!
I THINK SO, TOO.
RIGHT?
HE'S TWENTY-FOUR, BUT STILL DILLY-DALLYING ABOUT!
BUT YUMA-KUN IS WHO HE IS, AND IT'S LIKE HE TAKES ADVANTAGE OF THAT...
TRUE.
MY LATE HUSBAND WAS THE SAME.
THEY JUST DON'T KNOW HOW TO USE THEIR WORDS.
THERE'S THAT SCENE, THOUGH, WHERE SAKURA-KUN GATHERS UP ALL HIS COURAGE AND CHECKS HOW YUMA-KUN FEELS, RIGHT?
MM-HMM.
EXACTLY! HE SHOULD COME RIGHT OUT AND SAY IT!

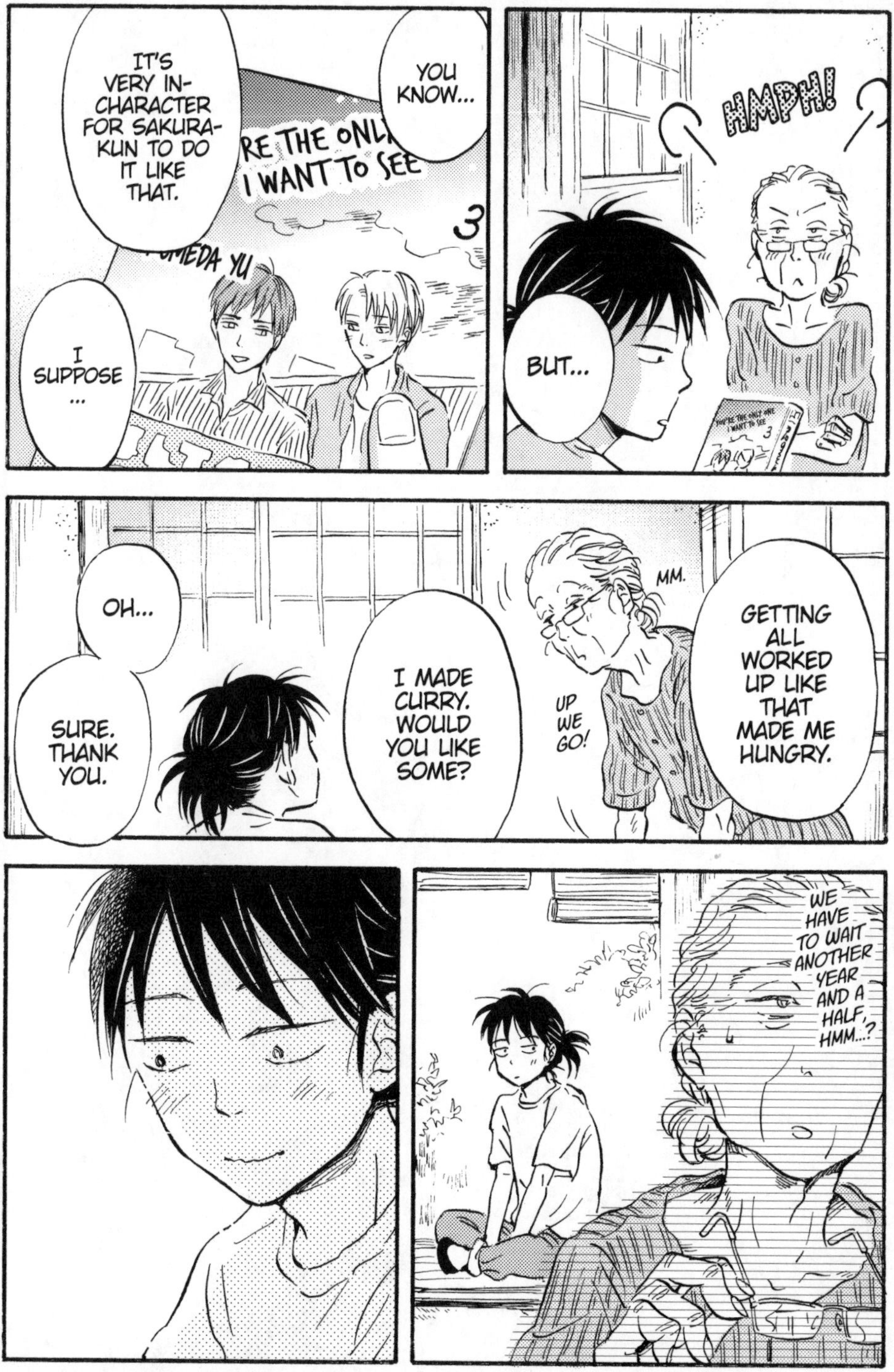
HMPH!
BUT...
YOU KNOW...
IT'S VERY IN-CHARACTER FOR SAKURA-KUN TO DO IT LIKE THAT.
I WANT TO SEE
I SUPPOSE...
GETTING ALL WORKED UP LIKE THAT MADE ME HUNGRY.
MM.
UP WE GO!
I MADE CURRY. WOULD YOU LIKE SOME?
OH...
SURE. THANK YOU.
WE HAVE TO WAIT ANOTHER YEAR AND A HALF, HMM...?

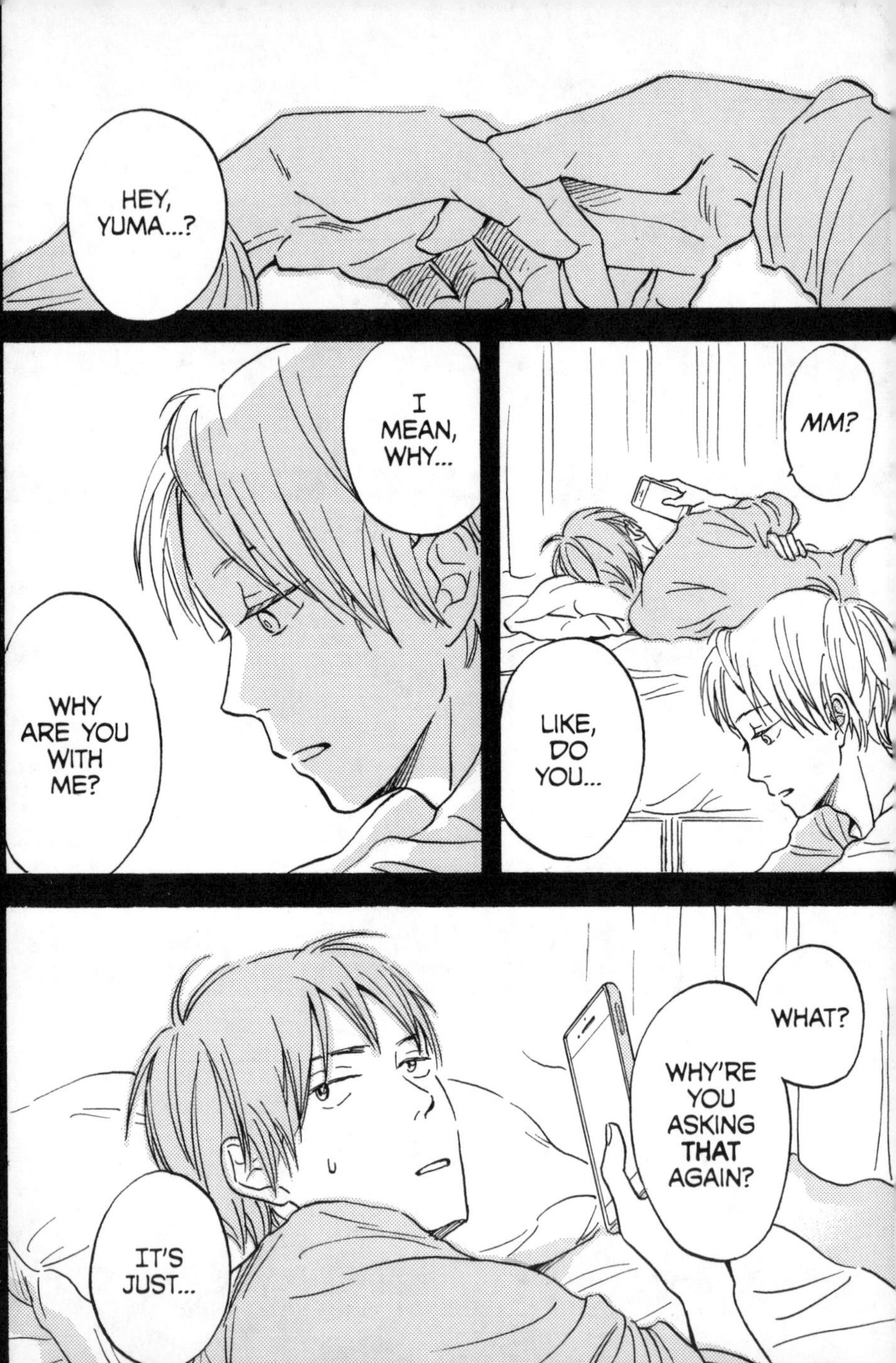
HEY, YUMA...?
MM?
LIKE, DO YOU...
I MEAN, WHY...
WHY ARE YOU WITH ME?
WHAT?
WHY'RE YOU ASKING **THAT** AGAIN?
IT'S JUST...

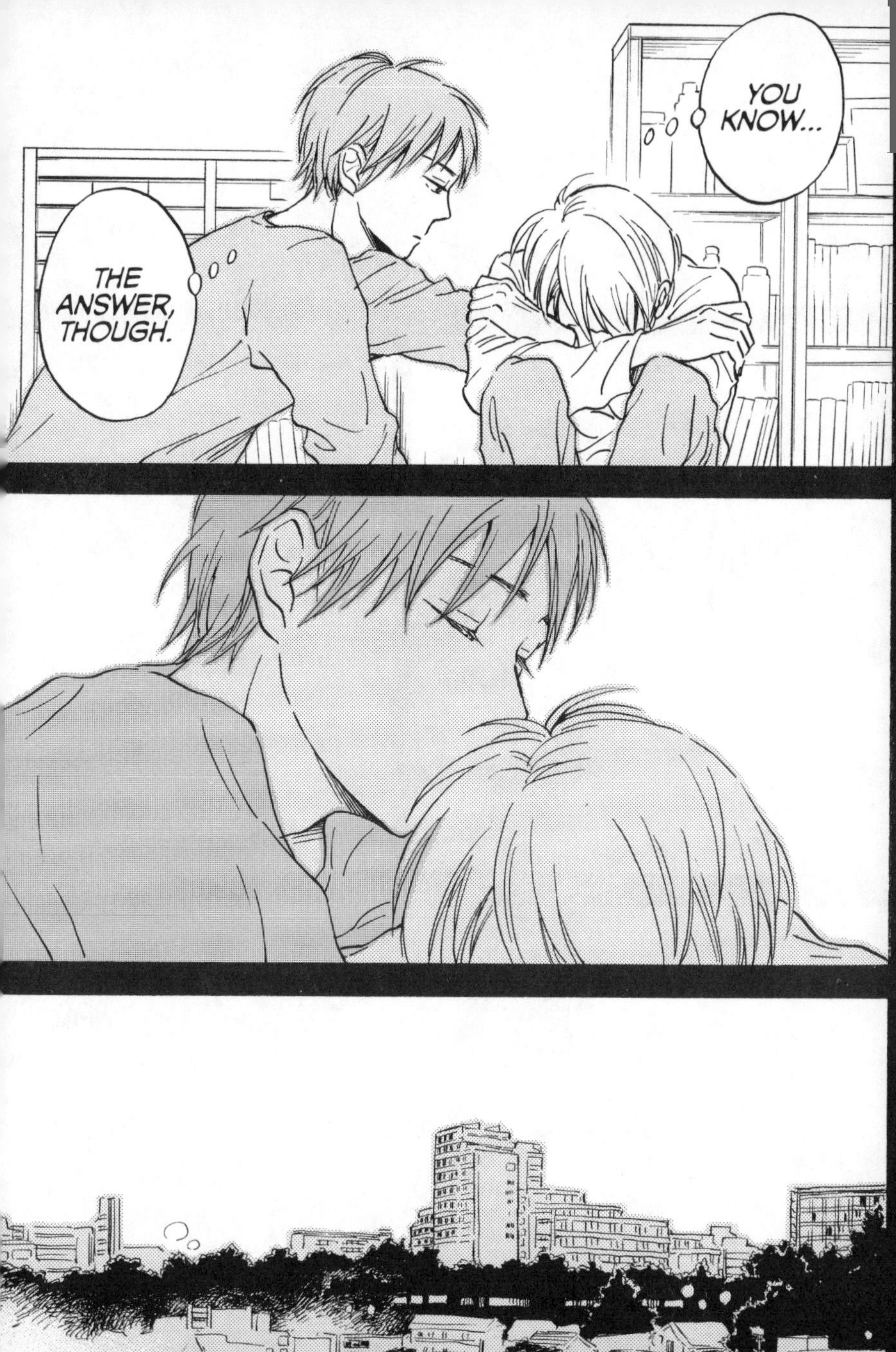
YOU KNOW...
THE ANSWER, THOUGH.

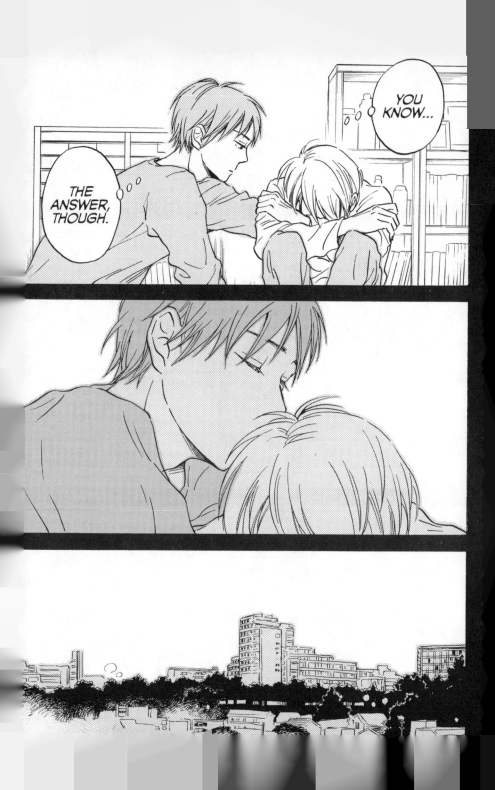

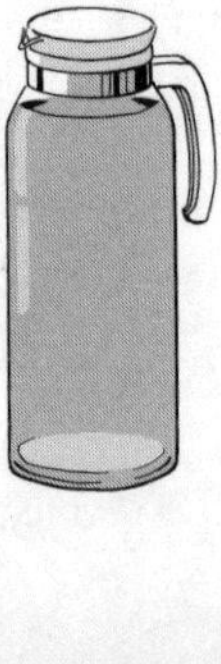

metamorphosis

Chapter 8

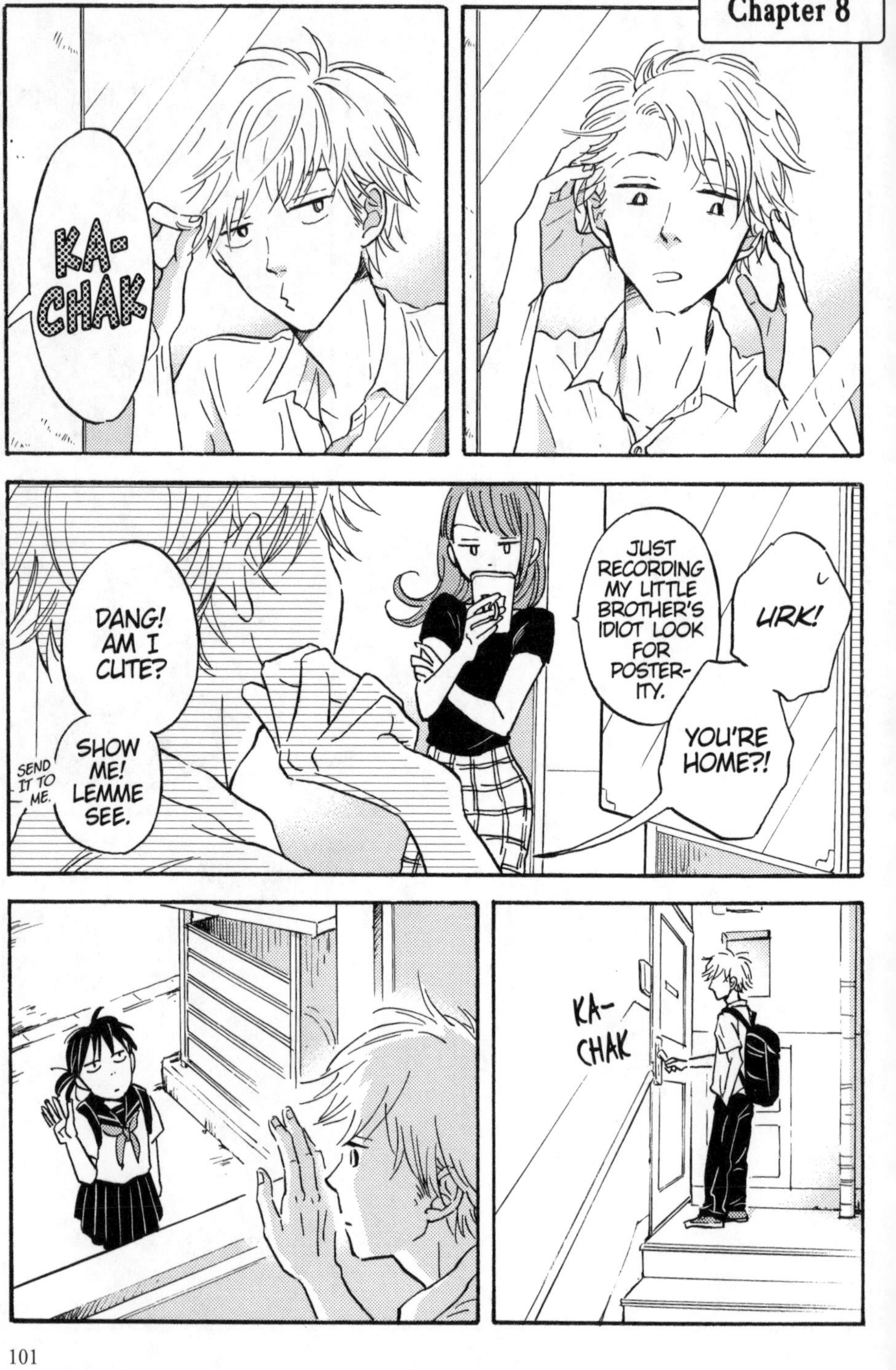
KA-CHAK
URK!
YOU'RE HOME?!
JUST RECORDING MY LITTLE BROTHER'S IDIOT LOOK FOR POSTER-ITY.
DANG! AM I CUTE?
SHOW ME! LEMME SEE.
SEND IT TO ME.
KA-CHAK

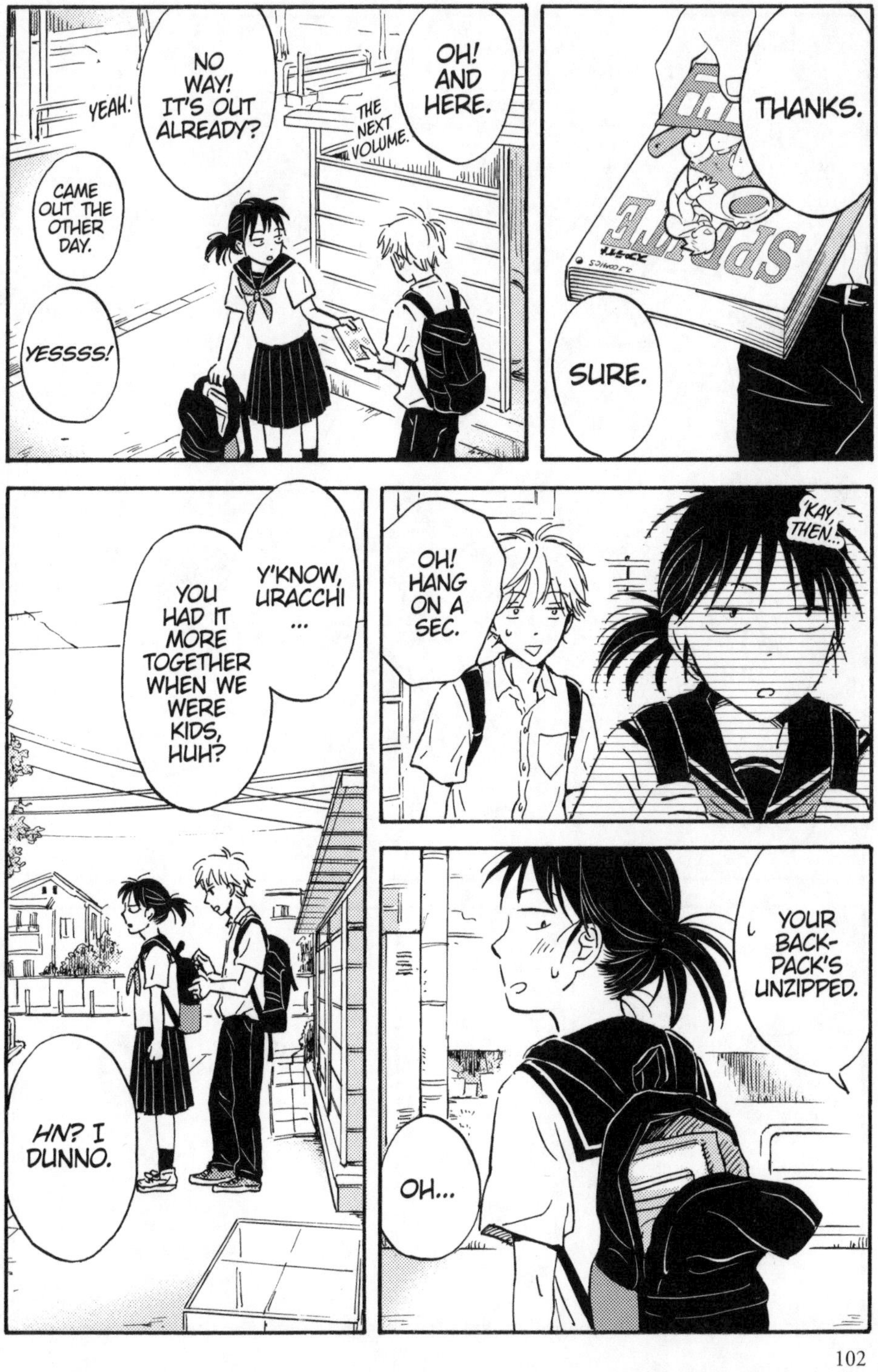
THANKS.
SURE.
OH! AND HERE.
THE NEXT VOLUME.
NO WAY! IT'S OUT ALREADY?
YEAH.
CAME OUT THE OTHER DAY.
YESSSS!
'KAY, THEN...
OH! HANG ON A SEC.
YOUR BACK-PACK'S UNZIPPED.
OH...
Y'KNOW, URACCHI ...
YOU HAD IT MORE TOGETHER WHEN WE WERE KIDS, HUH?
HN? I DUNNO.

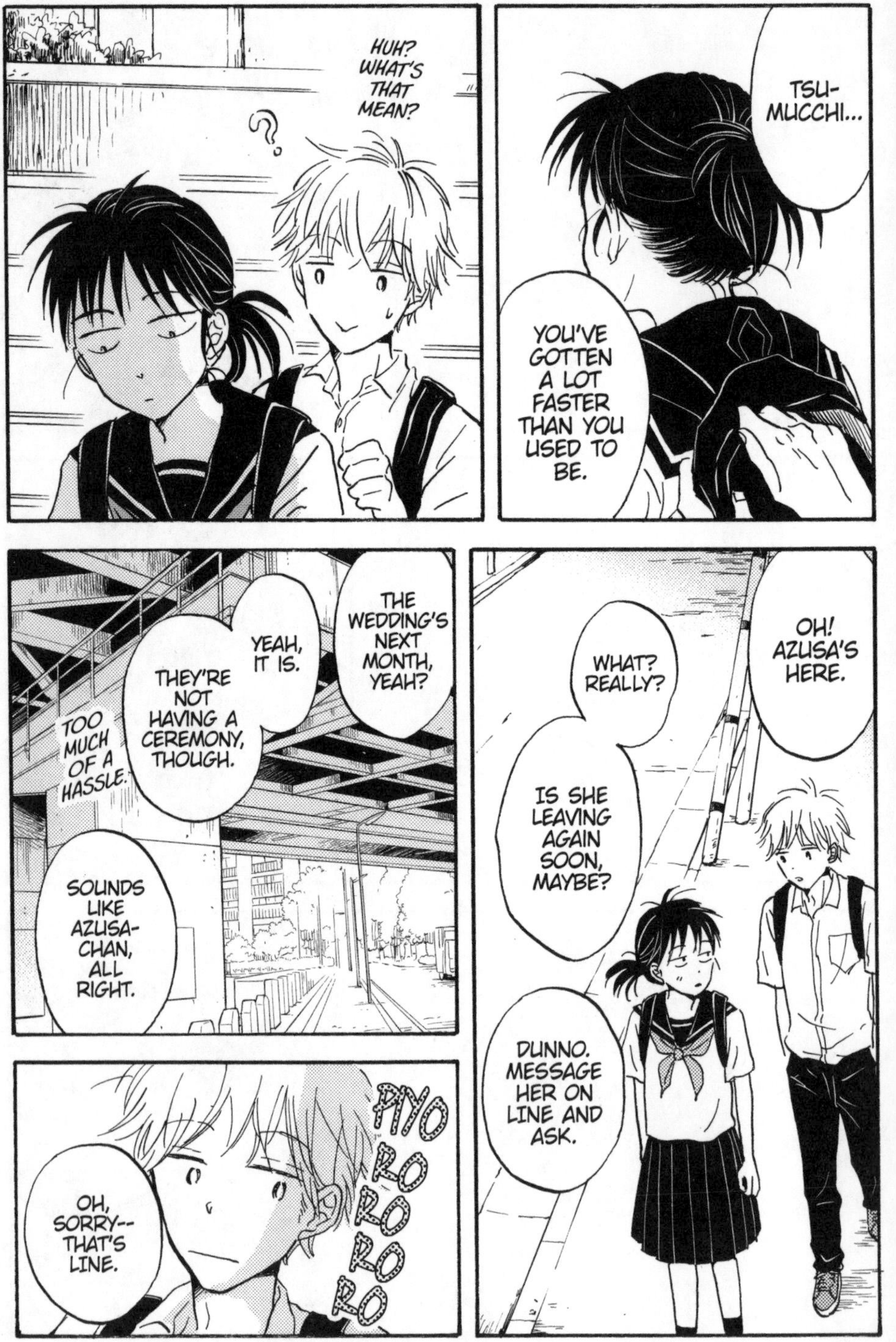
TSU-MUCCHI...
YOU'VE GOTTEN A LOT FASTER THAN YOU USED TO BE.
HUH? WHAT'S THAT MEAN?
?
OH! AZUSA'S HERE.
WHAT? REALLY?
IS SHE LEAVING AGAIN SOON, MAYBE?
DUNNO. MESSAGE HER ON LINE AND ASK.
THE WEDDING'S NEXT MONTH, YEAH?
YEAH, IT IS.
THEY'RE NOT HAVING A CEREMONY, THOUGH.
TOO MUCH OF A HASSLE.
SOUNDS LIKE AZUSA-CHAN, ALL RIGHT.
PIYO RO RO RO RO RO
OH, SORRY-- THAT'S LINE.

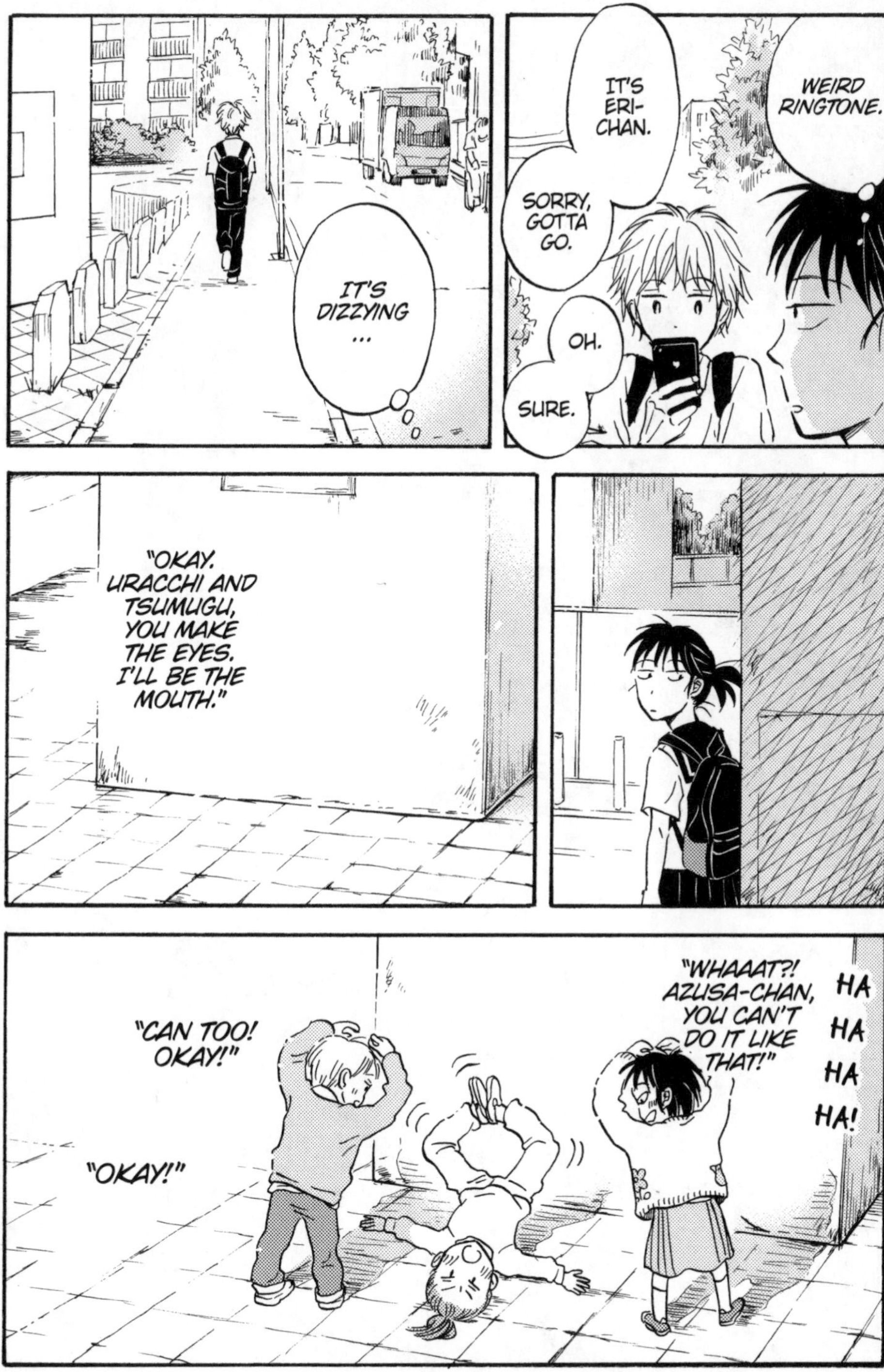
WEIRD RINGTONE.
IT'S ERI-CHAN.
SORRY, GOTTA GO.
OH.
SURE.
IT'S DIZZYING ...
"OKAY. URACCHI AND TSUMUGU, YOU MAKE THE EYES. I'LL BE THE MOUTH."
HA HA HA HA!
"WHAAAT?! AZUSA-CHAN, YOU CAN'T DO IT LIKE THAT!"
"CAN TOO! OKAY!"
"OKAY!"

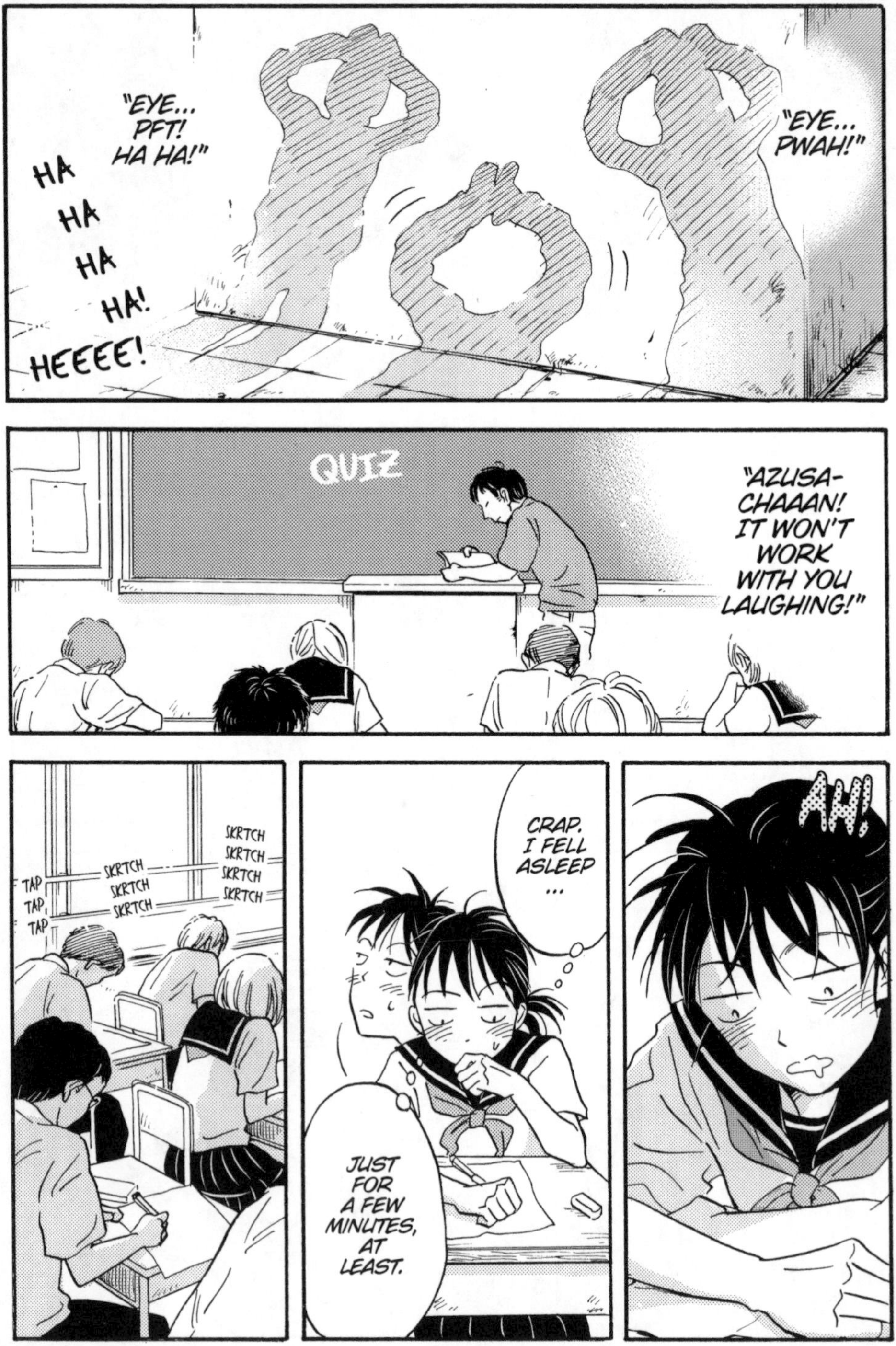
"EYE... PWAH!"
"EYE... PFT! HA HA!"
HA HA HA HA!
HEEEE!
QUIZ
"AZUSA-CHAAAN! IT WON'T WORK WITH YOU LAUGHING!"
AH!
CRAP. I FELL ASLEEP ...
JUST FOR A FEW MINUTES, AT LEAST.
SKRTCH SKRTCH SKRTCH SKRTCH
SKRTCH SKRTCH SKRTCH
TAP TAP, TAP

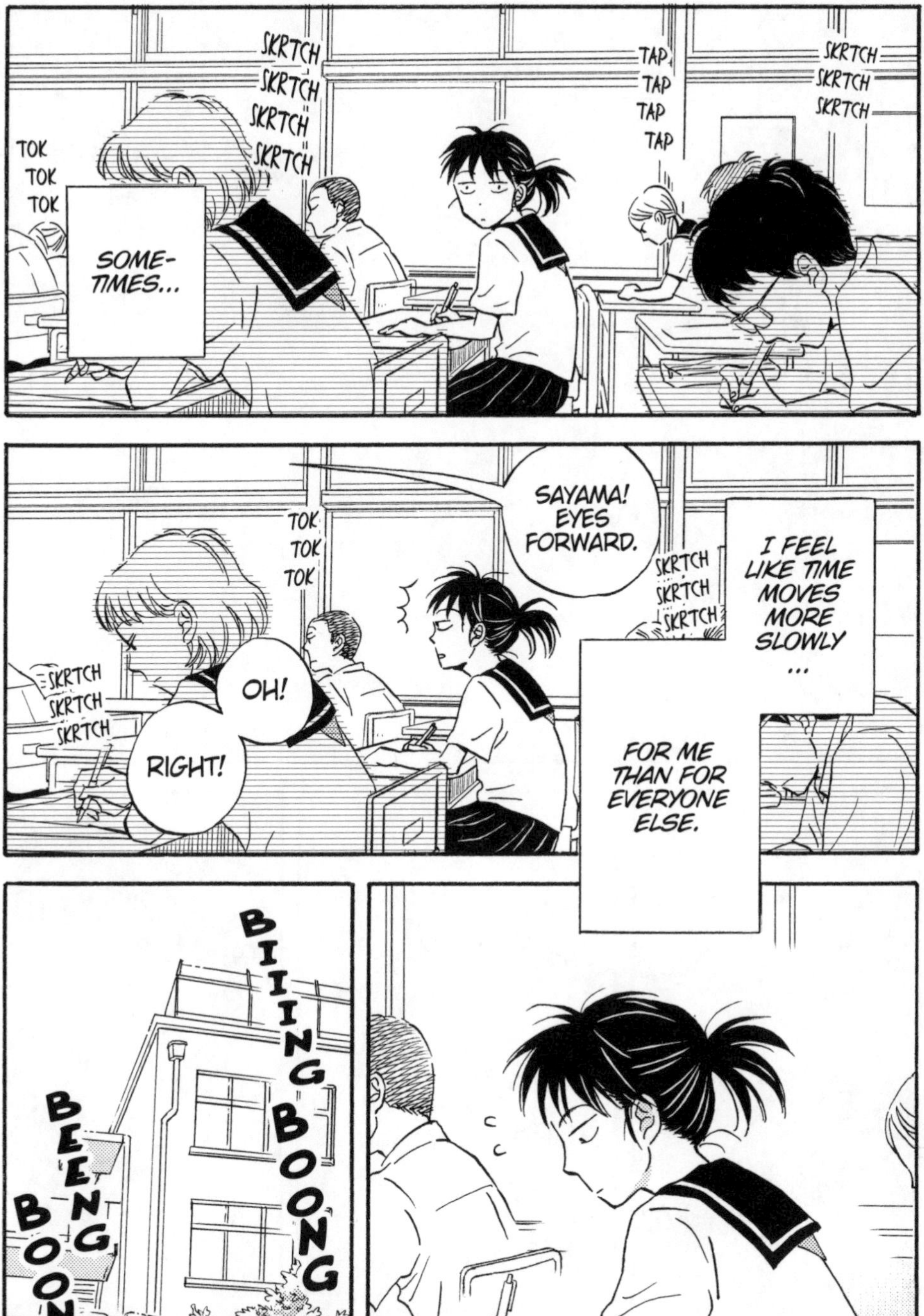

SKRTCH SKRTCH SKRTCH
TAP TAP TAP TAP
SKRTCH SKRTCH SKRTCH SKRTCH
TOK TOK TOK
SOME-TIMES...
SAYAMA! EYES FORWARD.
I FEEL LIKE TIME MOVES MORE SLOWLY ...
FOR ME THAN FOR EVERYONE ELSE.
SKRTCH SKRTCH SKRTCH
TOK TOK TOK
OH!
RIGHT!
SKRTCH SKRTCH SKRTCH
BIIING BOONG
BEENG BOONG

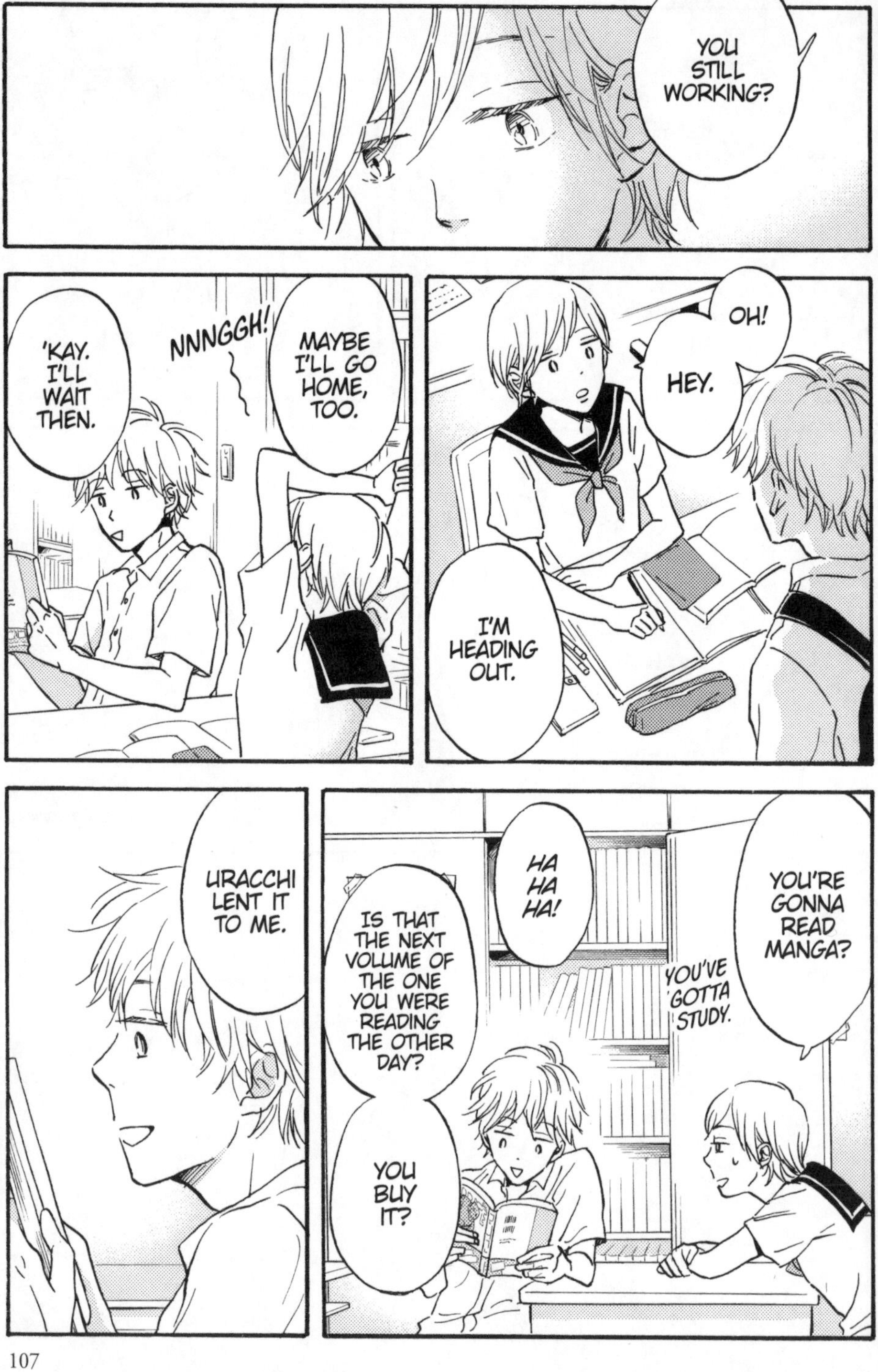
YOU STILL WORKING?
OH!
HEY.
I'M HEADING OUT.
MAYBE I'LL GO HOME, TOO.
NNNGGH!
'KAY. I'LL WAIT THEN.
YOU'RE GONNA READ MANGA?
YOU'VE GOTTA STUDY.
HA HA HA!
IS THAT THE NEXT VOLUME OF THE ONE YOU WERE READING THE OTHER DAY?
YOU BUY IT?
URACCHI LENT IT TO ME.

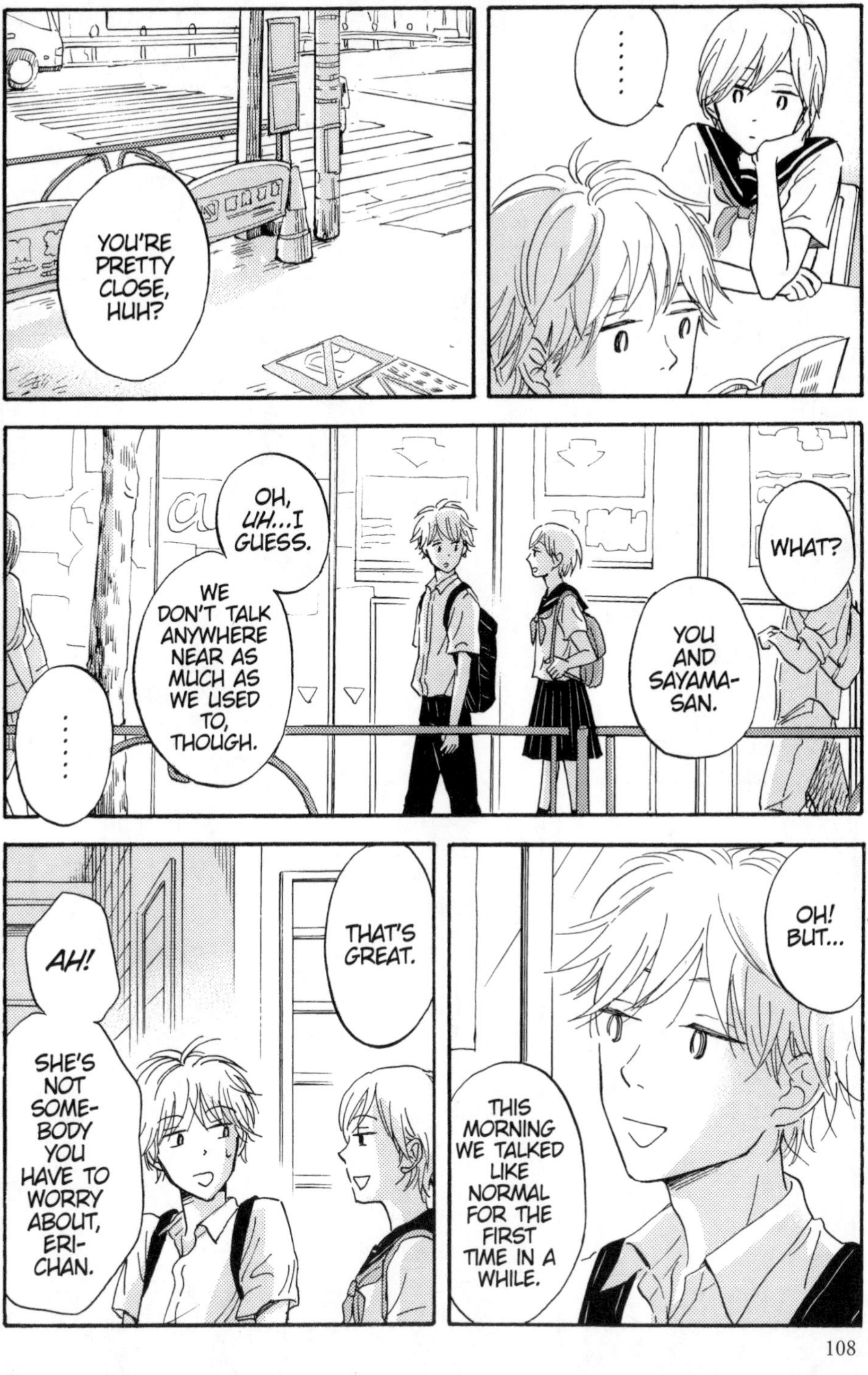
……
YOU'RE PRETTY CLOSE, HUH?
WHAT?
YOU AND SAYAMA-SAN.
OH, UH...I GUESS.
WE DON'T TALK ANYWHERE NEAR AS MUCH AS WE USED TO, THOUGH.
……
OH! BUT...
THIS MORNING WE TALKED LIKE NORMAL FOR THE FIRST TIME IN A WHILE.
THAT'S GREAT.
AH!
SHE'S NOT SOMEBODY YOU HAVE TO WORRY ABOUT, ERI-CHAN.

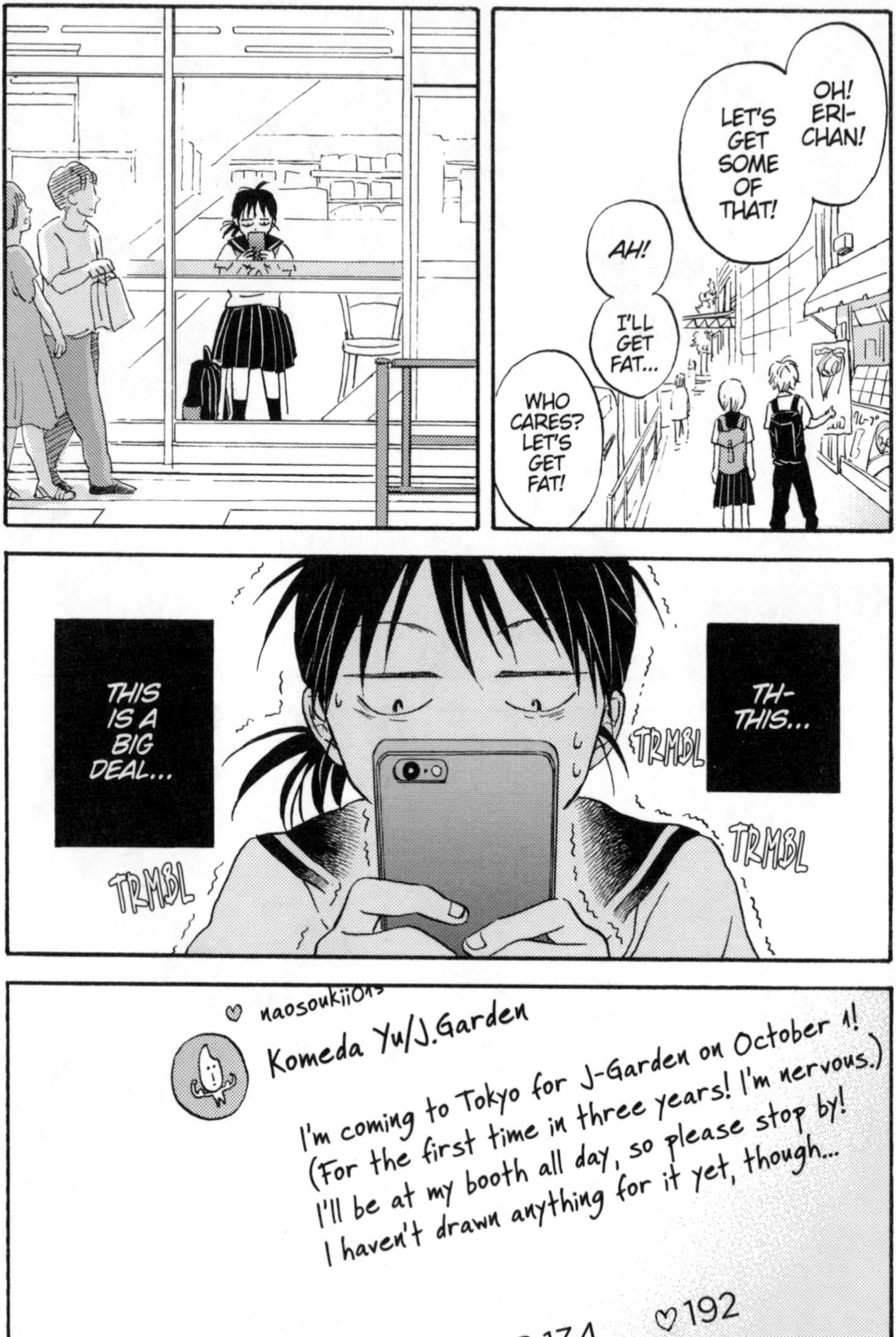
OH! ERI-CHAN!
LET'S GET SOME OF THAT!
AH!
I'LL GET FAT...
WHO CARES? LET'S GET FAT!
TH- THIS...
TRMBL
TRMBL
THIS IS A BIG DEAL...
TRMBL
naosoukii01
Komeda Yu/J.Garden
I'm coming to Tokyo for J-Garden on October 1!
(For the first time in three years! I'm nervous.)
I'll be at my booth all day, so please stop by!
I haven't drawn anything for it yet, though...
192
134

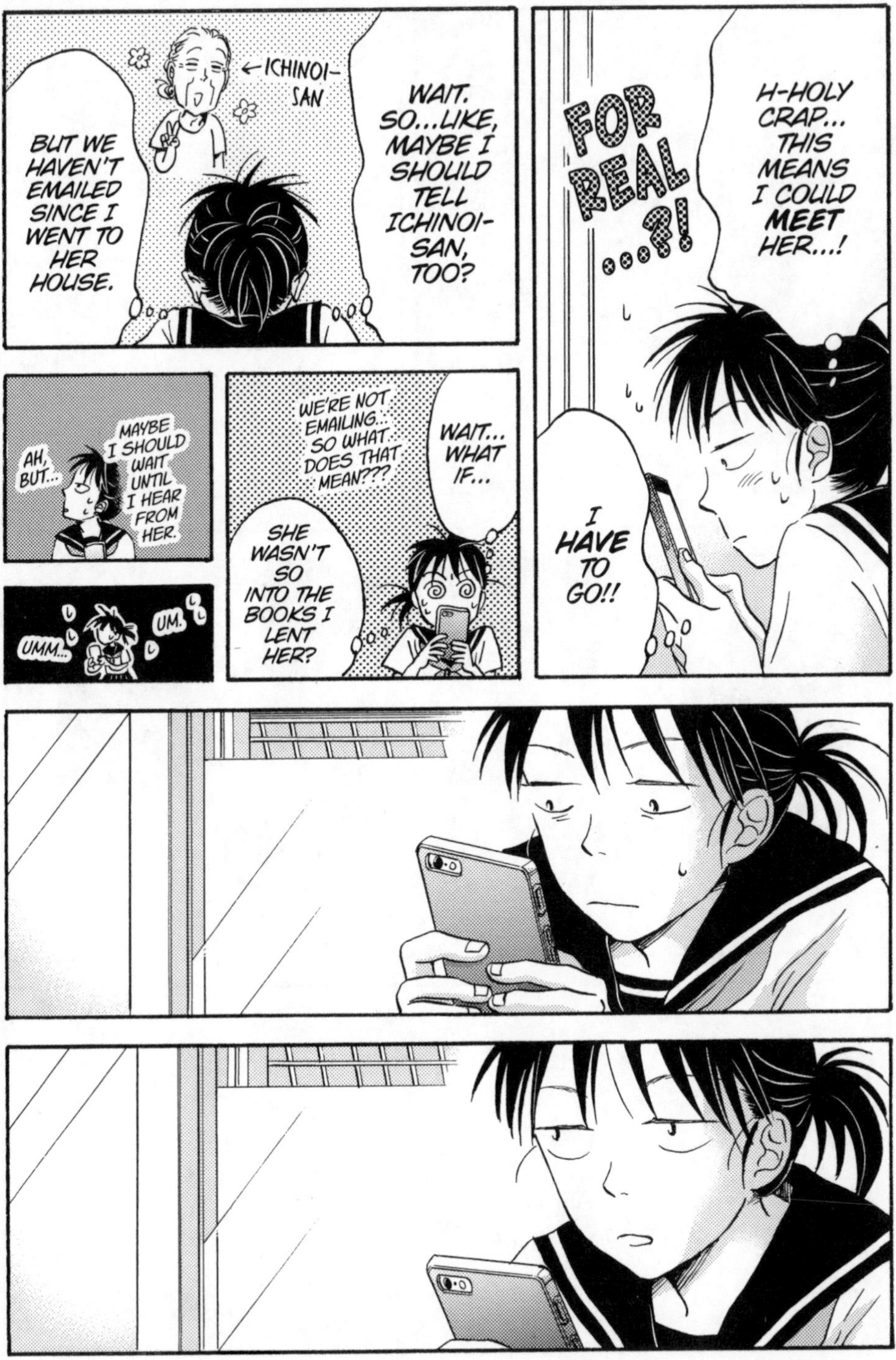
H-HOLY CRAP... THIS MEANS I COULD MEET HER...!
FOR REAL...?!
I HAVE TO GO!!
WAIT. SO...LIKE, MAYBE I SHOULD TELL ICHINOI-SAN, TOO?
←ICHINOI-SAN
BUT WE HAVEN'T EMAILED SINCE I WENT TO HER HOUSE.
WAIT... WHAT IF...
SHE WASN'T SO INTO THE BOOKS I LENT HER?
WE'RE NOT EMAILING... SO WHAT DOES THAT MEAN???
AH, BUT...
MAYBE I SHOULD WAIT UNTIL I HEAR FROM HER.
UMM...
UM.

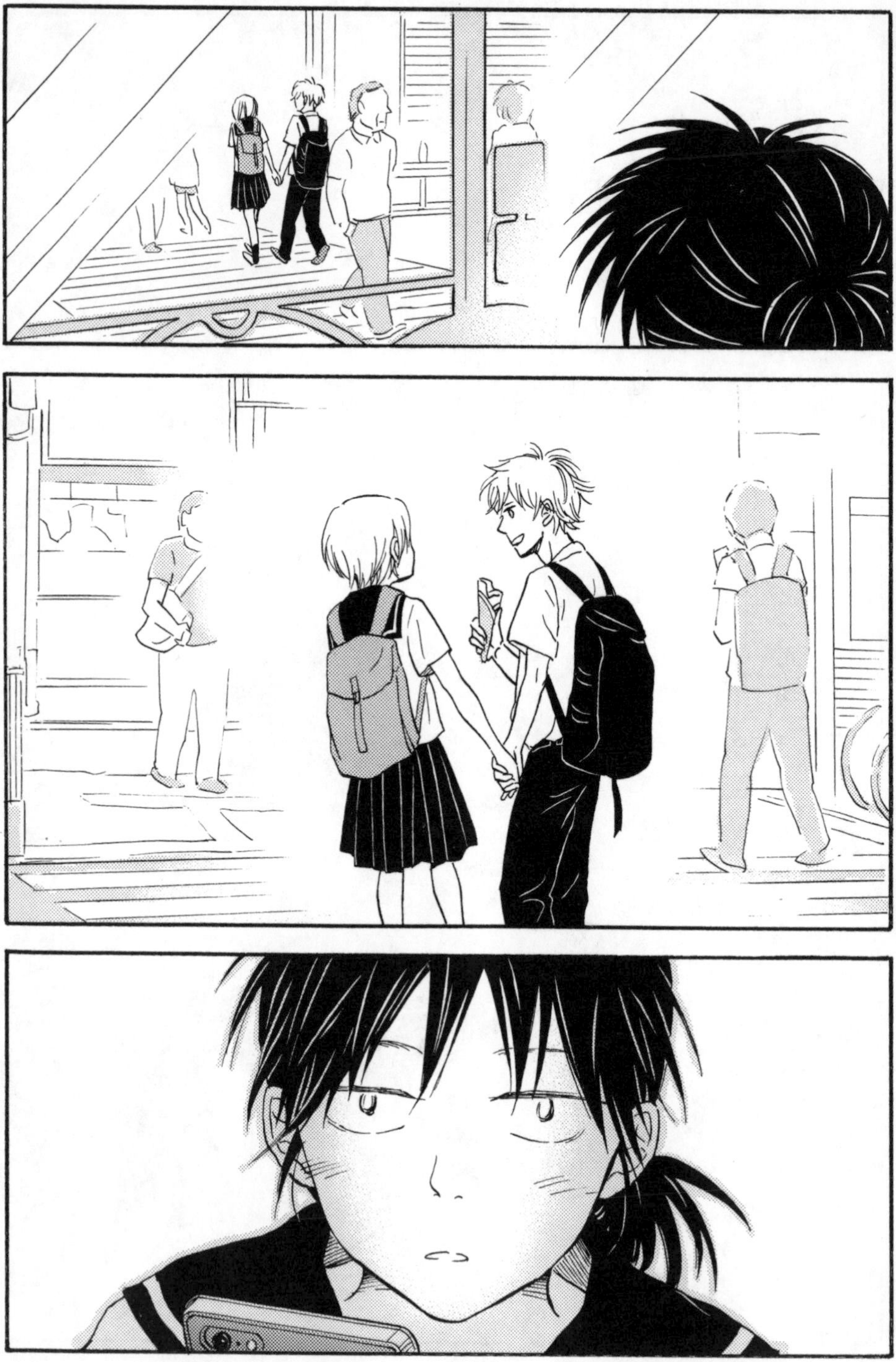

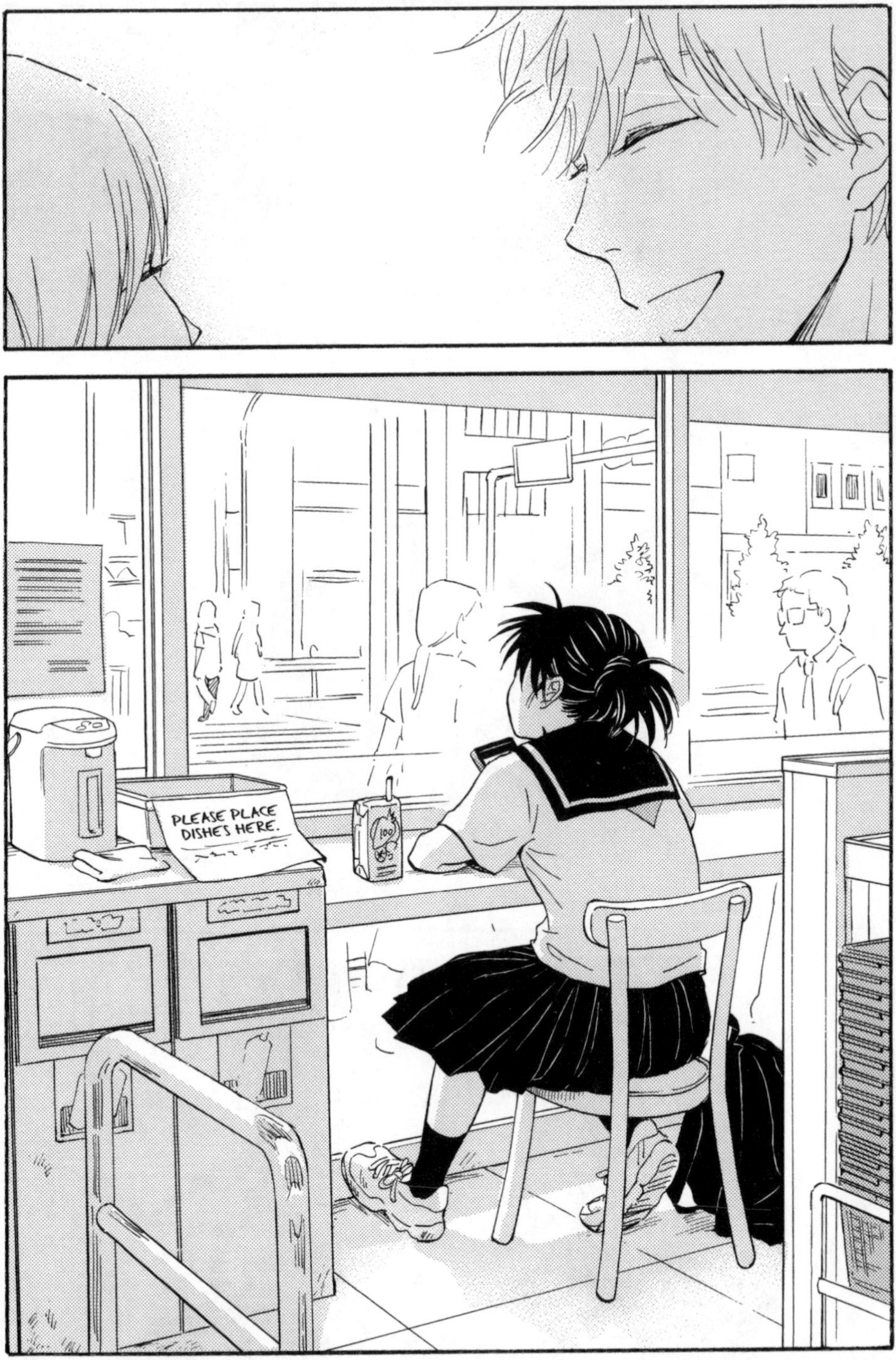
PLEASE PLACE DISHES HERE.

Chapter 8/END

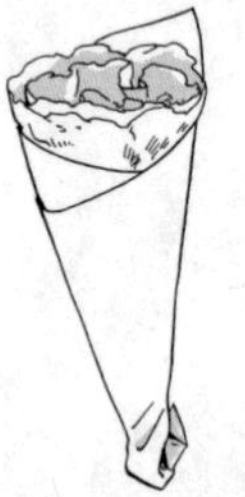

Metamorphosis

Chapter 9

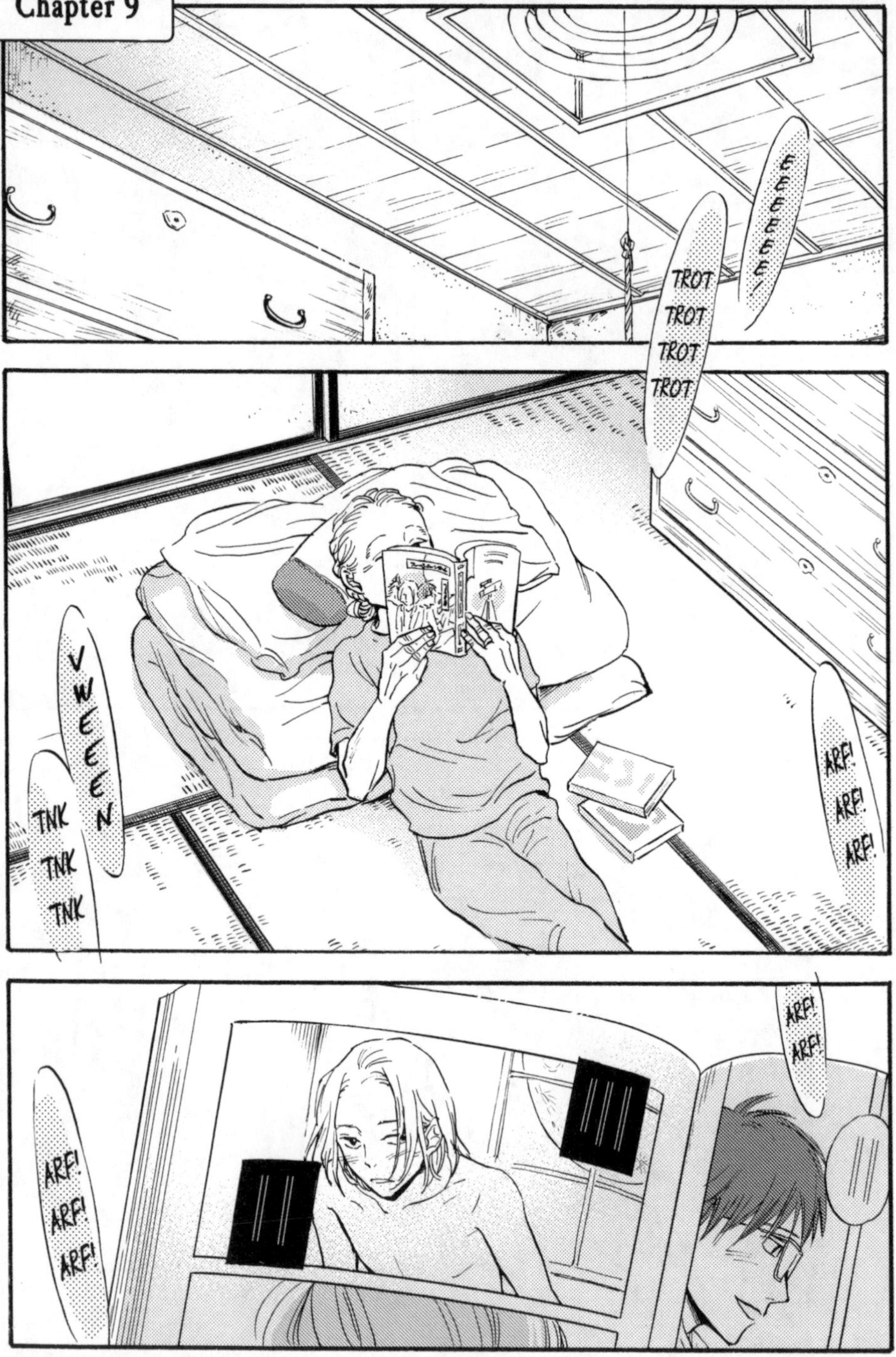
EEEEEEE!
TROT TROT TROT TROT
ARF! ARF! ARF!
VWEEEEN
TNK TNK TNK
ARF! ARF!
ARF! ARF! ARF!

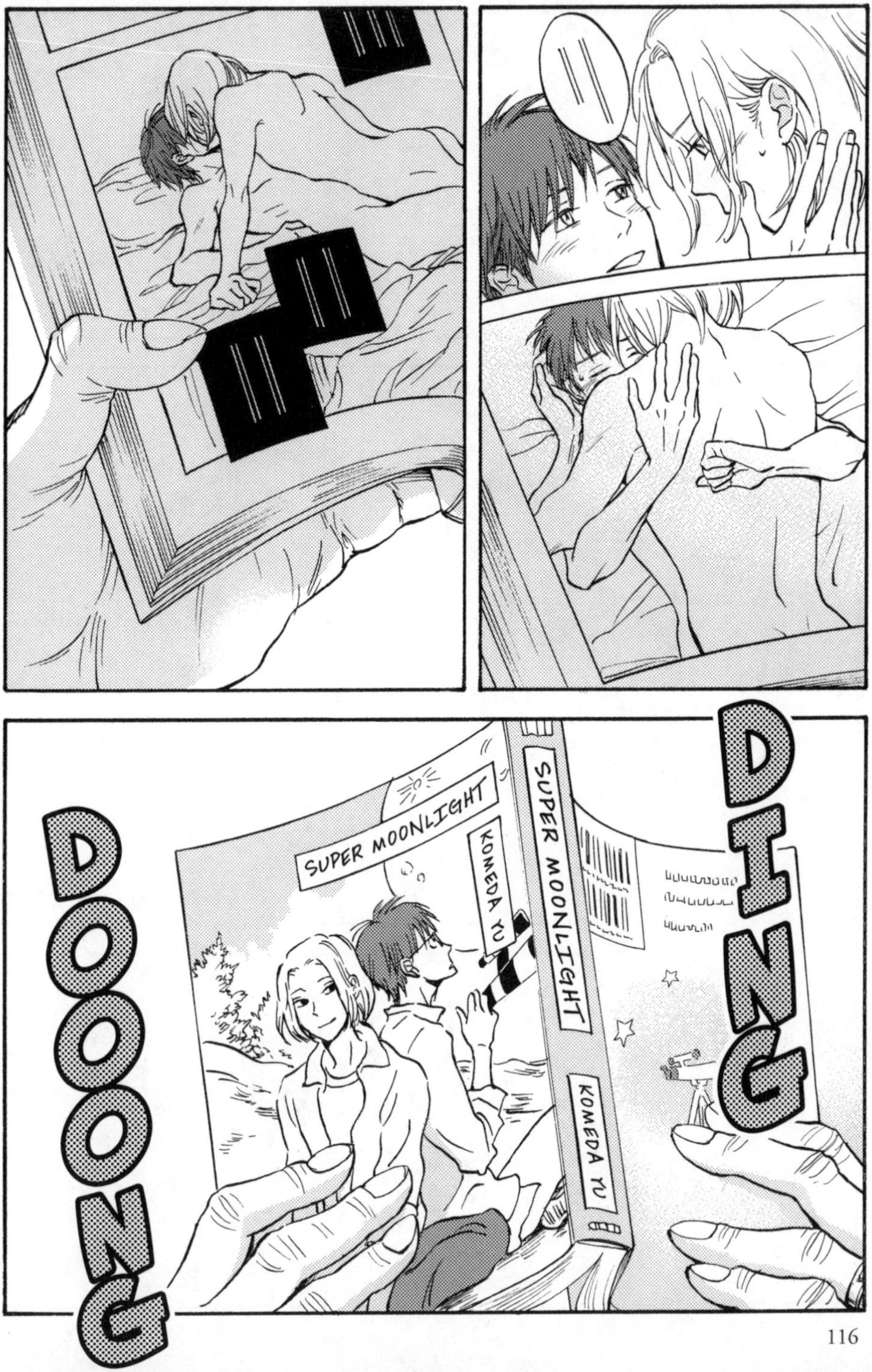
SUPER MOONLIGHT
KOMEDA YU
SUPER MOONLIGHT
KOMEDA YU
DING
DOOOONG

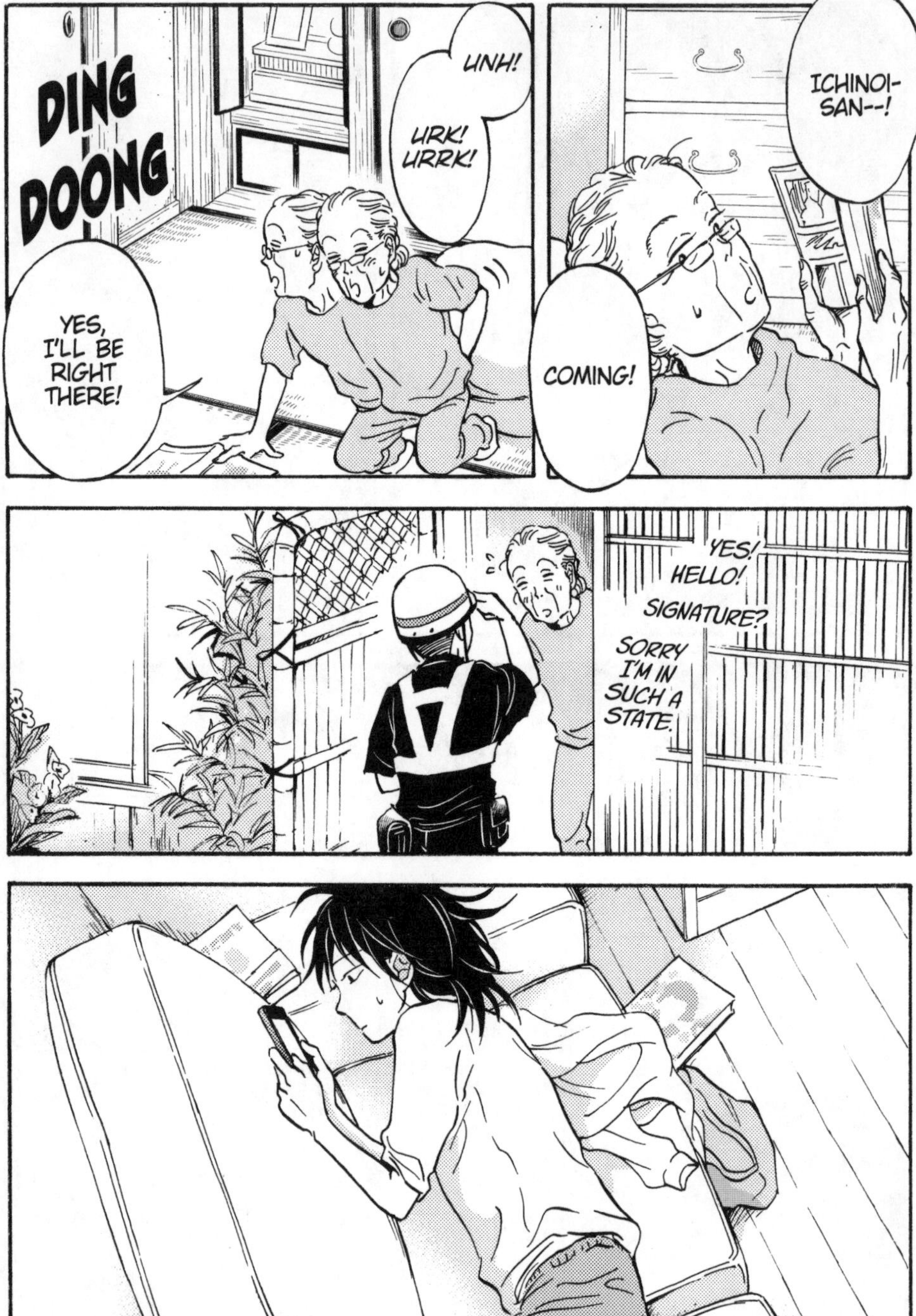
ICHINOI-SAN--!
COMING!
UNH!
URK! URRK!
DING DOONG
YES, I'LL BE RIGHT THERE!
YES! HELLO!
SIGNATURE?
SORRY I'M IN SUCH A STATE.

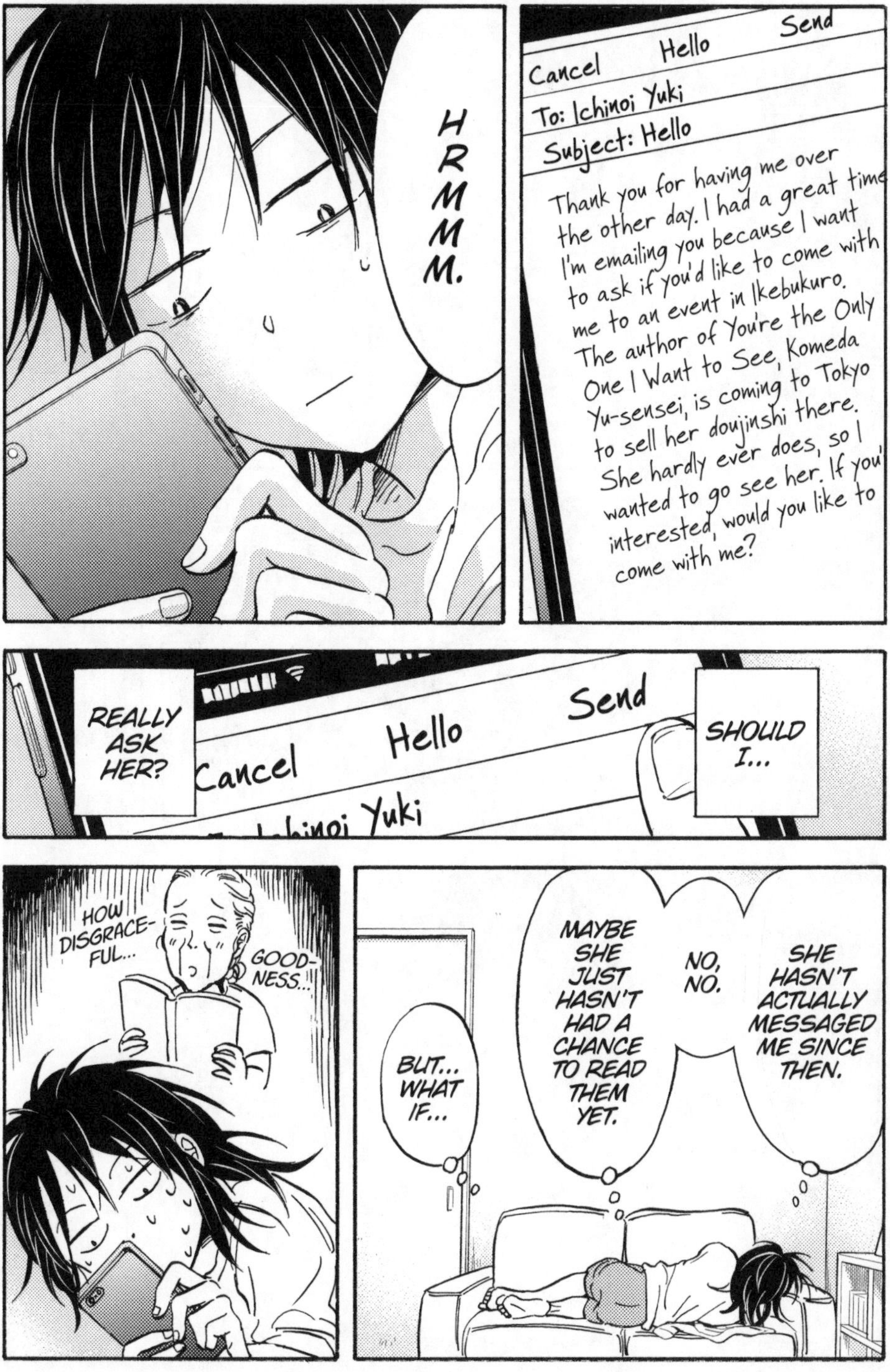
Cancel
Hello
Send
To: Ichinoi Yuki
Subject: Hello
Thank you for having me over
the other day. I had a great time
I'm emailing you because I want
to ask if you'd like to come with
me to an event in Ikebukuro.
The author of You're the Only
One I Want to See, Komeda
Yu-sensei, is coming to Tokyo
to sell her doujinshi there.
She hardly ever does, so I
wanted to go see her. If you'
interested, would you like to
come with me?
HRMMMM.
SHOULD I...
REALLY ASK HER?
Send
Hello
Cancel
Ichinoi Yuki
SHE HASN'T ACTUALLY MESSAGED ME SINCE THEN.
NO, NO.
MAYBE SHE JUST HASN'T HAD A CHANCE TO READ THEM YET.
BUT... WHAT IF...
GOODNESS...
HOW DISGRACEFUL...

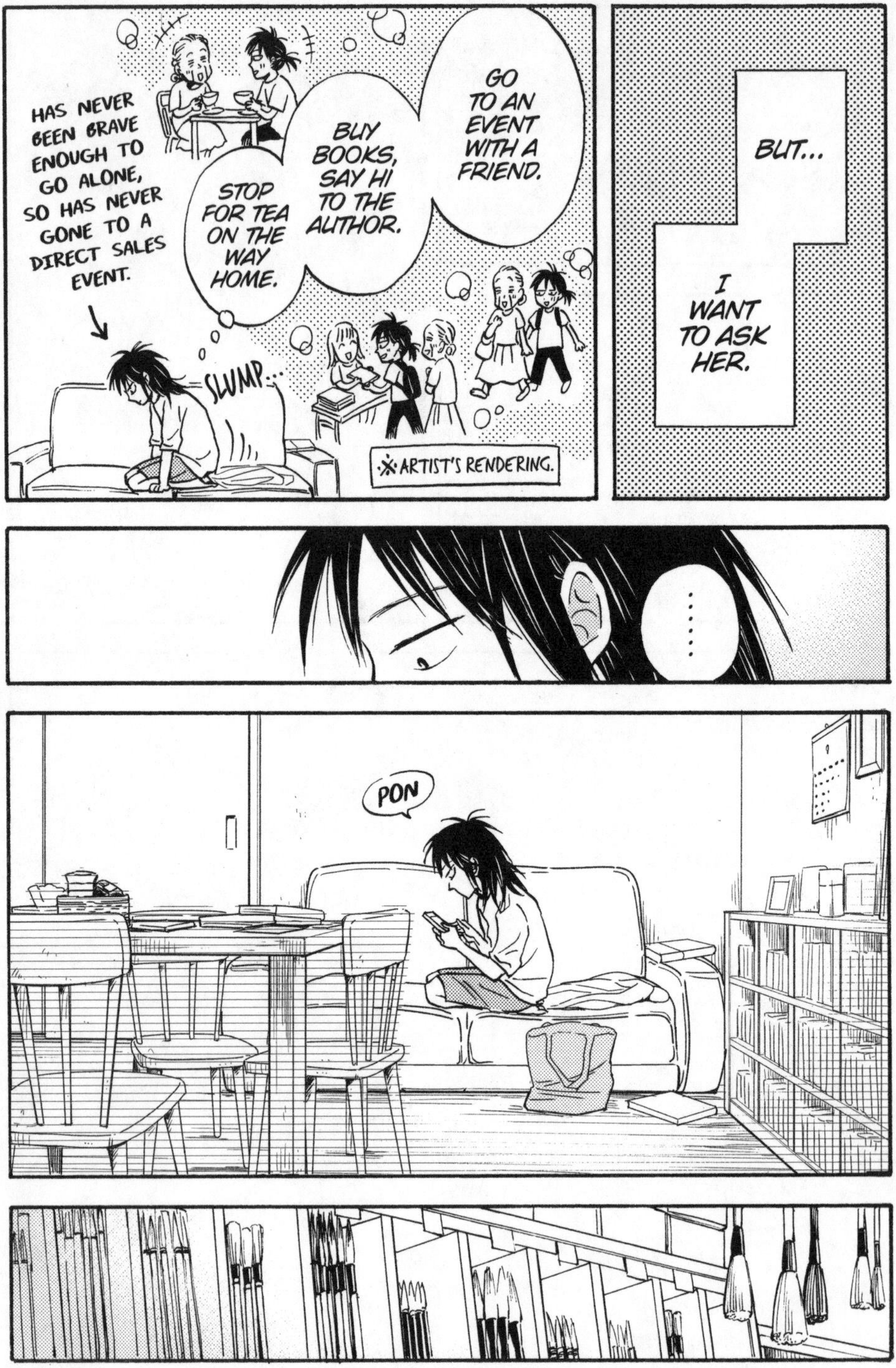
BUT...
I WANT TO ASK HER.
GO TO AN EVENT WITH A FRIEND.
BUY BOOKS, SAY HI TO THE AUTHOR.
STOP FOR TEA ON THE WAY HOME.
HAS NEVER BEEN BRAVE ENOUGH TO GO ALONE, SO HAS NEVER GONE TO A DIRECT SALES EVENT.
SLUMP...
※ARTIST'S RENDERING.
......
PON

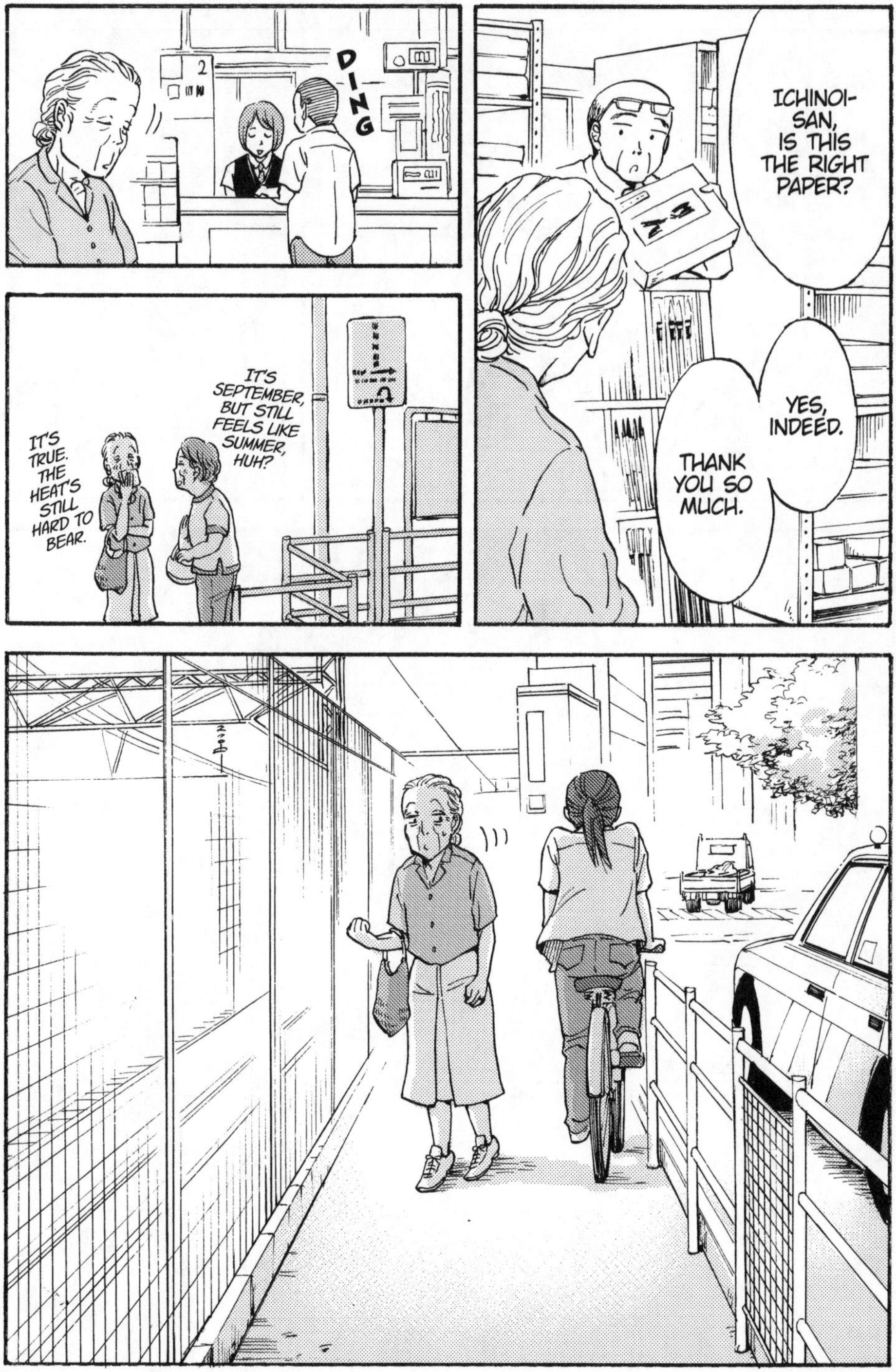
ICHINOI-SAN, IS THIS THE RIGHT PAPER?
YES, INDEED.
THANK YOU SO MUCH.
DING
IT'S SEPTEMBER, BUT STILL FEELS LIKE SUMMER, HUH?
IT'S TRUE. THE HEAT'S STILL HARD TO BEAR.

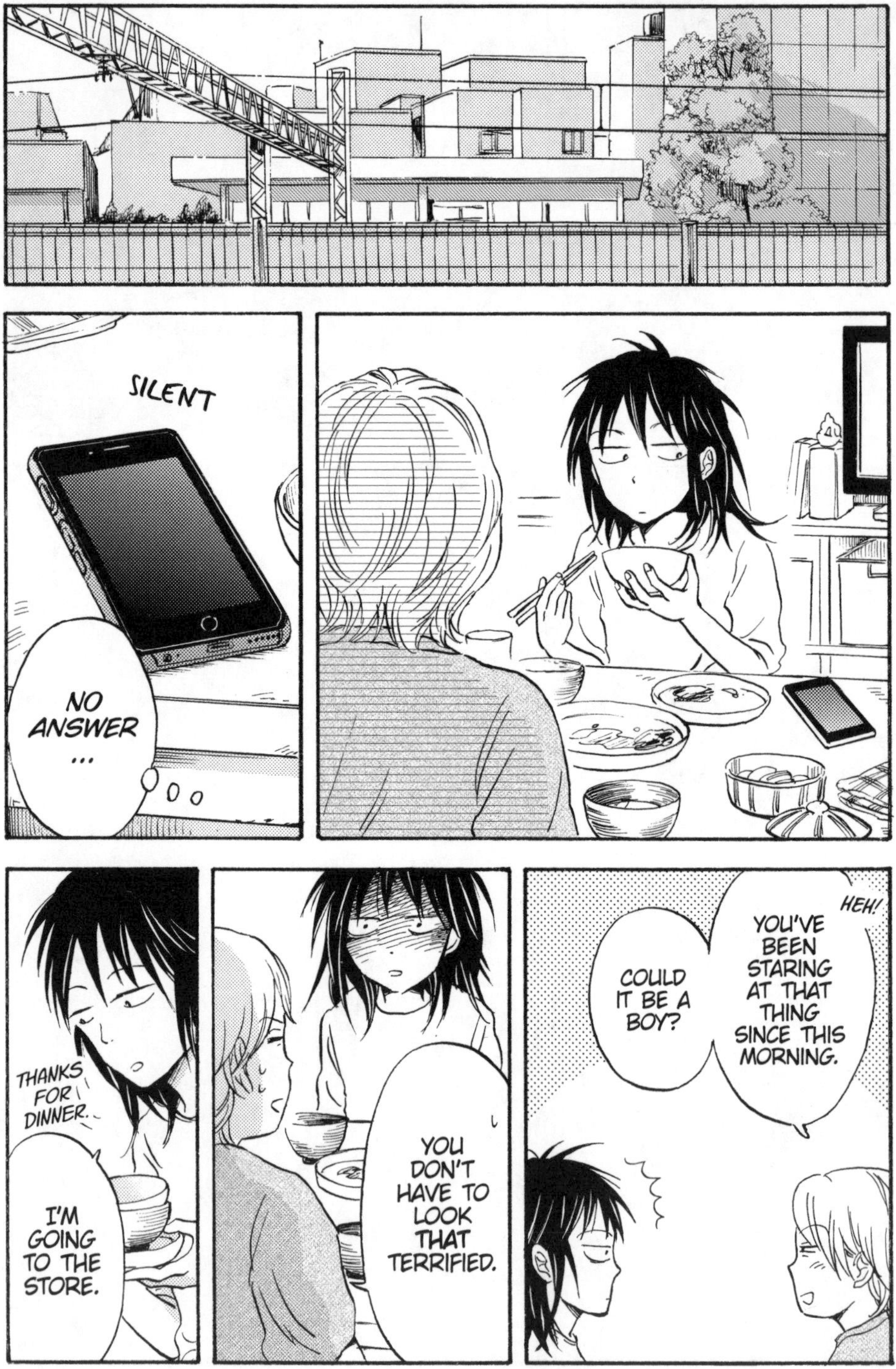
SILENT
NO ANSWER ...
HEH!
YOU'VE BEEN STARING AT THAT THING SINCE THIS MORNING.
COULD IT BE A BOY?
YOU DON'T HAVE TO LOOK THAT TERRIFIED.
THANKS FOR DINNER.
I'M GOING TO THE STORE.

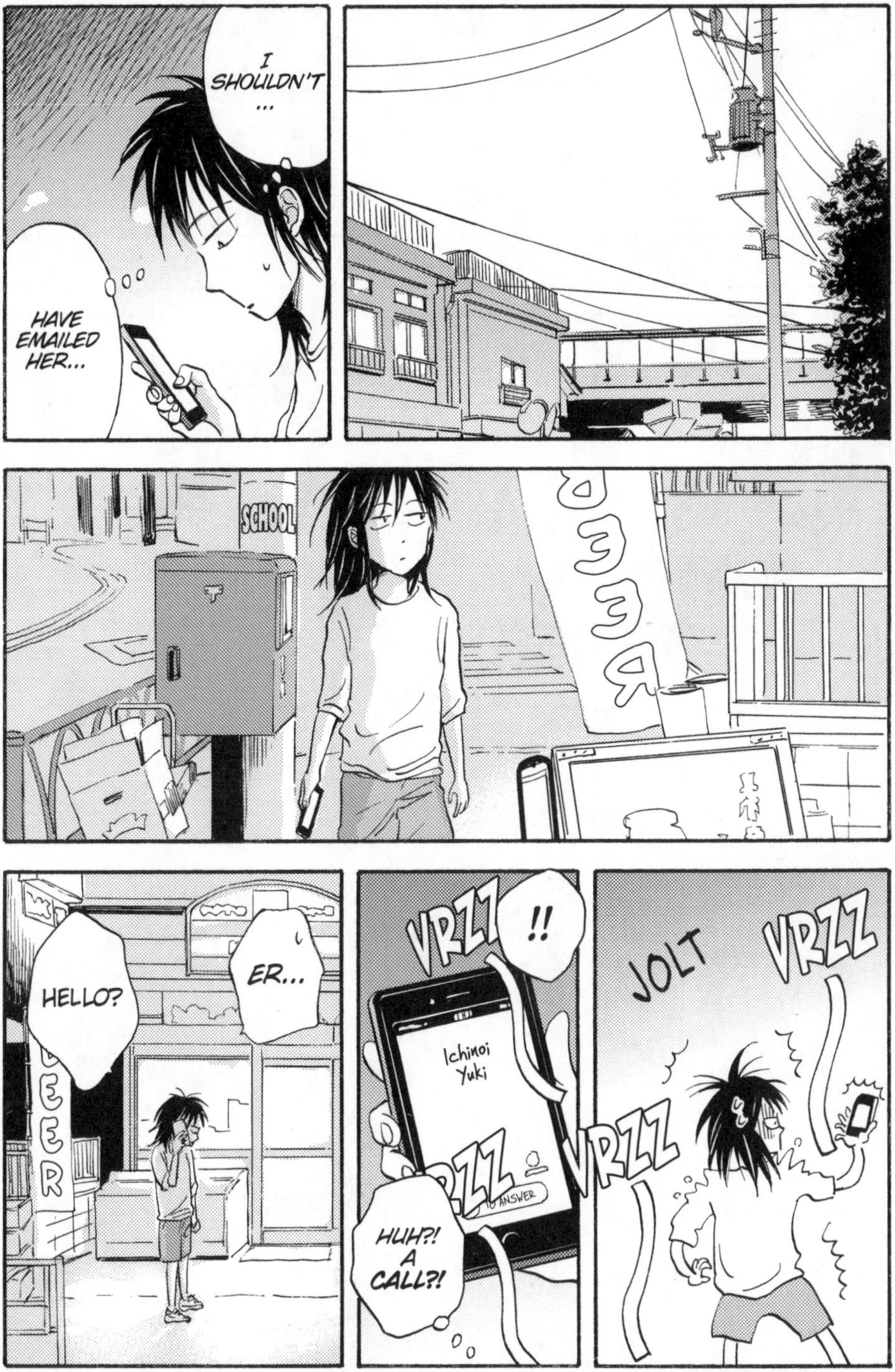
I SHOULDN'T ...
HAVE EMAILED HER...
SCHOOL
VRZZ
JOLT
VRZZ
!!
VRZZ
Ichinoi Yuki
VRZZ
HUH?! A CALL?!
ER...
HELLO?

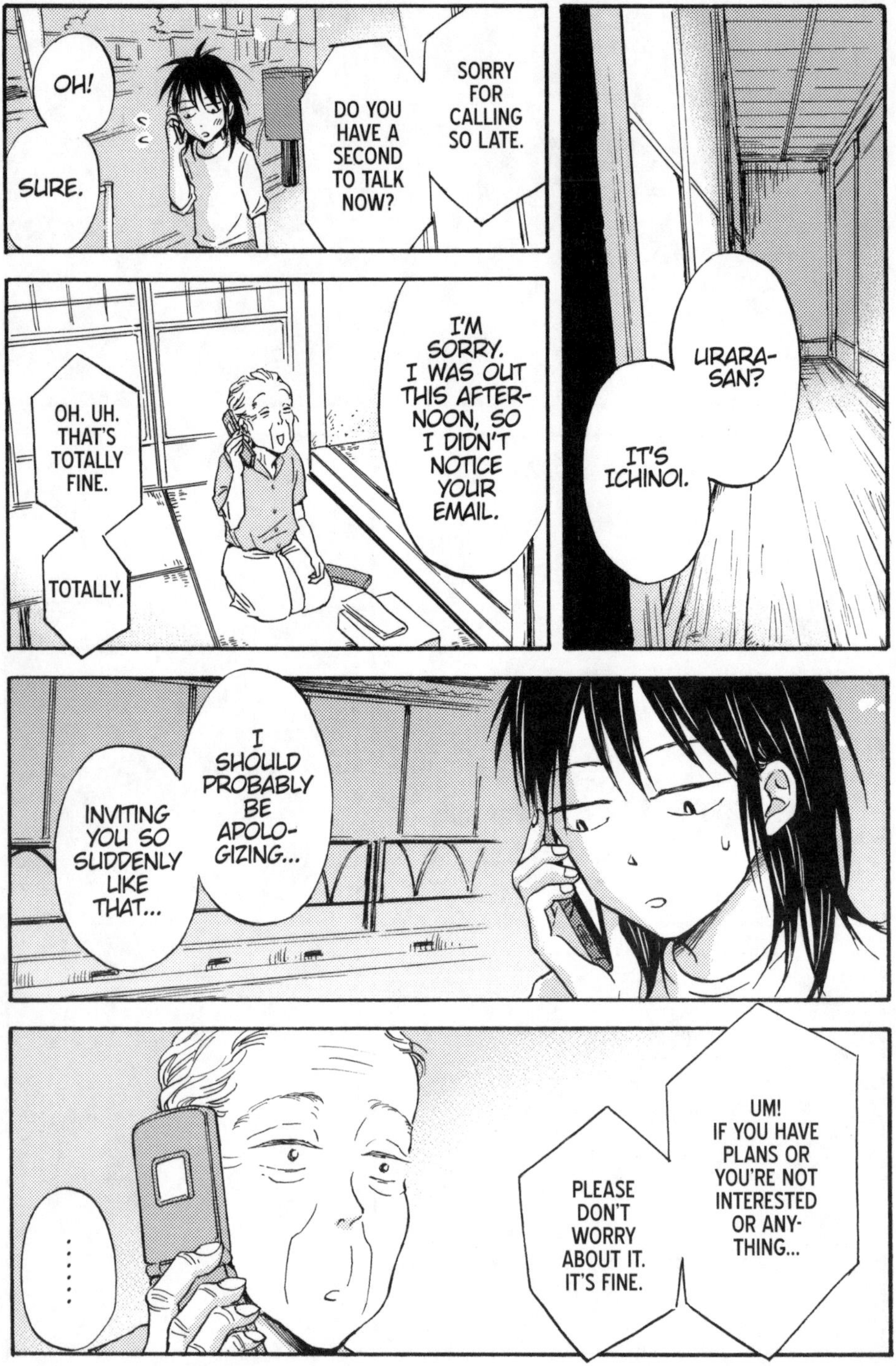
URARA-SAN?
IT'S ICHINOI.
SORRY FOR CALLING SO LATE.
DO YOU HAVE A SECOND TO TALK NOW?
OH!
SURE.
I'M SORRY. I WAS OUT THIS AFTER-NOON, SO I DIDN'T NOTICE YOUR EMAIL.
OH. UH. THAT'S TOTALLY FINE.
TOTALLY.
I SHOULD PROBABLY BE APOLO-GIZING...
INVITING YOU SO SUDDENLY LIKE THAT...
UM! IF YOU HAVE PLANS OR YOU'RE NOT INTERESTED OR ANY-THING...
PLEASE DON'T WORRY ABOUT IT. IT'S FINE.
......

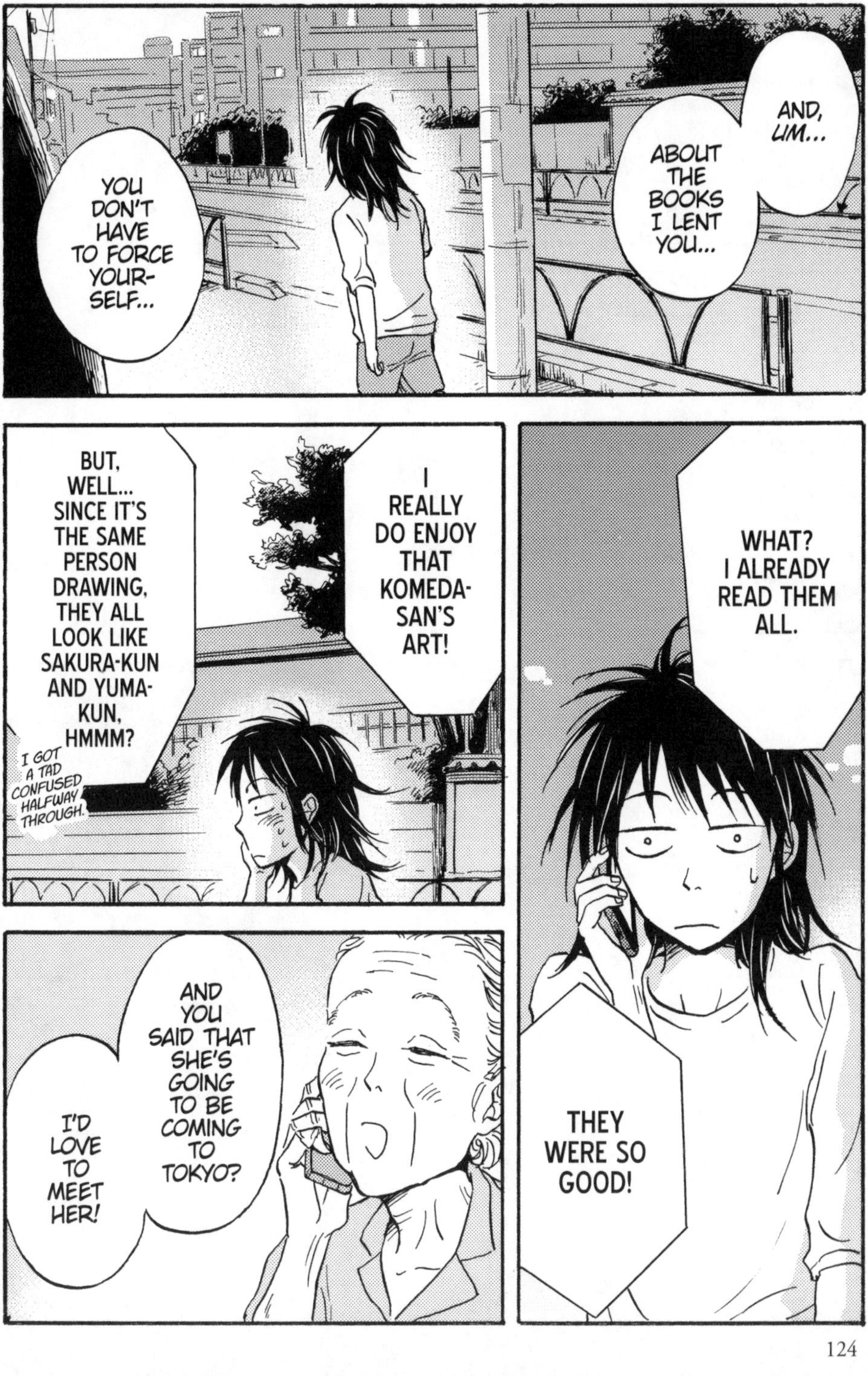
AND, UM...
ABOUT THE BOOKS I LENT YOU...
YOU DON'T HAVE TO FORCE YOURSELF...
WHAT? I ALREADY READ THEM ALL.
THEY WERE SO GOOD!
I REALLY DO ENJOY THAT KOMEDA-SAN'S ART!
BUT, WELL... SINCE IT'S THE SAME PERSON DRAWING, THEY ALL LOOK LIKE SAKURA-KUN AND YUMA-KUN, HMMM?
I GOT A TAD CONFUSED HALFWAY THROUGH.
AND YOU SAID THAT SHE'S GOING TO BE COMING TO TOKYO?
I'D LOVE TO MEET HER!

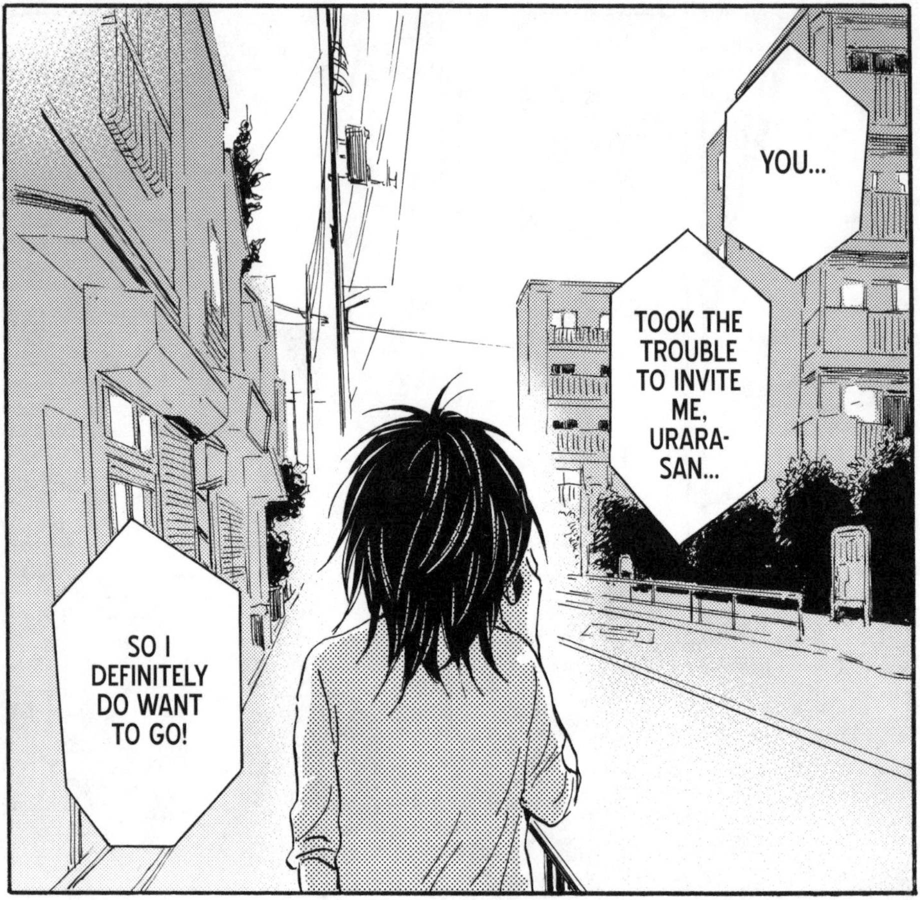
YOU...
TOOK THE TROUBLE TO INVITE ME, URARA-SAN...
SO I DEFINITELY DO WANT TO GO!

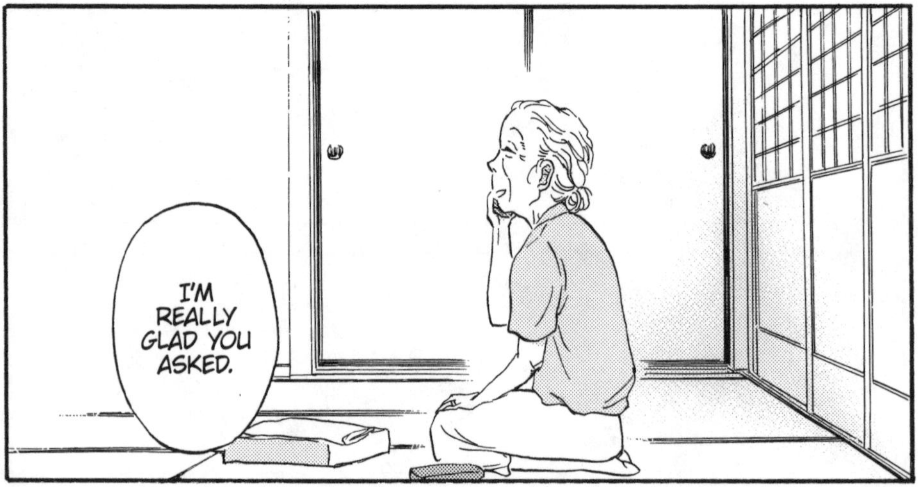
I'M REALLY GLAD YOU ASKED.

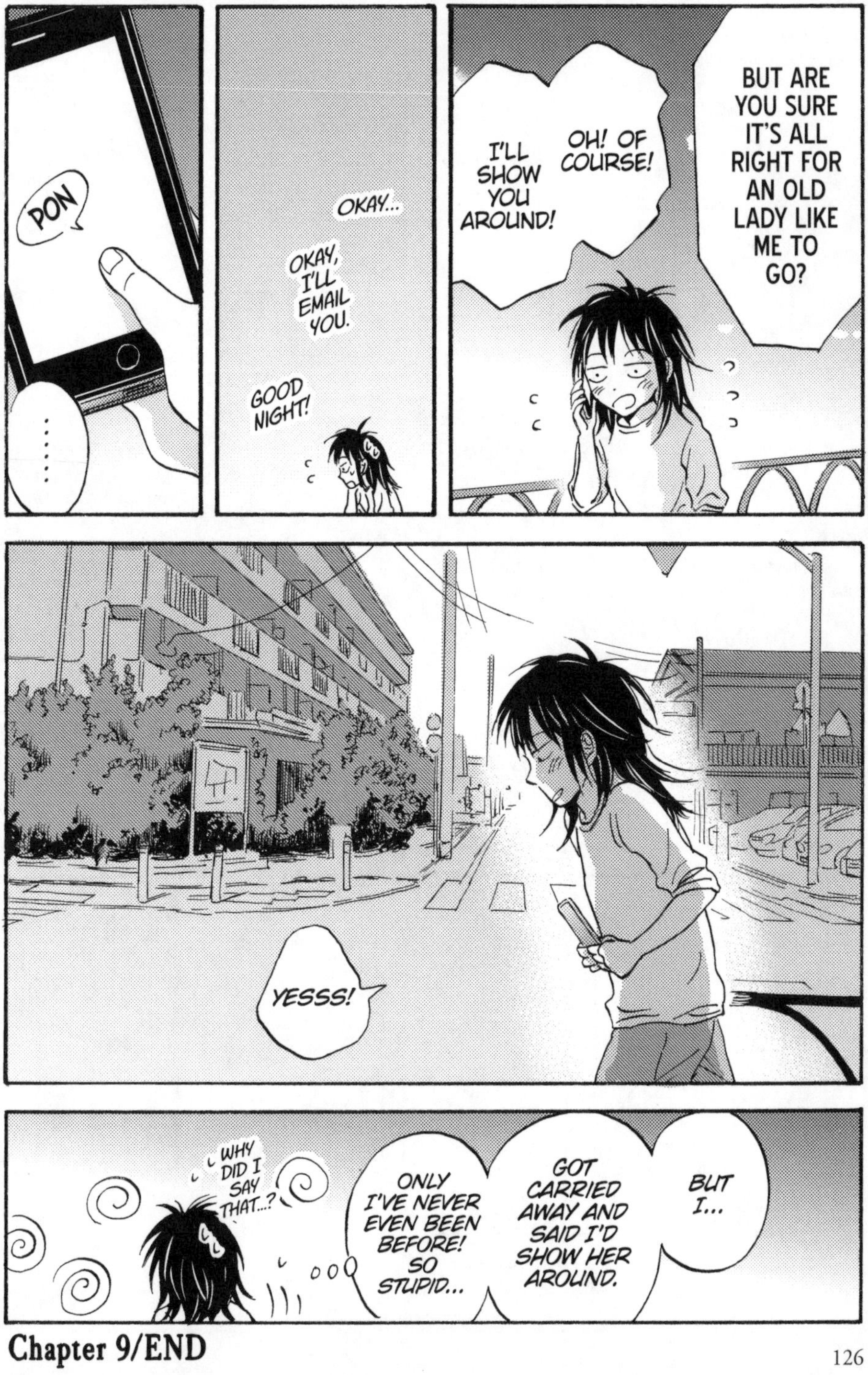
BUT ARE YOU SURE IT'S ALL RIGHT FOR AN OLD LADY LIKE ME TO GO?
OH! OF COURSE!
I'LL SHOW YOU AROUND!
OKAY...
OKAY, I'LL EMAIL YOU.
GOOD NIGHT!
PON
......
YESSS!
BUT I...
GOT CARRIED AWAY AND SAID I'D SHOW HER AROUND.
ONLY I'VE NEVER EVEN BEEN BEFORE! SO STUPID...
WHY DID I SAY THAT...?

Chapter 9/END

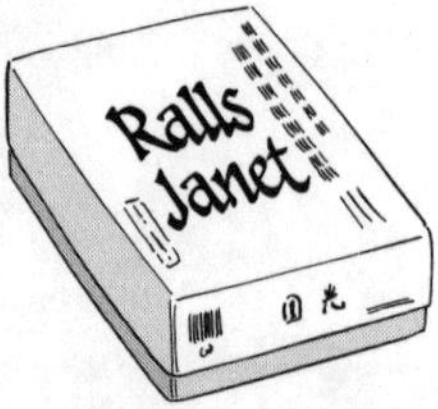
Ralls
Janet

metamorphosis

Chapter 10

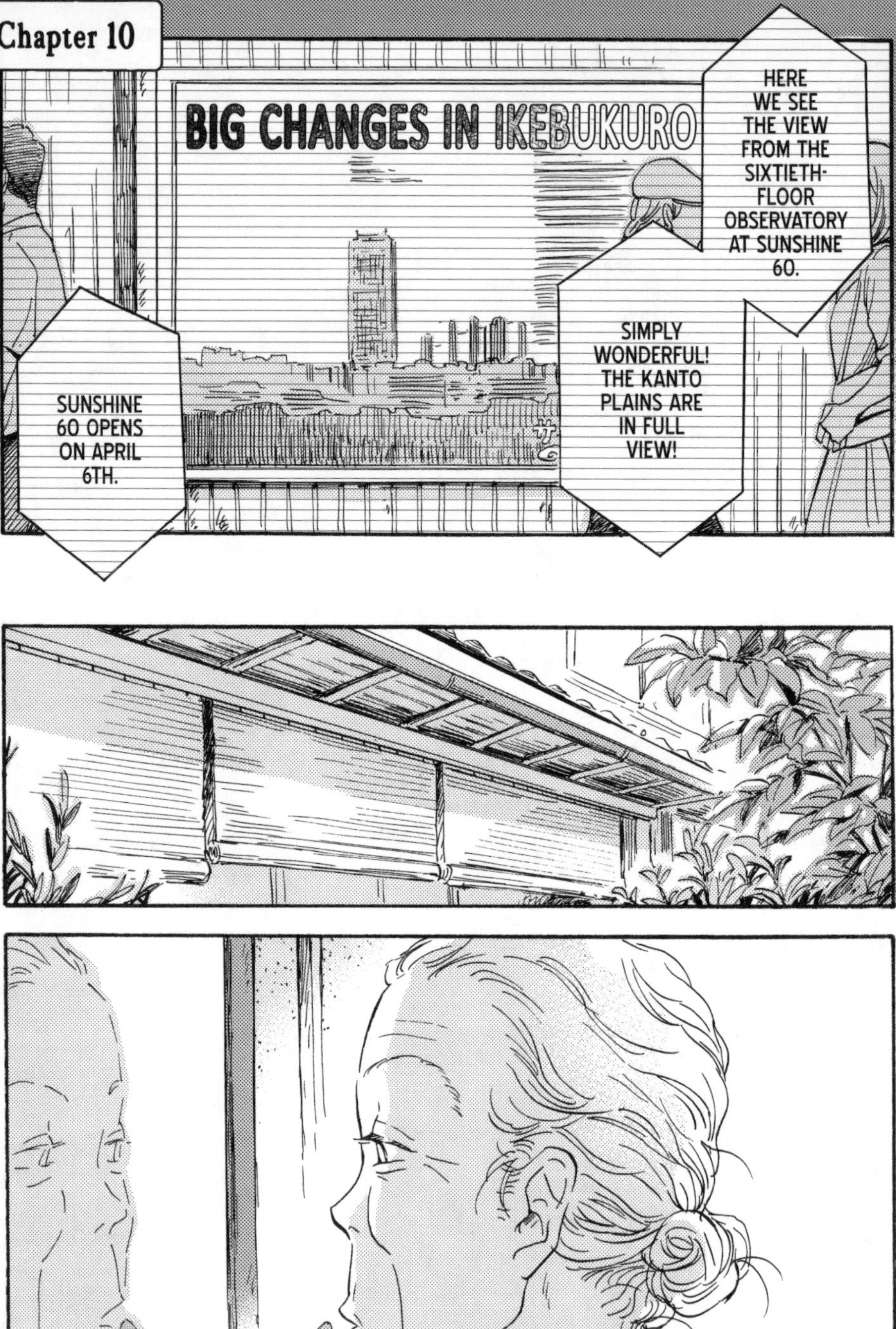
HERE WE SEE THE VIEW FROM THE SIXTIETH-FLOOR OBSERVATORY AT SUNSHINE 60.
BIG CHANGES IN IKEBUKURO
SIMPLY WONDERFUL! THE KANTO PLAINS ARE IN FULL VIEW!
SUNSHINE 60 OPENS ON APRIL 6TH.

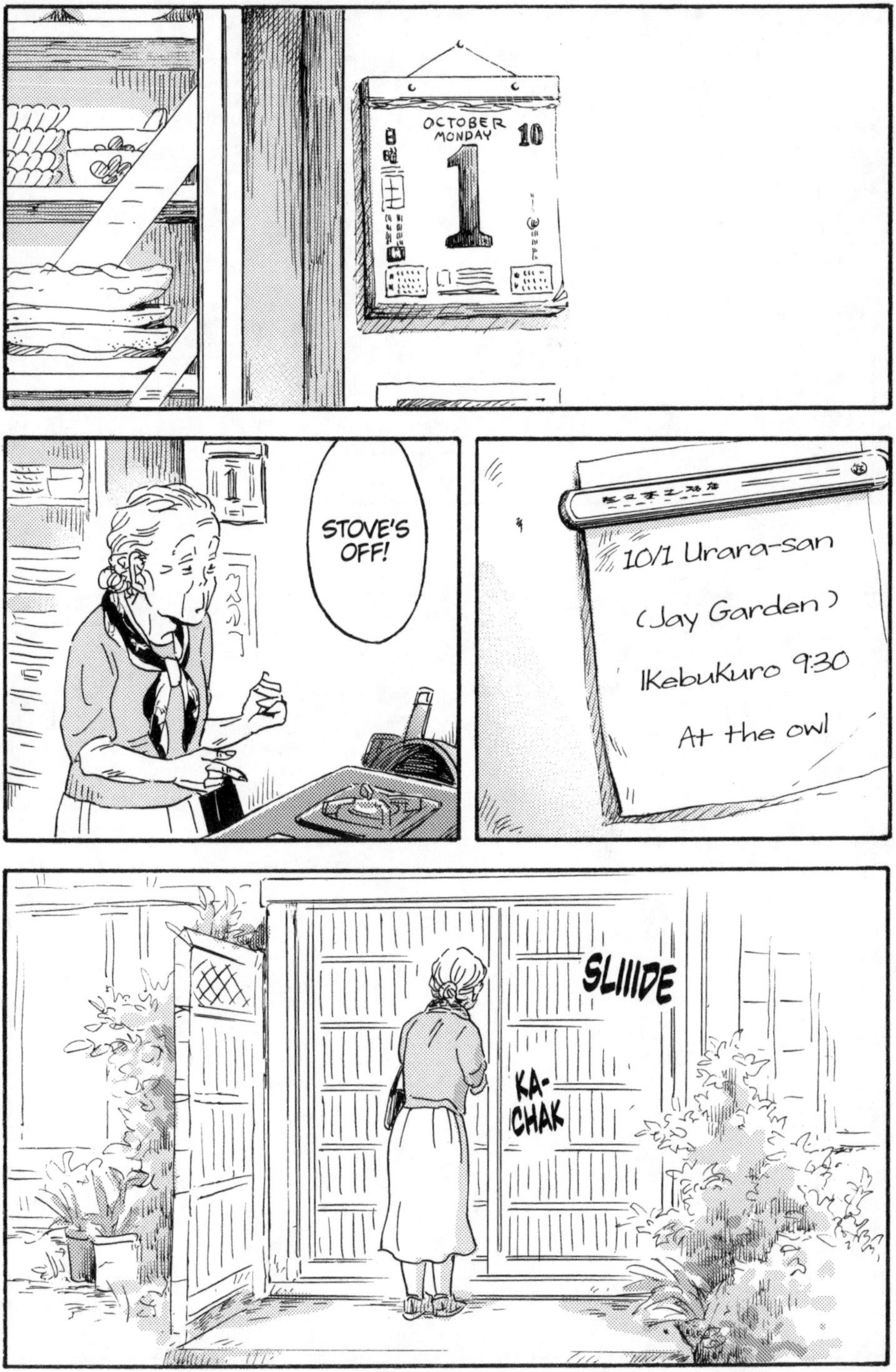
OCTOBER
MONDAY
10
1
10/1 Urara-san
(Jay Garden)
IkebuKuro 9:30
At the owl
STOVE'S OFF!
SLIIIDE
KA-CHAK

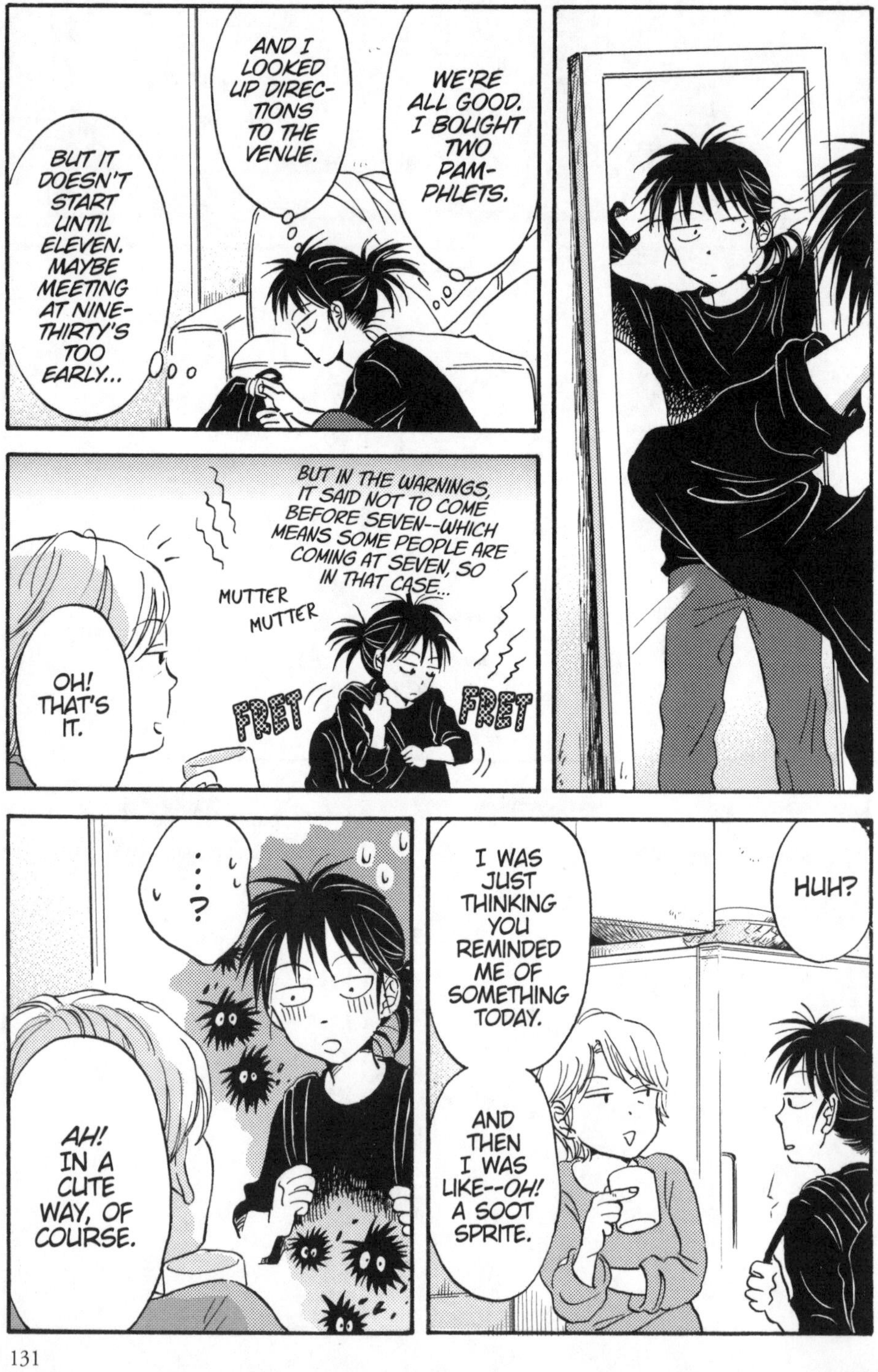
WE'RE ALL GOOD. I BOUGHT TWO PAMPHLETS.
AND I LOOKED UP DIRECTIONS TO THE VENUE.
BUT IT DOESN'T START UNTIL ELEVEN. MAYBE MEETING AT NINE-THIRTY'S TOO EARLY...
BUT IN THE WARNINGS, IT SAID NOT TO COME BEFORE SEVEN--WHICH MEANS SOME PEOPLE ARE COMING AT SEVEN, SO IN THAT CASE...
FRET
MUTTER MUTTER
FRET
OH! THAT'S IT.
HUH?
I WAS JUST THINKING YOU REMINDED ME OF SOMETHING TODAY.
AND THEN I WAS LIKE--OH! A SOOT SPRITE.
...?
AH! IN A CUTE WAY, OF COURSE.

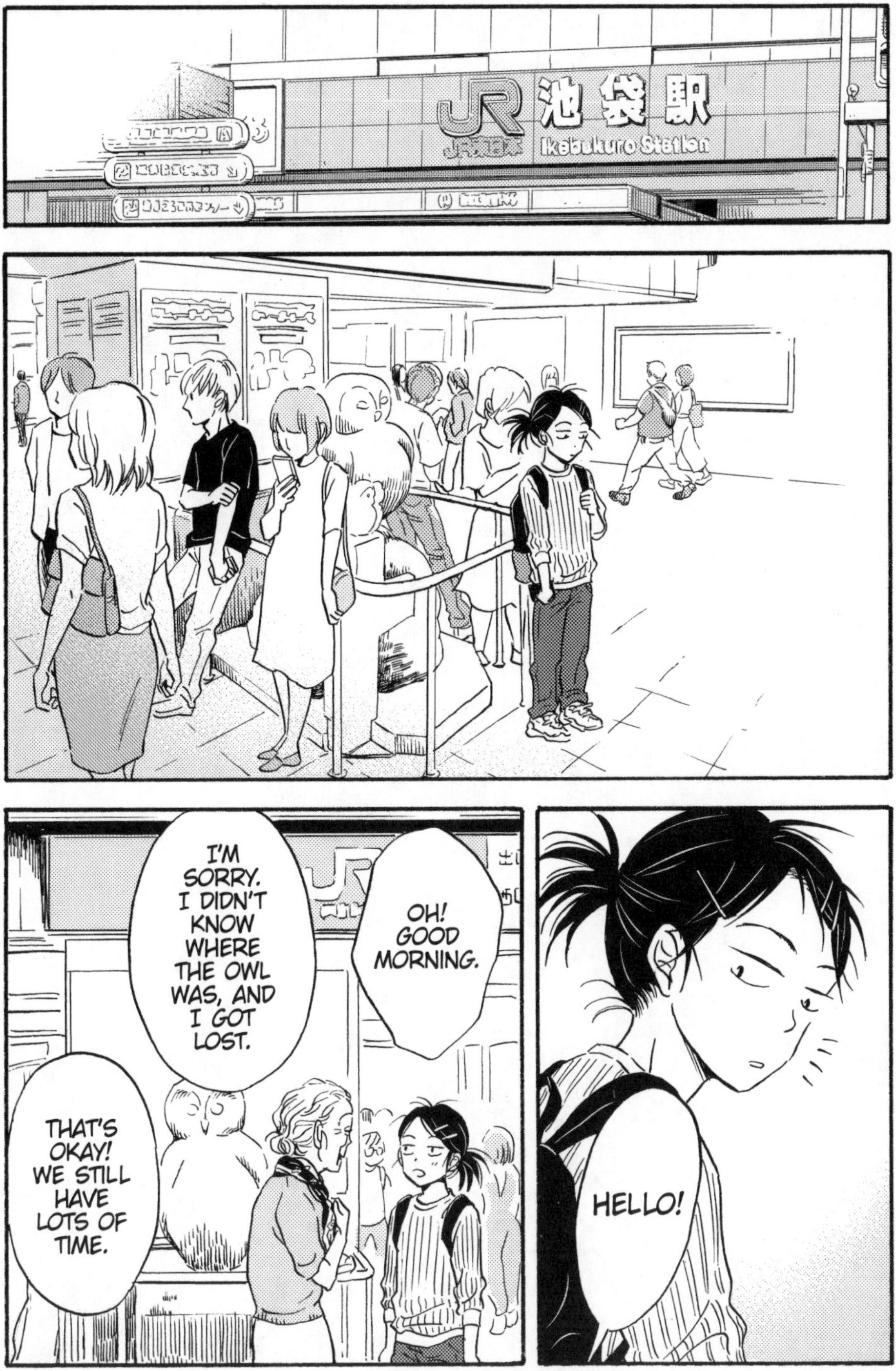
JR
池袋駅
Ikebukuro Station
HELLO!
OH! GOOD MORNING.
I'M SORRY. I DIDN'T KNOW WHERE THE OWL WAS, AND I GOT LOST.
THAT'S OKAY! WE STILL HAVE LOTS OF TIME.

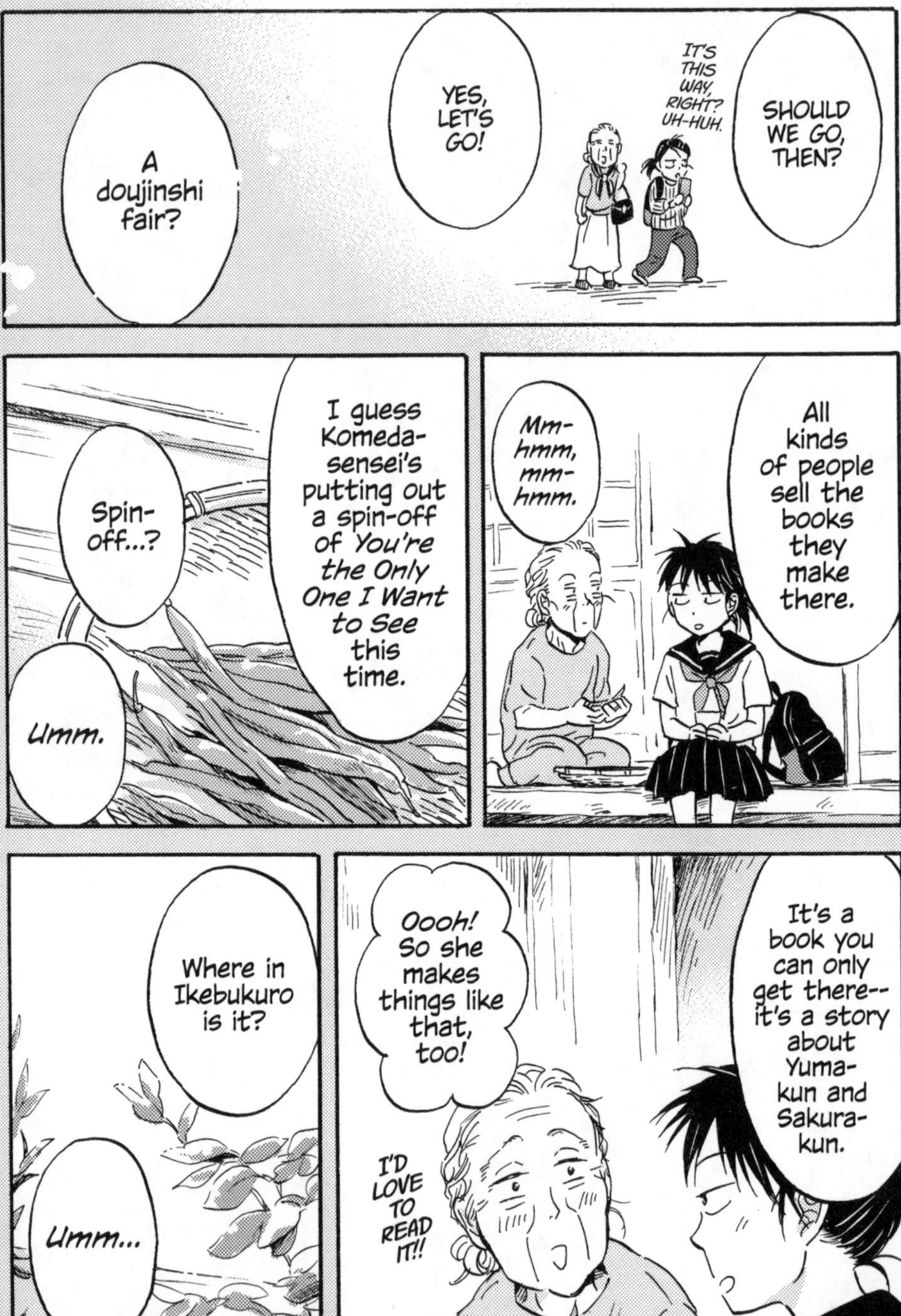
SHOULD WE GO, THEN?
IT'S THIS WAY, RIGHT? UH-HUH.
YES, LET'S GO!
A doujinshi fair?
All kinds of people sell the books they make there.
Mm-hmm, mm-hmm.
I guess Komeda-sensei's putting out a spin-off of *You're the Only One I Want to See* this time.
Spin-off...?
Umm.
It's a book you can only get there--it's a story about Yuma-kun and Sakura-kun.
Oooh! So she makes things like that, too!
I'D LOVE TO READ IT!!
Where in Ikebukuro is it?
Umm...

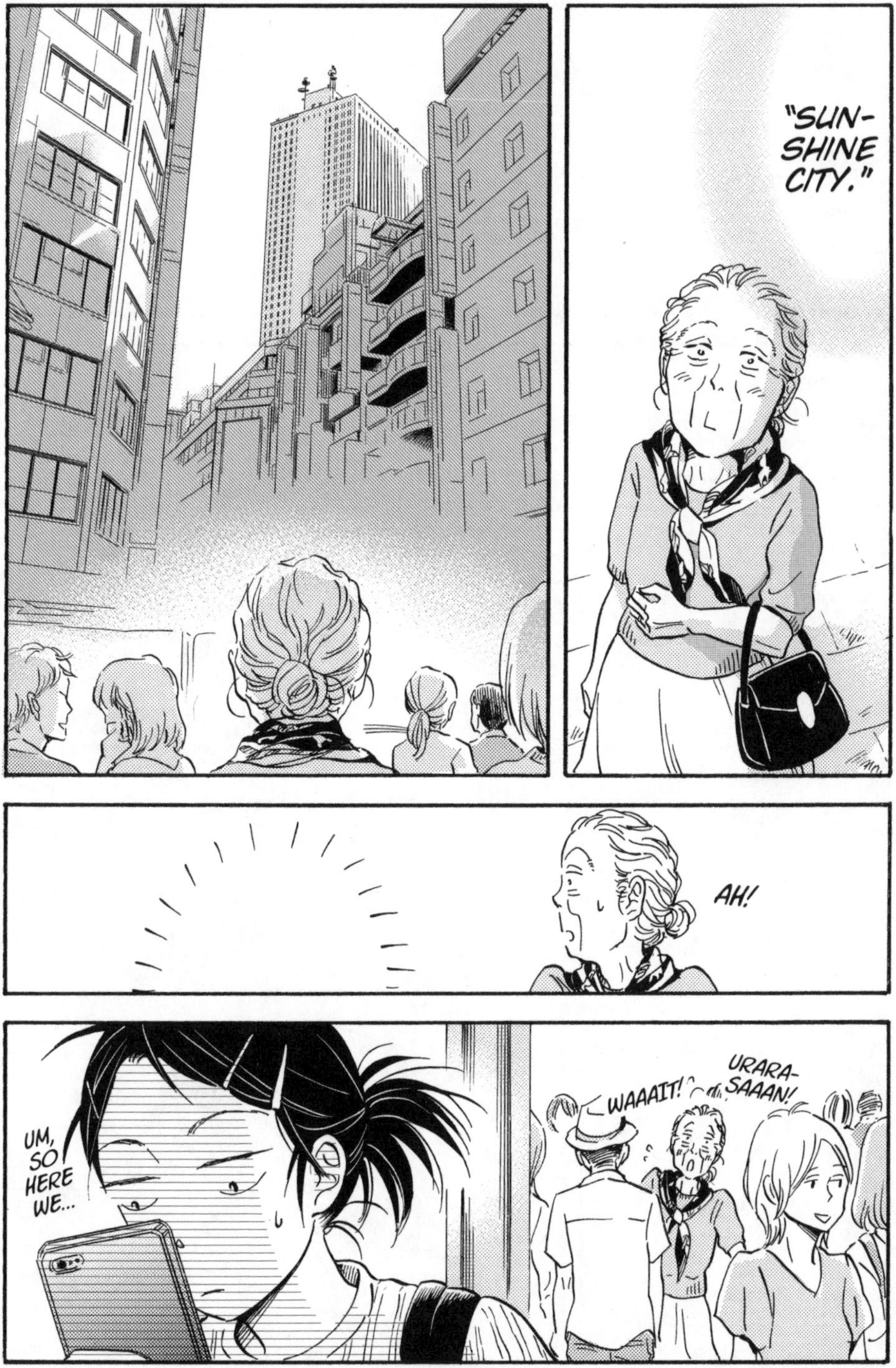
"SUN-SHINE CITY."
AH!
URARA-SAAAN!
WAAAIT!
UM, SO HERE WE...

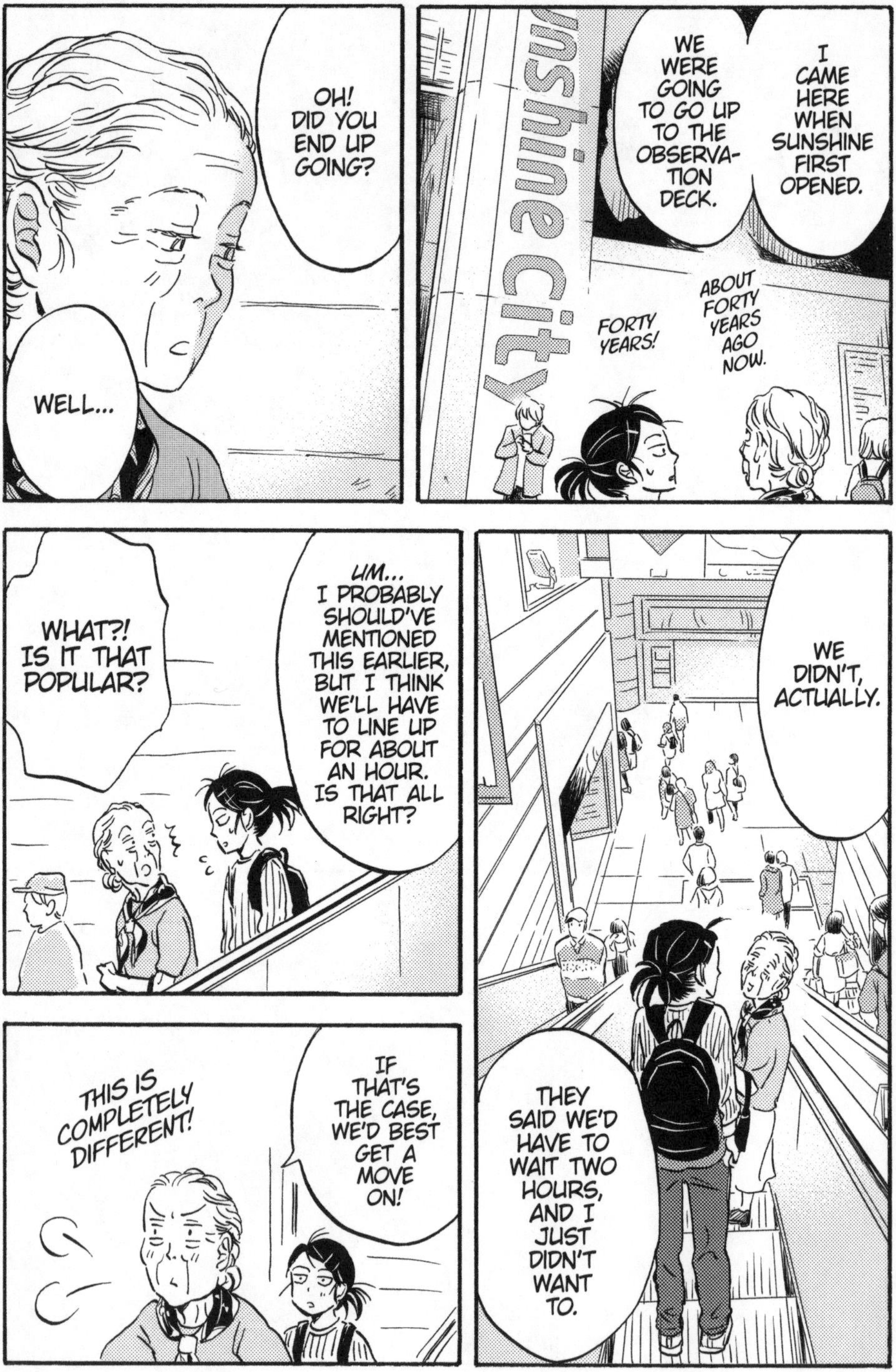
I CAME HERE WHEN SUNSHINE FIRST OPENED.
WE WERE GOING TO GO UP TO THE OBSERVATION DECK.
ABOUT FORTY YEARS AGO NOW.
FORTY YEARS!
OH! DID YOU END UP GOING?
WELL...
WE DIDN'T, ACTUALLY.
THEY SAID WE'D HAVE TO WAIT TWO HOURS, AND I JUST DIDN'T WANT TO.
UM... I PROBABLY SHOULD'VE MENTIONED THIS EARLIER, BUT I THINK WE'LL HAVE TO LINE UP FOR ABOUT AN HOUR. IS THAT ALL RIGHT?
WHAT?! IS IT THAT POPULAR?
IF THAT'S THE CASE, WE'D BEST GET A MOVE ON!
THIS IS COMPLETELY DIFFERENT!

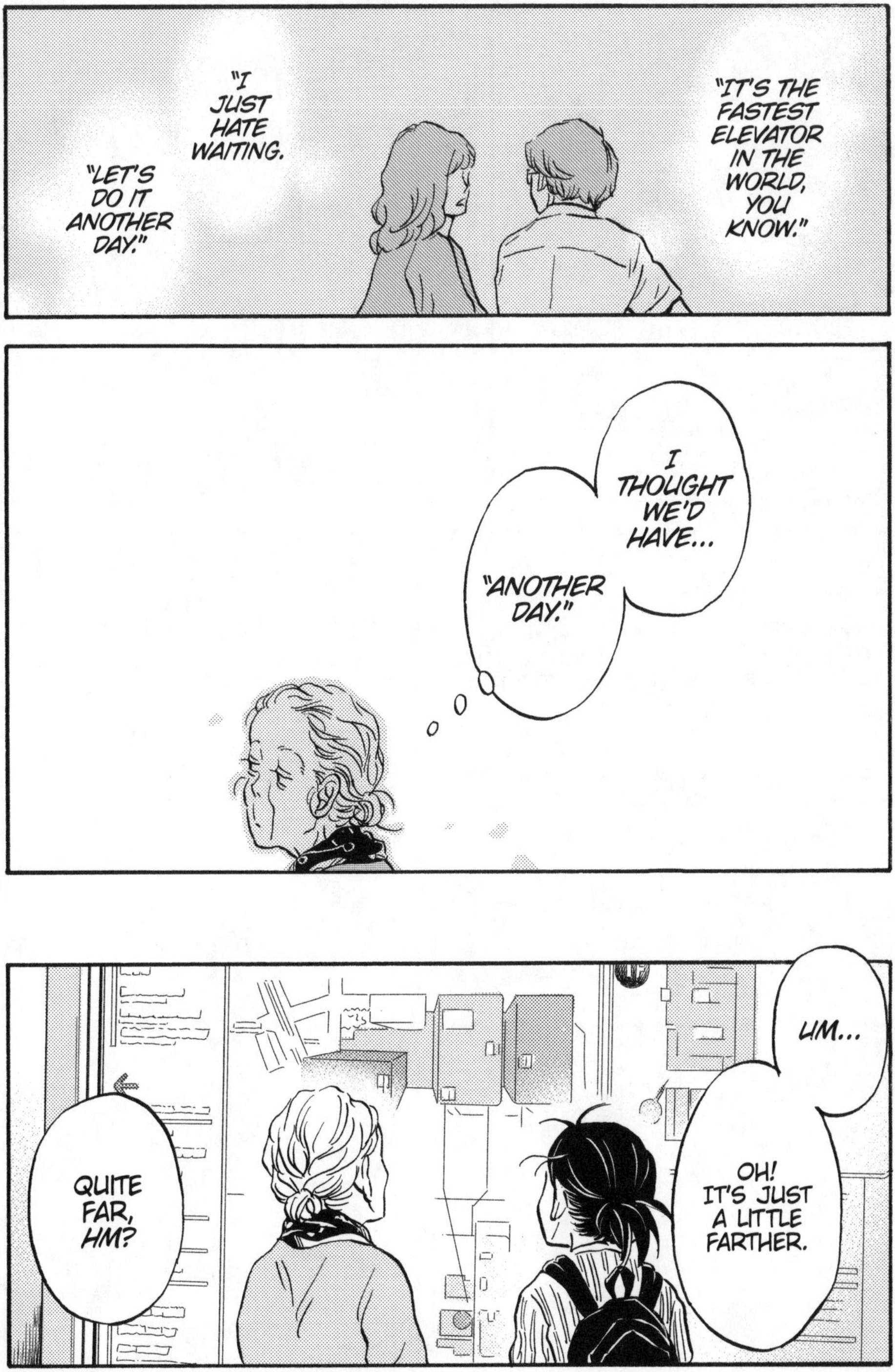
"IT'S THE FASTEST ELEVATOR IN THE WORLD, YOU KNOW."
"I JUST HATE WAITING.
"LET'S DO IT ANOTHER DAY."
I THOUGHT WE'D HAVE...
"ANOTHER DAY."
UM...
OH! IT'S JUST A LITTLE FARTHER.
QUITE FAR, HM?

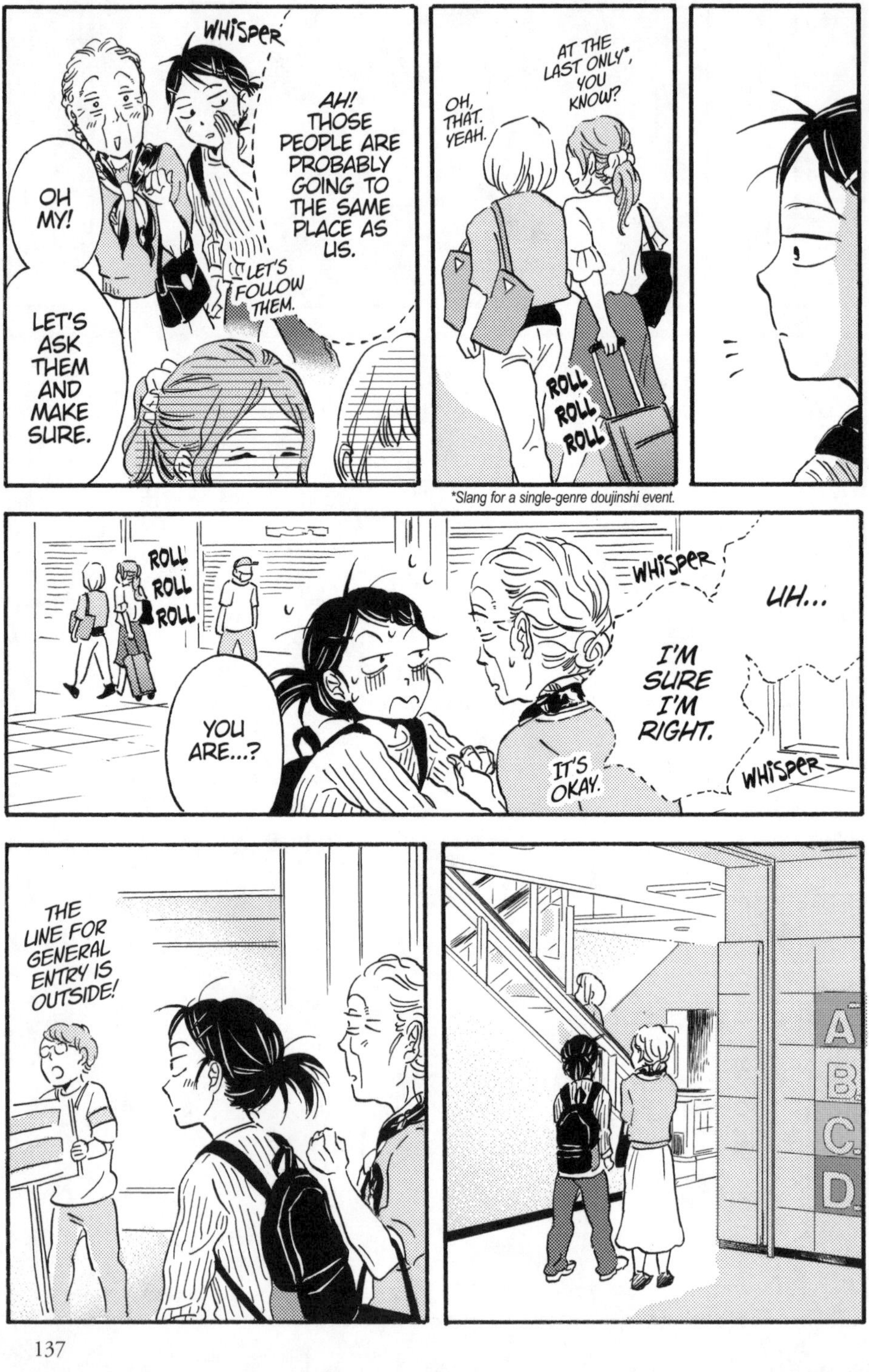
AT THE LAST ONLY*, YOU KNOW?
OH, THAT. YEAH.
ROLL ROLL ROLL
WHISPER
AH! THOSE PEOPLE ARE PROBABLY GOING TO THE SAME PLACE AS US.
LET'S FOLLOW THEM.
OH MY!
LET'S ASK THEM AND MAKE SURE.
WHISPER
UH...
I'M SURE I'M RIGHT.
WHISPER
IT'S OKAY.
YOU ARE...?
ROLL ROLL ROLL
A
B
C
D
THE LINE FOR GENERAL ENTRY IS OUTSIDE!

*Slang for a single-genre doujinshi event.

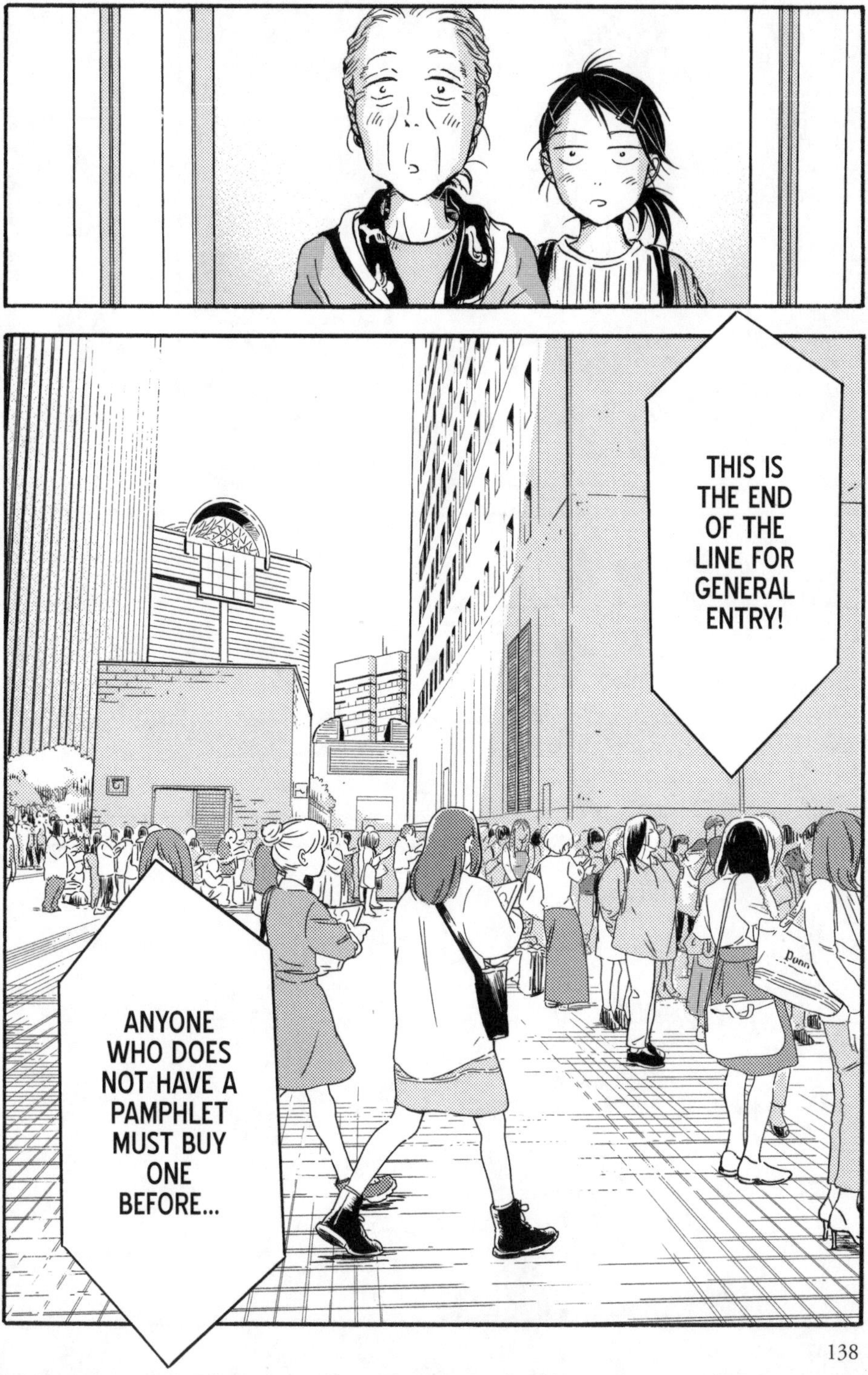
THIS IS THE END OF THE LINE FOR GENERAL ENTRY!
ANYONE WHO DOES NOT HAVE A PAMPHLET MUST BUY ONE BEFORE...

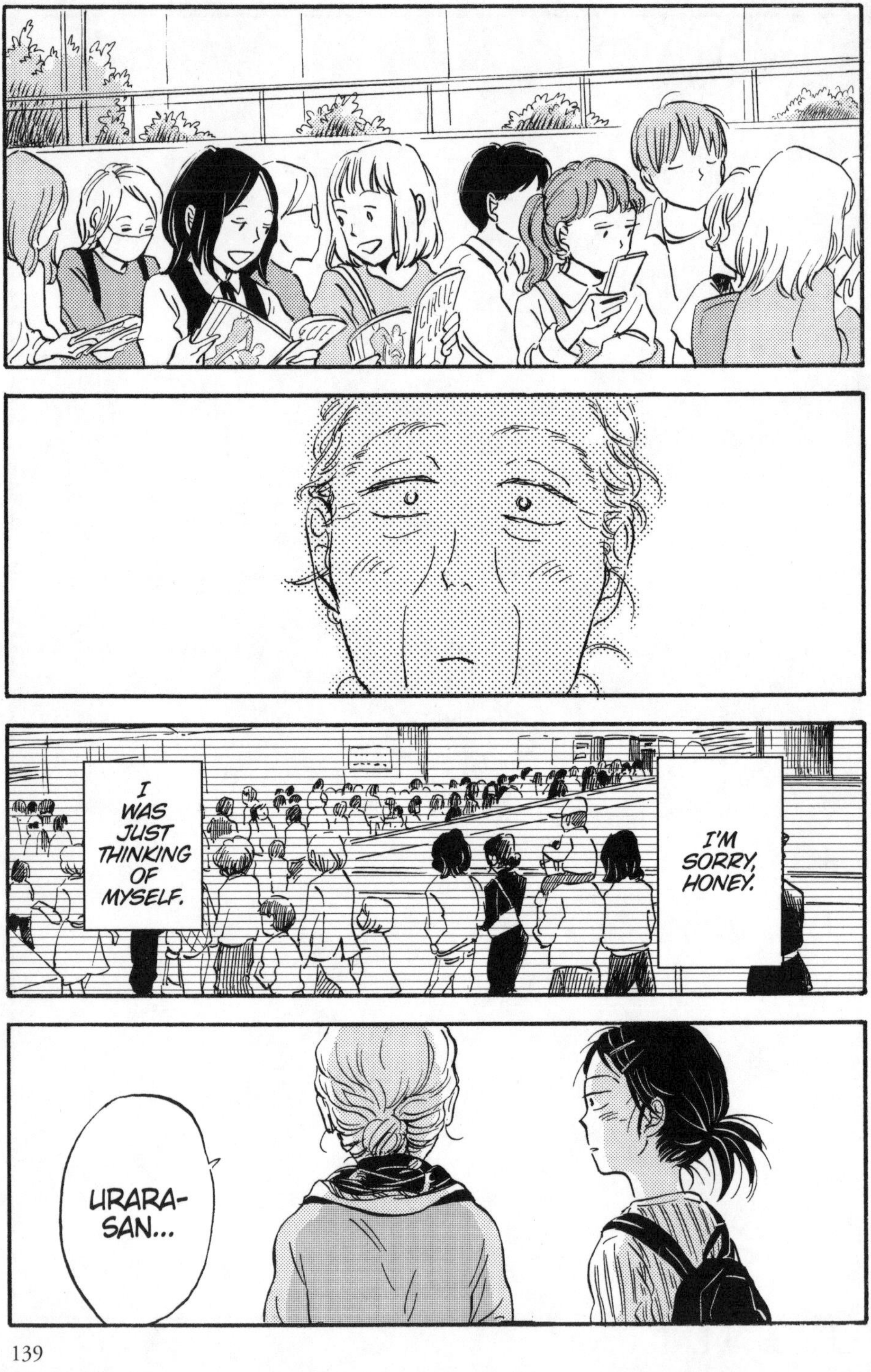
I'M SORRY, HONEY.
I WAS JUST THINKING OF MYSELF.
URARA-SAN...

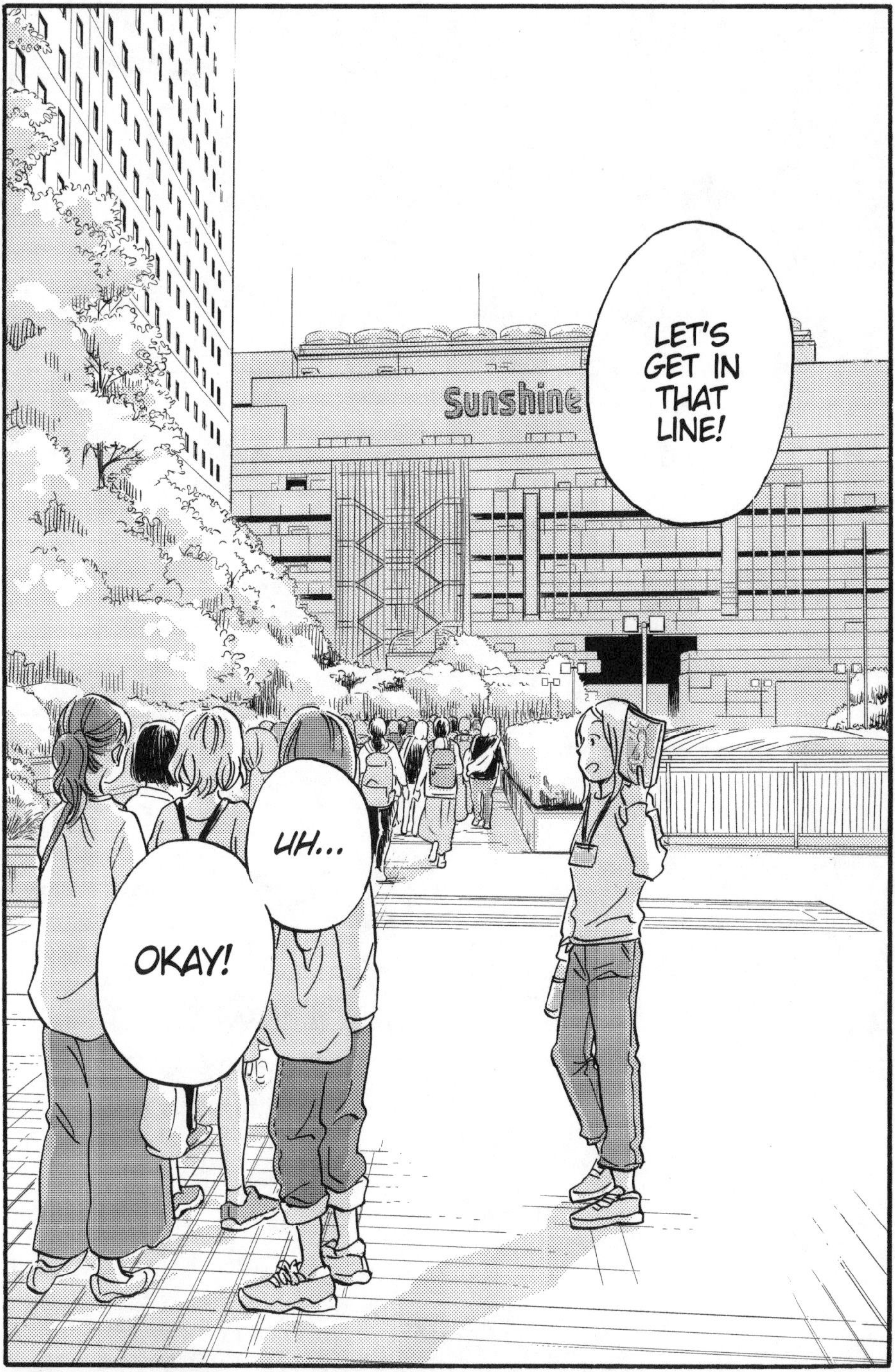
LET'S GET IN THAT LINE!
Sunshine
UH...
OKAY!

Chapter 10/END

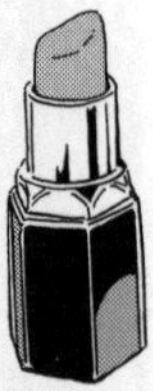

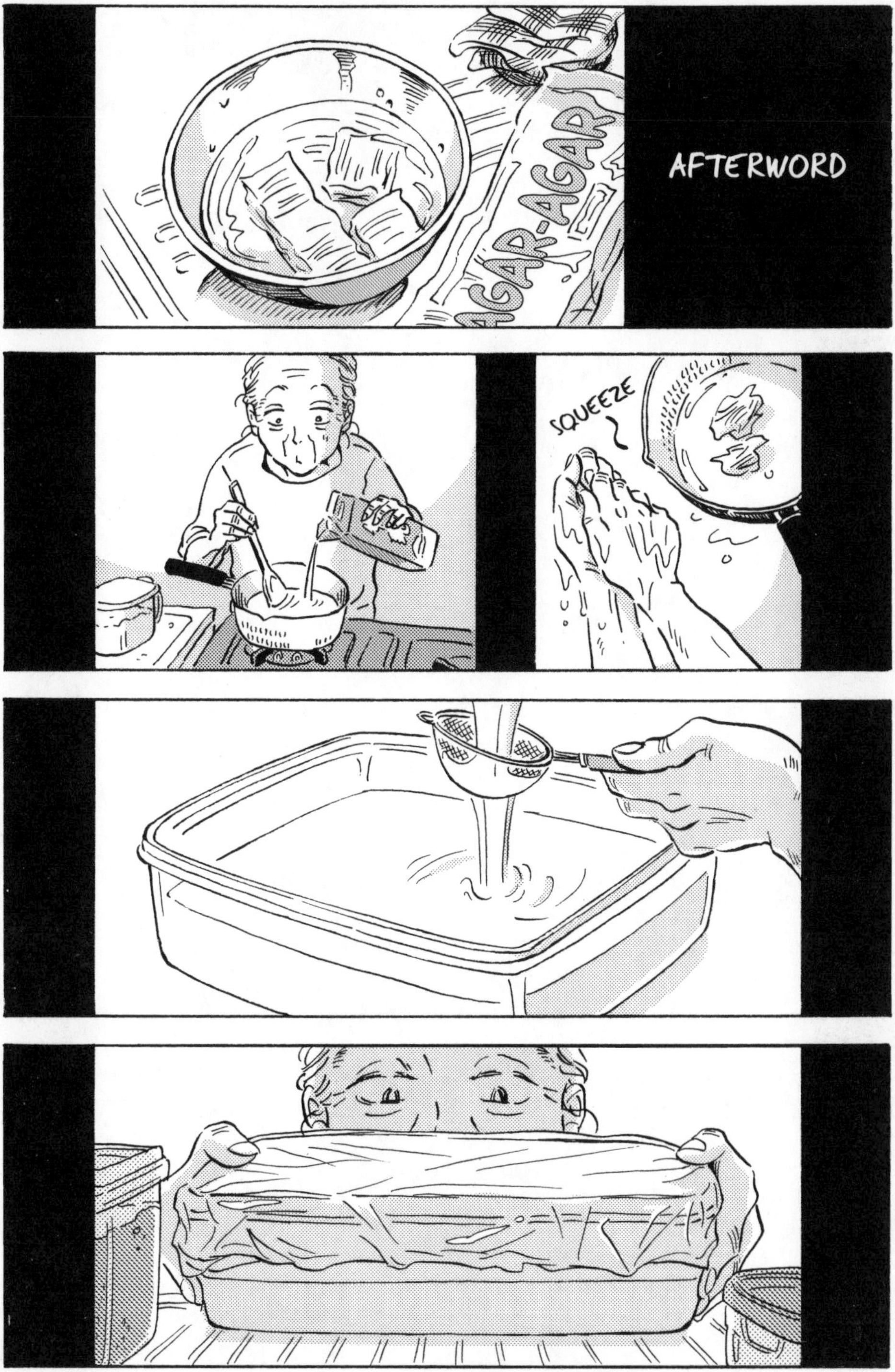
AFTERWORD
AGAR-AGAR
SQUEEZE

FROZEN GRAPES
SO COLD!
PUT THE MILK JELLY AND THE GRAPES IN A DISH.
TOP WITH SYRUP.

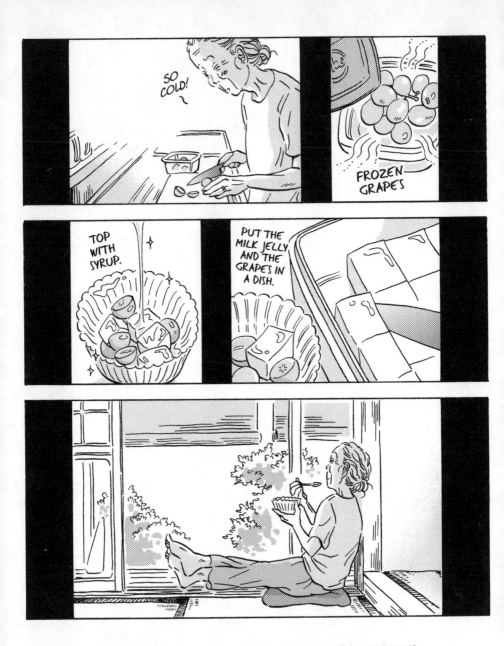

IT WAS WINTER THE WHOLE TIME I WAS DRAWING THIS. WHEN SUMMER COMES, I WANT TO MAKE SOME MILK JELLY AND EAT IT. THANK YOU SO MUCH FOR READING!

KAORI TSURUTANI, MARCH 2018

COVER DESIGN
Kohei Nawata Design Office

STAFF
Naomi Harada
Fumi Iwasaki
Nagatomo Keiko

EDITOR
Masayasu Noguchi

SPECIAL THANKS
Kemono
J. Garden
Shogaku Asagaya branch
Kazuharu Suzuki

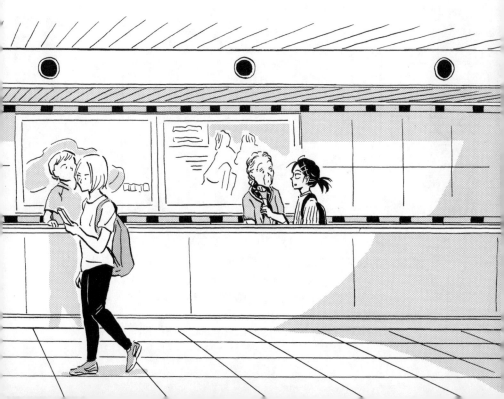

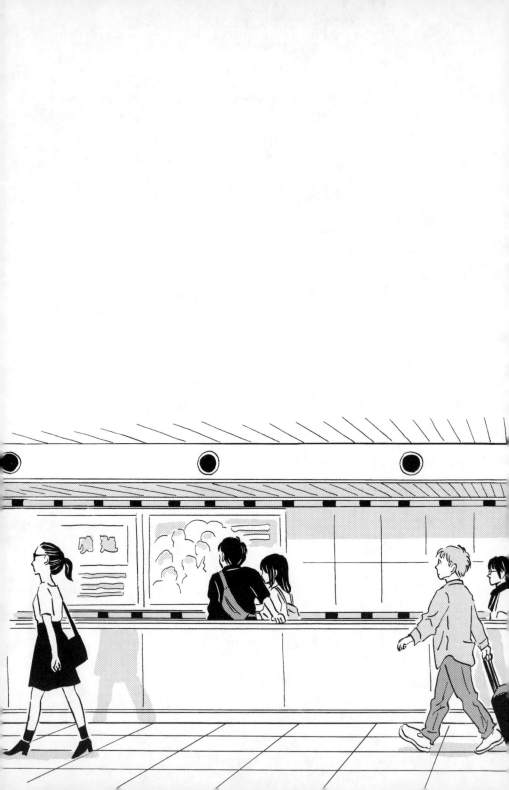

SEVEN SEAS ENTERTAINMENT PRESENTS

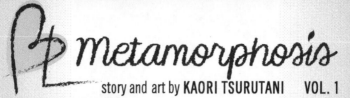

BL metamorphosis

story and art by KAORI TSURUTANI   VOL. 1

TRANSLATION
Jocelyne Allen

ADAPTATION
Ysabet MacFarlane

LETTERING
Ray Steeves

COVER DESIGN
KC Fabellon

LOGO DESIGN
Ki-oon

PROOFREADER
Danielle King

EDITOR
Jenn Grunigen

PREPRESS TECHNICIAN
Rhiannon Rasmussen-Silverstein

PRODUCTION MANAGER
Lissa Pattillo

MANAGING EDITOR
Julie Davis

ASSOCIATE PUBLISHER
Adam Arnold

PUBLISHER
Jason DeAngelis

METAMORPHOSE NO ENGAWA Vol. 1
© Kaori Tsurutani 2018
First published in Japan in 2018 by KADOKAWA CORPORATION, Tokyo.
English translation rights reserved by Seven Seas Entertainment
under the license from KADOKAWA CORPORATION, Tokyo.

Seven Seas press and purchase enquiries can be sent to Marketing Manager Lianne Sentar at press@gomanga.com. Information regarding the distribution and purchase of digital editions is available from Digital Manager CK Russell at digital@gomanga.com.

Seven Seas and the Seven Seas logo are trademarks of Seven Seas Entertainment. All rights reserved.

ISBN: 978-1-64505-295-1

Printed in Canada

First Printing: April 2020

10 9 8 7 6 5 4 3 2 1

W9-BNB-024

FOLLOW US ONLINE: *www.sevenseasentertainment.com*

READING DIRECTIONS

This book reads from *right to left*, Japanese style. If this is your first time reading manga, you start reading from the top right panel on each page and take it from there. If you get lost, just follow the numbered diagram here. It may seem backwards at first, but you'll get the hang of it! Have fun!!

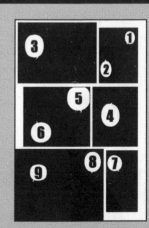